A *WESTERN HORSEMAN* BOOK

Bacon & Beans

Ranch-Country Recipes

Written By Stella Hughes

Edited by Brenda Goodwin

Bacon & Beans
RANCH-COUNTRY RECIPES

Published by
WESTERN HORSEMAN® magazine

2112 Montgomery Street
PO Box 470725
Fort Worth, TX 76147-0725

www.westernhorseman.com

Design, Typography, and Production
Western Horseman
Colorado Springs, Colorado

Printing
Branch Smith
Fort Worth, Texas

© 1990 by Western Horseman
a registered trademark of
Morris Communications Corporation
725 Broad Street
Augusta, GA 30901

Eleventh Printing: June 2006

ISBN 0-911647-20-1

DEDICATION

To Mack, my husband, who can do *anything*,
and thinks I can, too.
And to Robert Denhardt, a former editor of *Western Horseman*,
who bought my first story in 1950.
And to Dick Spencer III, who became editor in 1951.
He was my favorite and
faithful correspondent for the next 38 years.

Stella Hughes

STELLA HUGHES

INTRODUCTION

I'm not really a *good* cook. I'm a fast and nasty cook. That takes a bit of explaining. In cow country, a fast an' nasty cook doesn't necessarily mean a dirty cook; it means a competent one who can turn out a hearty meal in one big hurry, all without a lot of fuss and bother. It means a cook who is always on time and never stints on quantity.

This being on time and in a hurry I got from my dad, Lee Cox, who whistled while he worked and walked so fast his body got ahead of his feet. He had no patience at all with a dawdler or a procrastinator. I emulated him to the best of my ability.

Dad was always generous with praise when I did things fast enough and good enough. He bragged to friends that I could prepare breakfast for our family of six in 20 minutes. I busted a gut to break my record. My mother frowned on this heaping of praise on my head. "Lee, you're just going to *ruin* that girl, bragging on her all the time. She'll get the big head." I don't know if my head swelled, but all my 4 years attending Bell High School in southeast Los Angeles, I got up early every morning, prepared a big breakfast of bacon and eggs and sometimes hot cakes or biscuits, packed four sack lunches, cleaned the kitchen, and was on time for my 8 o'clock class.

Besides being a hurry-up cook, Dad loved outdoor cooking. When living on the farm in Oklahoma, we had fish frys on the lake and later, in California, he bought saltwater fish and prepared supper on the beach, our dinner music supplied by the ocean's roar. Even when attending distant rodeos or horse shows, we took our bedrolls and camp outfit and Dad cooked our meals over an open campfire. He seldom went to a lot of trouble stocking our chuck box. One big frying pan, a stew kettle or two, coffeepot and cups, tin plates, forks and knives, dishpan, and a water bucket were usually all he needed. His meals were simple and to his liking, meaning steaks or pork chops for supper, the ever-present bacon and eggs for breakfast, and always canned milk pan gravy. Dad was a big gravy eater.

If the weather was cool, he'd stir up a huge pot of chili and beans. He bought 1-pound blocks of compressed chili and suet and mixed this with cans of brown beans and served it hot with tons of crackers. He often made a mulligan stew and considered his the best in the world (in truth it *was* hard to beat), and his hospitality knew no bounds. Anyone wandering even close to our campfire was invited to share our bounty. If nothing else, he insisted they have a cup of hot, strong coffee. He made dozens of new friends this way.

Mother was a petite, black-eyed French Canadian and had grown up on a farm in North Dakota. Mother was never one to dawdle over her work either. She was a perfectionist and a wonderful cook. She followed recipe instructions to the letter, carefully measuring and mixing her ingredients. She fretted and stewed over her cakes and pies, and even her bread, which she baked twice a week, and hers was a baker's dream come true. But not in Mother's eyes. She never called anything she cooked as being perfect. Always, always she could find some tiny fault with her productions. They either needed a smidgen more salt (or less), needed a bit more sugar (or less), or were slightly overcooked (or not done enough).

When we kids were growing up, we learned early to stay out of the kitchen when her cakes were in the oven for fear we'd shake the floor and the cake would fall. The world would have promptly come to an end if Mother's cakes were ever a failure. I can never remember *anything* she cooked ever being a failure. She became famous for her sky-high, golden sponge cakes, and baked these prize-winners for every occasion, be it funerals, weddings, birthdays, holidays, or just for Sunday dinner.

When I was 14, my oldest sister married and moved away. Then Mother was ill for several years and I took over in the kitchen. I drove her completely up the wall by my slap-dash ways. The first time she saw me dumping *rounded* teaspoons of baking powder into my biscuit flour she almost fainted. I was supposed to carefully measure *level* teaspoons, she'd scold. I didn't listen to her. I'd already learned 1 rounded teaspoon was equivalent to 2 level teaspoons (more or less). My method was faster and the end results the same.

I wasn't entirely a nonconformist, and had learned a wonderful time-saver from watching Mother, and that was cleaning up as I worked. When I used sugar, the container promptly went back where it belonged. When finished with the flour or rolling pin, I returned it to the flour bin. While my creations were cooking, I washed all the dirty dishes in sight. If a pan needed soaking, I submerged it in hot soapy water at once. I always kept a dishpan, or sink, full of dishwater and cleaned the dirty pots and pans as I went. This made for a fast track.

I adopted any time-saver I thought to be a winner. When using thin-skinned potatoes with only minor blemishes, I merely scrubbed them with a stiff brush and cooked them in their skins. I never scraped or peeled young carrots either, and used the same stiff brush on them. They taste better and all the wonderful nutrients are saved. I learned exactly the correct amounts of flour and liquid to use in making pan gravy without wasting time measuring. When mixing pie dough, I went by feel and texture and always mixed more than needed for my pies. The surplus was rolled thin, sprinkled with sugar, spices, and dabs of butter and baked into tiny cinnamon rolls, which never made it to any table.

Planning ahead meant shaving off as much as a half-hour when preparing the next meal. Often I'd dash home during my lunch hour (the high school's back gate was only a block from our corrals) and prepare the makings for a pot roast. When school was out at 3:30, all I had to do was shove the roaster into the oven, catch and saddle my horse, and take off. I was able to ride until the last possible moment I had to return to finish supper.

Weekends were the same. I had my regular chores to perform, and they durned well better be done thoroughly, as Mother was as good a housekeeper as she was a cook. When I finished to her satisfaction, I was free to ride.

When I was 22, I married Mack Hughes, a handsome young cowboy, and moved to a faraway ranch in northern Arizona. It was 30 miles to the nearest town over rutted dirt roads and our only neighbors were Navajo Indians. I thought I was pretty well prepared to be a ranch cook, but I soon found there was a lot I didn't know. But I learned. At first it was hard to cope with no refrigerator, and a balky wood-burning stove. Also, I packed water in buckets from the windmill, never had any fresh fruit or vegetables, and learned to use canned green chilies in everything except my pies. Cooking with Dutch ovens on campfires was my greatest challenge. It took me years to master this art, but I was fortunate to have superb teachers.

In 1944, we moved to the Apache Indian Reservation in eastern Arizona where Mack served as manager of their remote tribal herd. The headquarters ranch was 80 rough miles from the Indian Agency at San Carlos and over 100 miles to Globe, the nearest town. Roundups were held twice a year, spring and fall, usually lasting from 2 to 3 months each. After the fall roundup came the 100-mile trail drive to the railroad shipping pens with 1,400 to 1,800 head of cattle. For 13 straight years I rode with them, the only woman, white or red, to ever do so. I made a hand horseback and was given no quarter nor did I ask for any. I did offer up fervent prayers the cook wouldn't quit until the drive was over, and miracle of miracles none ever did. After all, we *were* headed in the direction of their village. Almost all hands quit the night we arrived at the stockpens. By then I didn't care, for I could take over.

Cooking in a stationary camp was duck soup to me even though our camp was most primitive. The only shelter was a long brush arbor, or *jacal*, with the fire pit open to the elements. For years the one luxury item was a lone water hydrant 50 feet from camp. Down by the tracks were two outdoor toilets, one lettered "Jake" and the other "Jill." Mack and I slept on cots in a 10 by 12-foot tent. Much later we had electric lights and a tin roof over the cooking area. By that time, Mack and I also had a small camper-trailer that we parked near the "kitchen." No other improvements were ever made during the 30 years we were there.

It took a week of long, hard work to class the cattle into uniform lots and then they were sold at auction. Mack took pride in accomplishing the entire sale, without a hitch, often in less than 4 hours.

Meanwhile, I was in charge of the sale dinner. I learned to barbecue deep-pit style. The burlap-wrapped bundles of prime beef were put into the pit before midnight. By noon the next day they were resurrected and no tastier, more tender meat could be had. Besides dishpans of salads, I cooked 20 pounds of beans, made 20 gallons of coffee, and the piece de resistance was three 16-inch Dutch ovens of cobblers, one cherry and the others apple and apricot. I'd ordered 24 dozen individual sourdough rolls from the bakery in Globe and they were delivered the 40 miles to the stockpens early that morning.

Despite the adverse conditions, we managed a spotless dining area with long, oilcloth-covered tables for serving. Food was kept hot on a raised area that held hot coals and everybody served themselves. An average sale day crowd was 200. After all the cowboys, cattle buyers, visiting government dignitaries, truck drivers, and the train's crew were fed, the "bucket brigade" descended on the food like vultures. These were mostly women, many elderly, from the nearby village of Bylas and all carried some type of container, some so brave they brought water buckets. On days when I'd had the forethought, I squirreled away food for myself and my two hard-working flunkies, otherwise we'd have gone hungry.

The moment the dinner was over, Mack and his crew began loading stock cars for the waiting train. At the same time, huge 18-wheeler possum-belly trucks were loading and roaring off to destinations as far away as Iowa, Oklahoma City, Fort Worth, and even Florida. It often took a week, for we didn't dare leave the stockpens until every cow was shipped. Then the big ranch truck was loaded high with all our gear and lumbered away to the home ranch. The remuda was headed up the trail to be turned out for the winter in the big horse pasture.

My knowledge of barbecuing was put to the supreme test in 1972, when the Apache tribe hired me to feed more than 2,000 people for a big powwow to vote on a land deal. Mack, our son Skeeter, two other good hands, and myself cut and wrapped 1,600 pounds of prime beef in one evening, and had the bundles in the long pit by 1 a.m. Early the next morning we put on 100 pounds of pinto beans to cook, made tubs of tossed green salads, 10 gallons of barbecue sauce, and ordered enough bakery bread to feed an army. We brewed a dozen 10-gallon milk cans of strong coffee. That it was a hot day in June made no difference. The Apaches love their coffee.

At high noon the gigantic feed came off without a hitch. It was later when all hell broke loose. I was never real sure what started the riot, but someone said afterwards it happened when several dozen watermelons were offered free, first-come, first-served. The rush was on! Instantly it was out of control, and a horde of scavengers rushed to carry off bottles of ketchup, sacks of sugar, loaves of bread, butter, pots and pans, ladles—anything loose and not weighing over 100 pounds. As soon as the Indian police established some sort of order, a blinding sandstorm roared in off the river bottoms and in nothing flat there wasn't a human in sight—except a few of us less fortunates. Two thousand paper plates took flight like sea gulls and hours later some were still floating back to earth.

It was several years before the mental scars healed and I contracted to "put on" another big feed. In later years Mack and I barbecued for our local cattlemen's association, seldom feeding more than a hundred or so appreciative cowmen and their families. This is a fun event, and the "burying party" the night before, when we lay the bundles of beef to rest in the big pit, is so popular we never fail to have plenty of enthusiastic helpers. We grill all the T-bones and have potluck under the stars, savoring not only the tender steaks but sniffing the warm night air for threat of rain, and saying two prayers—one that it *does* rain and the other that it waits until the barbecue is over.

Many of the recipes contained in this book have been sent to Stella over the years by people who enjoy her columns and want her to try their favorite recipes. We have tried to give credit to these people where possible, but in many cases recipes were either sent in by a number of people, or were not clearly identified. If you find "your" recipe in here—with or without your name—thanks for sending it in.

CONTENTS

1 THE UNCROWNED KINGS

Cookie was an important person despite the lack of credit he receives in history books.

Some years ago when I began writing a book on chuck-wagon cooking, I wanted to pay tribute to that extraordinary person, the cow-camp cook, who often was referred to as "czar of the chuck wagon" or "tyrant of the pots and pans." I wanted to describe the kind of food that trail drivers ate, how it was prepared, the kind of utensils used, and how the food was stored and preserved for the long treks.

I also wanted to portray a true picture of the kind of man who served as cook on the cattle drives. Was he usually black? Or Mexican? What kind of background qualified him for such an arduous chore, and one demanding such an array of talents?

I needed to research a period of barely 50 years, beginning with the great cattle drives from Texas to northern markets in 1866, and ending with the fencing of the

There's no caption on this old photo, but it was most likely taken in Texas.

Photo Courtesy of Texas and Southwestern Cattle Raisers Association Foundation, Fort Worth, Texas.

open range. Well, boy howdy, did I receive a shock when delving into western history books!

Our local library had about a dozen books on the taming of the wild and wooly West. These books were of recent vintage, written or compiled by armchair historians who had never gotten out of New York. All are filled with beautiful illustrations by capable artists, along with authentic photographs covering subjects from cattle stampedes, wicked trail towns, barroom brawls, painted women, branding scenes, and cowboys riding bucking broncos . . . but not one picture of a chuck-wagon cook *cooking* something.

One great tome of a book never gives a clue as to what the trail drivers ate, who prepared it, or how. On one page the author says, "Fort Worth was the next stop on the trail, and there a drover could replenish his foodstuffs, six-shooters, and saddles."

Another book, claiming to give the "whole" story of the American West, gives the trail-driving cook even less acclaim. In one paragraph the author writes, "The makeup of the outfit consisted of a chuck wagon which carried the food, bedding, and tents. From its tailboard was served food, which had been prepared over an open fire." Son of a gun! Nowhere does he give Cookie credit for how he prepared the food, and kept the wagon organized so it didn't all fall by the trail side.

If this is the whole story, it's like forgetting the Alamo in Texas history, or leaving Arizona's Grand Canyon off the map. Or, you might say, they plumb forgot to salt the beans.

The Book of the American West, by Jay Monaghan, has some really well-known co-authors helping out. Ramon F. Adams did a fine job authoring the chapter on cowboys, but he pulls up short when writing of the cook's duties. In almost 600 pages, there's a single lone engraving of cowboys eating at a chuck wagon. Yet, there's page after page of skillful drawings by Jo Mora of spurs, boots, cowboy hats, chaps, slickers, bedrolls. The book even shows neckerchiefs, with minute details right down to the type of cloth, the proper knots, and the hankie's many uses.

Even at that, Adams does the best job of describing what the cowboys ate and how the cook prepared it, compared to most books. But, it seems to me, ol' Cookie

and his pots and pans deserved as much time as a bandanna.

Another book, authored by a highly touted historian, says the food on the trail drives was meager and just plain bad. He believed this to the extent he said it twice. It's a cinch that writer never drove drags behind a herd from sunup till sundown, or he would know any food that satisfies hunger is good. Think about that for a moment. I've seen the time when a cold mashed potato sandwich would have tasted like pure ambrosia.

That same author spends some time in telling of the cook's disposition and character, saying he was "an unsociable individual with a temperament that was pugnaciously independent as well as uniquely eccentric." Well, no wonder! That's pretty strong language, and besides, if I didn't get anymore credit than poor ol' hard-working Cookie, I'd have shot the heels off any cowboy who looked crosswise at me.

Although some of the books failed miserably in telling the story of the trail-driving cooks, there are some that do a creditable job. The more successful ones were authored by men wise enough to rely heavily on authentic diaries kept by "men on the spot." For example, the editors of *Before Barbed Wire* relied on the superb photographs taken by L.A. Huffman. Now, there was a true artist with a camera. Huffman appreciated cooks, and was wont to call them the uncrowned kings. He then had the good sense to photograph the uncrowned king at work, surrounded by the tools of his trade.

The really accurate source of material on the old-time cooks is the old-timers themselves. The early trail drivers, in their memoirs, told about the different cooks, remembering certain individuals fondly or bitterly. They described the kind of food they had and how the cook prepared it, because meals were important to them. Cowboys didn't have a heck of a lot of comforts to look forward to, and so after a long day in the saddle, supper and that brief hour around the cook's fire were of utmost importance.

Not so with our modern historian, compiling data from periodicals and books written long ago. He sits in a comfortable chair in his warm office, with a full belly, and forgets simple things like food and the humble man who cooked it. Instead, he latches onto the more sensational aspects

Although some of the books failed miserably in telling the story of trail-driving cooks, there are some that do a creditable job.

Cooks were a diversified assortment of older men. Many were ranch-raised, but others were tenderfeet, and there are records of immigrants, newly freed Negroes, white Confederate veterans, and family men serving as cooks on cattle drives north.

of trail driving and plays up the wild stampedes, Longhorns swimming swollen rivers, cattle rustlers, and Indian massacres.

Some writers, in describing the trail-driving cooks, made the mistake of molding them all alike, when in truth they were a diversified assortment of older men. Many were ranch-raised, but others were tenderfeet, and there are records of immigrants, green as gourds, serving as cooks on the drives north. After the Civil War, many were Negroes, newly freed and seeking work. Many were white Confederate veterans, bitter and calloused to suffering and killing. Others were family men, desperate to earn some money in order to feed and clothe the wife and kiddies. A few of the cooks were fairly well-educated for the times, while others were illiterate. So, it would seem that each cook was an individual in his own right, and in no way did cooks conform to a mold.

Fred Gipson, in his *Trail Drivin' Rooster,* tells a true story of a black cook, Sam Goodall, packing four frying chickens in a crate atop the chuck wagon, awaiting the opportune time to serve the trail hands a supper of fried chicken. Sam is no unsocial or eccentric grouch the author proves as he spins his yarn of the relationship between the good-natured cook and the trail hands. The book is a simple tale of a runty, fighting rooster named Dick, and the touching account of how the cook saved his pet from ending up in the pot.

J.R. Williams, the cowboy's cartoonist, is the only person who came close to portraying a true picture of a ranch cook. Williams' "Sugar," a stove-up ex-cowhand full of comments abrasive as a rasp, was featured for three generations in the famous cartoon strip, *Out Our Way.*

Ol' Sugar might not have always lived up to all his name implied, but he had a wonderful sense of humor, and never fell down on the job. The cowboys working "out Wickenburg way" knew, come mealtime, that ol' Sugar would serve the best he could with what he had to "do" with. Sugar stood for every pot wrestler who ever built a batch of biscuits or boiled a pot of frijoles.

Andy Adams' *Log of a Cowboy,* as well as Teddy Blue Abbotts' *We Pointed Them North,* have been quoted from so often they are probably the best known of trail-driving days. Yet, even they left a lot to be desired to any researcher. I've found

The Trail-Drivers of Texas, published by the University of Oklahoma Press, a treasure trove of genuine, little-known facts on cooks and the kind of food the trail drivers ate. Another valuable source is regional publications by historical societies in the western states.

One such publication told the story of Baylor Johnson, who took on the job of cooking for a trail crew driving a mixed herd of Longhorns from San Antonio to Abilene, in 1869. Johnson knew nothing of cattle, but he'd been, at various times, a butcher in New York, a cook on a sailing vessel, a grocery clerk in New Orleans, and for the previous 2 years he had worked for a freight outfit between Corpus Christi and San Antonio.

Johnson goes into marvelous detail when writing of outfitting his chuck wagon. Although he had yet to see a chuck wagon as used by the trail drivers, he built his to the specifications of one of the cowboys who had been "up the trail" the year before. The wagon box measured 42 inches by 12 feet overall, and its sides had been raised to 4 feet in height. It was caulked and made as waterproof as possible. Then Johnson built a sleeping bunk in the wagon bed, with storage space beneath. No other account have I ever read where the cook had such comfort.

The chuck box was built 4 feet high to contain drawers and shelves roomy enough to contain eating implements and cooking utensils for 12 men. Johnson lined the inside of this box with thin sheets of metal like that used in covering certain types of steamer trunks. The box fit exactly in the rear of the wagon. The door of the chuck box was hinged and could be lowered; resting on a folding leg, it served as a work table. However, first the tailgate of the wagon had to be taken out; it was another handy work table around camp.

Another compartment, called a "boot," also had a hinged door. It hung below the chuck box and contained two Dutch ovens, a flat-bottomed kettle with bail, a heavy cast-iron skillet with a long handle, a pot with a lid that Johnson called a "coffee boiler," fire irons, fire hooks, and a pothook. (Johnson did not name this pothook, used in lifting a Dutch oven by the bail when removing it from the fire. The pothook was also used in removing the heavy lid from the Dutch oven. In the Southwest today, we call this indis-

A cook who could turn out light, delectable cakes was a sure-fire hit with early day cowboys like these fellers. This 1911 photo shows the vaquero wagon at Jerry Slough, also known as Tracy Camp, near Buttonwillow, California. The ID on the back of the photo is sketchy, but here it is. From left: Wrango, the Portugee Kid; Tex, later the cook; Theodore Graniv, cook; Emmet McAdam (behind Graniv), buckaroo; Bob Sharpe ("Pica"), buckaroo; Guadalupe Ortiz, top vaquero; Frank Riis ("Chico"), buckaroo; Joe Garcia (back to camera), vaquero; and Rafael Quin, range and vaquero boss. **Photo by Rolla Watt**

pensable tool a goncho or gonch hook.) Because the boot was so handy, the ax and short-handled, flat-bottomed shovel were also carried here.

A side platform was built, toward the front of the left side of the wagon box, to hold the wooden water barrel. Two compact tool boxes were attached to each side of the wagon for necessities likely to be needed before the long trip ended. In the front, just below the wagon seat, was another box with hinged lid called the jockey box. Always, without fail, this box contained the wagon iron, used in removing wheels. The driver rested his feet on this box and, as it was the handiest compartment on the wagon, he often carried some of his private "comforts," such as chewing tobacco, salve for chapped lips, and gloves. Rivets and a hammer would be some of the tools carried here, as well as axle grease for the wheels. Five hardwood wagon bows were attached by metal brackets to the wagon box, and over these was stretched a waterproof canvas,

generous enough to extend over the chuck box and work table during bad weather.

Johnson stocked this "home away from home" with some luxuries unheard of for a Texas cattle drive. He purchased tins of green tea, a keg of pickles, soaps and spices, salt, and saleratus (baking soda). Of these items, only salt was indispensable. He bought a coffee grinder with a side mount, and a good supply of roasted coffee beans.

Canned milk was not common on country-store shelves in Texas until after the war, and though it was considered outrageously expensive, Johnson stocked a number of Borden's hermetically sealed tins of milk, along with some baker's chocolate. Although other canned goods were available, such as tins of meat (also by Borden's) and some fruits and vegetables, canned corn was not found in the far West until the late 1870s. Johnson passed up the expensive vegetables, and finished stocking his wagon with commodities sold in bulk, such as dried apples, cereals, and

11

flour. Cornmeal was purchased by the barrel, as were beans and sugar.

Granulated sugar was a luxury, even though it was coarse and brown, and so hardened in the barrel or hogshead in which it was shipped that a special auger was needed to loosen it; a sugar grinder was also necessary to pulverize the lumps. Johnson bought some molasses as well as sugar.

Although Johnson's list is not complete, he says they not only took some dried beef, rolled in thin sheets which was called *charqui* (jerky), but also a good supply of smoked hams and slabs of home-cured bacon to supplement the diet of beef.

I think it's safe to say the young Texans "ate high on the hog" on this trip north, with Johnson slinging the pots and pans.

One other old-timer's diary from 1885, when trail driving had become very commonplace, tells how the cook made

cracklin' cornbread with pork cracklings brought along just for this purpose. This same writer remembers another meal, served as a banquet on the trail, when the cook fried a big mess of catfish he'd caught from a river, along with a plum duff made from wild sandhill plums.

Another account tells about the trail boss purchasing a keg of sweet pickles, mixed with chunks of cauliflower, tiny whole onions, and small sweet peppers. When spearing into the keg with a fork, the cowboys took what they got, first try, even though their favorite was the crisp cauliflower buds. Any trail driver who kept fishing until he found his preference was considered unmannerly and lacking in proper upbringing.

I refuse to believe that meals served on the trail were "meager and just plain bad." Monotonous, yes; a horror to nutritionists, certainly. But, the meat-eating Texans

A range cook was commonly called "Cookie" by the cowboys. There were other names, such as belly-robber, grub-spoiler, old woman, pot-rustler, dough-puncher, hash-burner, ol' slick an' greasy, or cossie (short for cocinero).

were accustomed to beef and beans, salt pork, and cornpone, and biscuits and gravy, and they would rather fight than change their diet.

A range cook was commonly called "Cookie" by the cowboys. There were other names for roundup cooks, such as belly-robber, grub-spoiler, old woman, pot-rustler, dough-puncher, hash-burner, ol' slick an' greasy, or cossie (short for *cocinero*). But, whatever they may have called the cook behind his back, he often was called Mister to his face, and certainly always in a respectful manner.

If there was an uncrowned king, it was the old-time roundup cook. He had to be good to qualify as a wagon cook; and also resourceful, versatile, and talented in a dozen different trades. Father-confessor, banker, doctor (for both man and beast), barber, tailor, laundryman, butcher, teamster, stake-holder for horse races and bronc rides, and arbiter to settle quarrels resulting from horse races and bronc riding. Those sum up some of a range cook's duties; is it any wonder he has become a legend?

He had to be an expert at scrounging and improvising when the chuck ran low; he could make do as long as the coffee didn't run out and he had flour. The mainstay of a range diet, then as well as now, was beef, and that was always on hand. All meals were built around some form of beef, with variations depending on the skill of the cook and local customs. There wasn't anything he couldn't cook under almost insurmountable difficulties, from lack of proper firewood to minor incidents like stampedes, blizzards (blue northers), dust storms, floods, and "gyppy" water.

The old-time cook was a very important person and he knew it. He ruled his chuck wagon and cooking area with an iron hand. There were (and still are) unwritten laws no self-respecting cowboy would dream of violating. Riding into camp, the cowboys *always* stayed down-wind. Woe betide the unfortunate rider dumb enough to dash by, stirring up a cloud of dust. There were camp rules of etiquette that only a greenhorn who didn't know better would break.

The rule against crowding around the cook's fire for warmth while the cook was at work was almost never broken. The space between the fire and chuck box was sacrosanct, and belonged to the cook alone. Cowboys provided separate wood and warming fires for themselves if the cook was at work. These were referred to as bull fires, and if wood was scarce, the cowboys never used the cook's precious supply. Nor did a cowboy walk into camp and help himself to a snack, or even a cup of coffee, until invited to do so by the cook. Most cooks, however, kept a coffeepot on a bed of coals so that any cowboy could help himself at all hours.

After finishing a meal, the cowboys scraped their plates clean and put them in a tub or pan provided by the cook. The receptacle was often called the wrecking barrel. Any careless rider who left a cup or plate lying around might find himself on the short end of the cook's serving spoon next meal.

No horses were tethered or hobbled near the chuck wagon, regardless of how many westerns or TV programs might show one practically drooling down the cook's neck. Oh, sure, there are any number of photos and paintings by famous artists showing horses in the cook's kitchen. Historians will point this out in argument, but I have an answer for them. Those old-time photographers (yeah, and the new-timers too) were famous for setting the stage. They were never satisfied with a cow-camp "as is," and weren't happy unless they could set the scene to what they *thought* a roundup camp should look like. So the cowboys on their horses were invited to crowd around the chuck wagon, lending color. The cowboys *knew* better, but after all, the photographer was their guest! No one dreamed of being impolite by suggesting the photographer might not know *his* business. So, whenever you see an old-time picture of a cowboy sitting on his horse or holding a horse smack dab in the cook's kitchen, please observe the silly look on that hombre's face.

If the cook didn't have a flunky, or the horse wrangler was unable to help, the cowboys themselves snaked in wood at the end of their saddle ropes for camp. When breaking camp, cowboys not immediately needed elsewhere hitched the horses to the wagon and loaded supplies and bedrolls.

Keeping the cookie happy paid off in wonderful dividends. Although not a gourmet, the cowboy liked good food. Just as an army travels on its stomach,

13

Runaway mules seemed to have played a big part in molding a cook's character.

whether a roundup was a success or failure depended on the skill of the cook and the largess of the outfit. A stingy owner who tried to cut costs at the expense of the cowboys' stomachs found himself short of hands come roundup time. Many men swore the success of a roundup depended entirely on a good cook and a competent horse wrangler. For what cowboy could be expected to do a hard day's work on an empty stomach, riding a gant horse?

The cook had many duties to perform aside from his regular chore of turning out two hearty meals—sometimes three— under adverse conditions. If wood was unavailable, the cook had to make do with cow chips. This fuel burns like paper, if it burns at all. When chips were damp they provided a smoke screen that would hover in the lowlands days after the chuck wagon moved on. Then there was the problem with water. If it was gyppy, that meant coffee tasted like a cross between lye and carbolic acid and chances were good of the crew coming down with an ailment that could immobilize them for days.

Dust and flies, scorching sun or freezing wind, cantankerous wagon mules, a lazy horse wrangler, burned thumb, and pesty blowflies—all could turn a cook into an antisocial cowboy-hater, wife-beater, and dog-kicker, dishing out meals under an atmosphere as gloomy as a wake.

Down through the history of the cattle industry comes the traditional belief that all cow camp cooks were temperamental, cantankerous, mean, antisocial cowboy- haters. These adjectives may have applied to some, but from all accounts as gathered from old-timers, it would seem that cow- country cooks came in a wide range of personalities and temperaments.

Mack Hughes, who started out working for the Hashknife outfit in northern Ari- zona when he was 12 years old and spent the next 65 years cowboying and riding the ranges of Arizona and Nevada, says he knew only one really vile-tempered cook during all those years.

"Bill Woods was the meanest cook I ever knew," Mack remembers with a shake of his head. "He hated cowboys so bad he'd park his wagon over a red ant hill so no one could sit in the shade to eat."

Mack says another misconception peo- ple have was that all cooks were filthy and dirty. Mack admits he did know two

really unsanitary and downright nasty cooks in his life. The worst of the two was Dutch Joe, who later owned his own outfit on the mountain 50 miles south of Winslow, Arizona. This ranch became known as the Dutch Joe Place, and is known by that name today.

Dutch Joe was a little man with long, greasy whiskers that would have been white if he'd ever washed them. He smoked an evil-smelling pipe, so rank its odor rivaled that of the old man, who never bathed to anyone's knowledge.

Joe and another cook named Herman personified "Ol' Slick and Greasy," the name dirty cooks were called all over the West.

Mack says most cooks were passably clean, if they wanted to continue working, and Mack said he even knew of two cooks who were so clean they were almost fanat- ical. One such cook was Shorty Suthin, who not only was the cleanest cook Mack ever knew, but was possibly the most good-natured. Shorty simply didn't have an enemy in the world and was happy in his work.

Shorty spent all his working hours, when not actually cooking, tidying up his cooking area. He washed his dish towels every day and even had clothespins and a line strung up. His dish rags were boiled in lye daily and he scoured his pots and pans until they shone like new. He carried a garden rake in the wagon and raked the area clean. He even sprinkled water around the chuck box to keep down the dust. He dug a small pit a distance from the fire and insisted the cowboys scrape their tin plates clean before depositing them in the wrecking barrel—the tub of hot, soapy water provided by the cook.

No one seemed to mind Shorty's pen- chant for cleanliness, for the little cook was always grinning and cracking a joke. He seemed to always be in a good humor and was known to lose his temper only once. Mack remembers it well.

"Little Shorty was really short," Mack explained, "and he had a problem in that the high-wheeled wagon made his work table about chin high. Shorty got around this by digging trenches about a foot deep and backing the wagon into them, thereby lowering his table to a more comfortable position. To this wagon, Shorty drove a four-up team of black mules that were a shade boogery. One time Shorty got

**Illustration by
Bill Culbertson**

carried away when digging his trenches in sandy soil to back his wagon into, and when he hitched up the blacks next morning and crawled to the high seat and chirped to his team, they couldn't budge the load. Shorty slapped his wheelers right smart with the lines and squalled. Still, the mules couldn't start the outfit."

Mack said Shorty was laughing and said they might have to unload before they could go on, but before anyone could do anything about it, Elmer Jones came riding up.

"Elmer was scatter-brained," Mack explained, "and the big dummy drew his six-shooter from his chaps pocket and shot right under them mules." Mack laughs in describing the scene that followed. "That dumb stunt got action, all right. Them mules run off. Poor Shorty nearly got his neck popped off, they left so fast. There wasn't a one of us that could catch them for a quarter of a mile, an' by that time

Shorty got them circling and under control. When we rode up, we saw Shorty was mad, really mad. He called Elmer some terrible names. Ol' dumb Elmer didn't let it seem to faze him none and just sat there grinning sheepishly. Finally, he said, 'Well, I got 'em off their bed ground anyhow.'"

There's another story of a good-natured cook, John Devers, who had a pair of spoiled mules change his disposition. Runaway mules seemed to have played a big part in molding a cook's character.

John Devers' wife called him "Sugar," his daughters called him "Papa Darling," his hounds never left his side, and his neighbors swore he didn't have an enemy in the world. He was amiable, kind, soft-spoken, and had a heart as good as gold.

The outfit's wagon mules, named Jake and Jude, changed all that when Devers took the job cooking for the Hashknife outfit one spring roundup back in the

15

Despite the belief that all cow camp cooks were cantankerous, mean, antisocial cowboy-haters, it would seem they came in a wide range of personalities and temperaments.

1920s. Overnight, John Devers' sunny disposition changed to that of a sullen, snarling, sour human being. The cowboys eating at his wagon gave the surly cook a wide berth, and swore he was the most evil-tempered man alive.

Maybe the sorrel mules shouldn't receive all the blame for the change in Devers' personality. Some say the combination of bad weather, the general nature of a roundup cook's chores, and a siege of boils that John developed also contributed. Whatever, here are the facts.

As mentioned before, a roundup cook had to have various talents besides slinging Dutch ovens. For sure he had to be a teamster, and a good one. John Devers qualified, as he was in his mid-40s, rawhide tough, and had broke his share of bronc mules.

As a result, Bill Jim Wyrick, the red-headed wagonboss, welcomed the chance to get some good use out of Jake and Jude, as previous cooks had balked at using them on the chuck wagon. So, on that first morning, Bill Jim assigned two good cowboys, riding stout horses, to rope and lead the mules from the corral. Snubbing them close, the men put halters on them before handing the lead ropes to the cook and horse wrangler.

Both mules were big, sound, and handsome. But they were also snorty and rank, and had a bag of dirty tricks. Jude pulled the first one by jerking away from the wrangler and taking off with the lead rope snapping the breeze behind him. The two cowboys set spurs to their horses, shaking out their loops as they rode in hot pursuit.

Then Jake, tied to the front wheel of the wagon, reared back, breaking his halter. The sudden release threw him off balance and he fell backwards, sprawling flat on his back, all four feet flailing the air.

Hearing the ruckus, the cook came running around the rear of the wagon carrying Jake's collar. Jake sprang up, lashed out with both hind feet, and caught the cook square in the stomach. Devers let out a

whoosh of air that sounded like a boiler popping off steam, and staggered back. Luckily, the collar had taken the full impact of Jake's heels, saving the cook from serious injury.

The sun was high when Jake and Jude were brought back, not quite as fresh as earlier that morning, and hitched to the wagon. Satisfied with their fun, they settled down like good work mules.

Several days later, a chilling wind blew in from the north, bringing sleet and rain.

As if putting up with cold rain, ornery mules, wet wood, and flat sourdough starter wasn't enough, Devers had developed several painful boils on his posterior. Bill Jim was properly sympathetic, but had nothing to ease the misery. The cowboys suggested several kinds of hot poultices, but none offered to help apply them.

Meals became disasters, with the cook snarling at any cowboy who looked crosswise at him. He spent most of the night dozing on his feet, close to the campfire, as he swore it was impossible for him to sleep in his bed. He began serving breakfast practically in the middle of the night, telling Bill Jim that as long as he couldn't sleep he might as well be working. The unhappy cowboys spent their time waiting for daylight, rolling endless cigarettes, and consuming gallons of black coffee while casting hateful looks at the cook.

After working the Big Tank area, the outfit prepared to move to Chevelon Creek. The rain had ceased, but the wind blew harder than ever, howling around the wagon as Devers packed his gear and shouted angrily to the wrangler to bring on his mule team.

Just as the wrangler handed Jude's lead rope to Devers, the fury of the wind picked up a tin washbasin that had been lying on the ground. It sailed through the air and smacked Jude right between the eyes. Jude turned wrong side out and stampeded, with the cook hauling on the halter rope and yelling "whoa." Devers reared back and dug his heels into the shale rock, but he was dragged on the seat of his pants through the rocks and grass. He went about 50 feet in this manner before getting Jude to stop.

Standing up, Devers started to slap the dirt from the seat of his pants until he suddenly remembered—and his hand stopped in midair. Then he began to grin, and the grin turned to shouts of laughter that almost stampeded Jude again.

Grinning from ear to ear, the cook called out joyously, "That did it, boys. That *did* it. I'm well again. Yeah-hoo!" And he let out a cowboy squall in sheer exuberance.

After that, the weather turned fair, the hills greened up, spring flowers bloomed, and Jake and Jude were worked down to where they behaved like model wagon mules. John Devers became carefree and happy, whistling while he worked, baking cobblers and puddings for the cowboys, and catering to their every need.

Mack says the very first roundup cook he can remember was back in 1916, when he was only 7 years old. At that time, Mack's dad, Pat Hughes, worked for Wallace and Bly out of Holbrook, Arizona, and the Hughes family lived at the home ranch at Adamana. When gathering cattle in the fall, the outfit camped just below the Hughes' house.

"The cook's name was John Savage and we kids visited his camp the first morning. I guess Savage hated kids, because he ran us off and threatened to work our hind ends over with a wet rope if he caught us sneaking around again. Man, after that we stayed shy of his fire, and if we watched, it was from a safe distance.

"One morning we saw the cook pull a dirty trick on Bugger Red who was the bronc snapper for the outfit. We watched Bugger saddle a young sorrel horse called Number Three, and heard him talk soft as he eased into the saddle, so the sorrel wouldn't buck. Then Red rode past, a nice respectable distance from the chuck wagon an' down-wind, but it seemed to

irk the cook, because he stepped out from his fire and threw an empty water bucket under the colt's heels. I mean the bronc ride took place, but Bugger Red ruined the cook's fun by sitting tall in the saddle and spurring that sorrel until he quit bucking."

In later years, Pat told me about John Savage, and said he was just a "git-by" cook. He kept just clean enough to get by. Pat said there was a bunch of get-by cooks, and if he had his druthers, he'd take a cranky cook instead. Providing, Pat added, the cowboys spent so little time in camp that the main concern was to have good food and lots of it.

Mack told me the years he managed outfits, he had only one cook that was skimpy on grub. No matter if Mack supplied him with everything in the way of chuck and plenty of fresh beef, this certain cook never prepared enough. The last few cowboys in line would find only broth in the bean pot and soup left in the meat.

Mack let this stingy cook go, and the next one he hired wasted food by the ton, and Mack's cow dogs got so fat they refused to work cattle.

Mack tells about another unusual cook who worked for the Hashknives back in the 1920s by the name of Charley Farnsworth. Charley was young for a roundup cook, being only about 30 years old. "Farnsworth was the worst boot-licker I ever knew and catered to the boss something awful. He'd hover over Bill Jim Wyrick, our wagonboss, during meal times. He'd insist Bill Jim have a second helping of dessert and, all in all, made a fool of himself."

Mack told about the day they'd run out of meat, but Farnsworth had managed to save one steak, which he cooked and tried to serve to Bill Jim. When Bill Jim saw the rest of his men eating beans, while the cook handed him a plate with the lone steak, Bill threw a fit. He tossed the steak into the fire and told Farnsworth angrily, "When I eat steak, *my men* eat steak!"

A stingy owner who tried to cut costs at the expense of the cowboys' stomachs found himself short of hands come roundup time.

17

2 COOKIN' BY GUESS AND BY GOSH

"All the measuring and weighing was bad enough, but that book wasn't writ for no cow camp. There wasn't a receep in it that didn't call for some stuff no chuck box ever dreamed of havin'."

Blackie Clingman of Gila County, Ariz., was a good cowboy in his younger days, but had to resort to cooking after he lost a battle with a bronc in later years. One fall he cooked for Mack during the roundup of the Ash Creek Cattle Association on the San Carlos Indian Reservation. This was a temporary setup, because the Apaches thought Mack should hire Indians (except for bronc breaking) and this hiring of an Anglo was frowned on by the members of the board of directors.

So, while we could, we ate high on the hog, for Blackie was a real artist when it came to slinging Dutch ovens, and the cowboys found out what *real* sourdough biscuits were. The previous cook had made such awful bread, the crew had been in the habit of peeling off the top crust and throwing the rest into the brush for crows and coyotes to fight over after the outfit moved on.

Besides being such a good cook, Blackie was one of the rare clean ones. In fact,

Illustration by
Mike Craig

"—that looks like about 1³/₅ cup."

18

Blackie was so clean he was downright cranky when the cowboys didn't adhere to his high standards. I saw him threaten one young man with the gonch hook when Blackie saw the cowboy hadn't washed up before lining up at the pots. There was plenty of water, soap, and wash basins supplied by the outfit, and Blackie saw that they were used.

I'd been told about the time Blackie had gone to visit an old-timer by the name of Supel Hicks. Old man Hicks was notorious for his sloppy housekeeping. He lived alone in a faraway camp and when Blackie rode up, Supel greeted him like he was welcome. Blackie went to work trying to set the place in order. He got carried away in scrubbing the coffeepot, and wore a hole in it. Made old Supel so mad he ran Blackie off, and here Blackie was the first company he'd had in 6 months!

Blackie told me when he had to quit cowboying and hired out the first time to cook for an outfit, he wasn't too sure how he'd do. I'll let Blackie tell about it in his own words.

"I didn't have much confidence in my cookin', so bought me a 'receep' book. I was in trouble the very first thing. All them receeps said 'four servings.' Now, four servings for what? It didn't say if it'd feed four hungry cowboys or four office workers. If it meant them office workers, well *that* wouldn't come within a country mile of feeding four starvin' cowhands. An' I ain't never knowed any other kind.

"Well, I got bogged down tryin' to quadripple one-and-three-fourths cups of this an' that, an' one scant dessert spoonful of something else. I only went to school a few years an' didn't learn very high mathematics. By the time I 12-timesed a receep, a person needed a degree in triggerometry!

"Besides that, I didn't have nothin' that receep book called for to measure stuff in. The only cups we had was the tin ones we drank our coffee from, an' as for tablespoons, we was lucky if we had some big ladles for servin' beans and such. Then the book kept sayin' to use pounds of this and ounces of that, an' we bought flour by the barrel an' lard in 20-gallon cans, so I got lost there, too. An' how in heck do you 12-times a dash or pinch of something?

"All the measuring and weighing was bad enough, but that book wasn't writ for no cow camp. There wasn't a receep in it that didn't call for some stuff no chuck box ever dreamed of havin'. Take, for instance, a simple thing like a pot roast. This book said to sear it on both sides in some olive oil. Well, I didn't let that throw me. I just heats up my Dutch oven good an' hot, throws in some lard in place of olive oil, dumps in the meat, an' let 'er sear. Next, the book says to add a minced onion. So I chops up a Chihuahua big onion. Then the next ingreedy-ants throw me proper. It says a half-cup each of minced parsley, chives, shallots, 2 tablespoons Cognac and the same of sherry, a dash of Worcestershire sauce, 1 tablespoon prepared mustard, an' salt and pepper to taste. The salt and pepper was all I had, so I threw 'er in.

"Not a one of them cowboys knowed the difference, an et every bit of that pot roast an' called 'er good.

"After that I just throwed that receep book in the bottom of the chuck wagon, an' cooked by guess an' by gosh. That is, 'til the boys got to clammerin' for me to make a cake. Cowboys all got a sweet tooth. Several in fact. So I dug the book up, and cracks 'er open to see if it'd give me any pointers on how to build a cake. I nearly fainted when I read about the first one. Angel food cake, it said. Had to laugh, this angel food, intended for a bunch of hell-roarin' cowboys. But, I read on.

"Next it said to use *12* egg whites. An' it didn't say a word what was to be done with all them yolks. Then it went on to say to use a whisk in beatin' the eggs. Here all the time I thought 'whisk' was some old-maids card game! I did know we sure didn't have no whisk in the chuck box. For that matter, we didn't have no eggs neither.

"So I skipped some pages an' found another receep for a spice cake. We had pert nigh everything it called for, exceptin' the eggs, so I went ahead and built 'er that way. The hands said it was the best cake they ever et, an' after that I made 'er often. I named it Desperation Cake."

Mack and his crew enjoyed Blackie's tallow puddings (see Chapter 12), flaky biscuits, and luscious T-bone steaks (the last cook had boiled the steaks). But, as all good things must come to an end, Blackie had a run-in at the stock pens and quit. It happened this way.

The shipping pens at San Carlos were out to the edge of the village. The moment the Ash Creek outfit got in, the local

"I just throwed that receep book in the bottom of the chuck wagon, an' cooked by guess an' by gosh."

19

"Git you a cup of yeast . . . not too big a cup. Put in some sody or bakin' powder, whichever you got. You don't need to measure no sugar nor bakin' powder . . . just throw 'er in. The sugar is to kill the taste of the sody if you got too much."

bootleggers descended on the camp like vultures. (Selling liquor to Indians was illegal at that time.) In a short while, the entire crew was drunker than seven hundred dollars, including the cook's flunky.

Oddly enough, the flunky stayed on the job, but was far more of a hindrance than help to Blackie in preparing the noonday meal. Finally the flunky retired to his tent to sleep it off, and emerged unsteadily an hour or so later. He must have been a little more confused than usual, for he went over to where Blackie had the meat well wrapped in tarps, and began dragging it out and uncovering it. "We gonna have stew for supper," he informed Blackie.

"Leave that beef alone," Blackie spoke calmly. "I already got steaks cut for supper."

The Apache helper completely ignored Blackie, and kept right on removing the tarp from the meat. Blackie simply picked up his gonch hook and flattened the flunky to the ground.

From the stock pens, Mack just happened to witness this by-play, and by the time he got to the camp the flunky had recovered and was hot-footing it to call the Indian police.

Blackie had removed his apron and was rolling his bed when Mack rode up. He grinned somewhat sheepishly.

"Hell, I've had my fill cookin' for a spell," Blackie said. "I hate to quit you in a tight, but I ain't hankerin' to spend time in no Indian calaboose. Maybe you'd better run me in to Globe."

Eve Ball wrote a good book about an early day family in Lincoln County, N.M., the Heiskell Jones family. They had nine sons and one daughter, and I suspect all the boys learned to cook to some degree. In Ms. Ball's book, *Ma'ma Jones of the Pecos*, she writes down Sammie Jones' recipe for sourdough biscuits. Sam was an excellent cook, and Ma'ma said with pride that he could make better sourdough biscuits than she could, and hers were famous. I think Sam's recipe is a classic of cooking by guess and by gosh, and here it is. (Reprinted by permission from *Ma'ma Jones of the Pecos*, by Eve Ball, Tucson; University of Arizona Press, copyright 1969.)

When asked for his recipe, Sam said, "Why, they ain't nothin' to makin' biscuits; anybody can do it. 'Course you got to have some salt yeast. Git yourself 'bout a quart to a half-gallon o' buttermilk, if you got it, and if you ain't, git some sweet milk and let 'er sour. If you ain't got no milk, you can use water by maybe throwin' in a chunk o' tater, or two or three if they're little. It's better to throw in a chunk of sourdough if you got it, pretty good size. Let it work two or three days, however long it takes. Then thin 'er down 'bout like buttermilk. Pour out enough for your biscuits, an' thin 'er down some more. This here's yore starter.

"Git you a cup of that there yeast . . . not too big a cup. Put in some sody or bakin' powder, whichever you got. You don't need to measure no sugar nor bakin' powder . . . jest throw 'er in. The sugar is to kill the taste of the sody if you got too much. But maybe you ain't. Put in a little salt and a little grease. Bacon grease if you got it. Can use taller but it ain't so good. Put in 'nough flour to make a soft dough with blisters in. Git it as soft as you can, an' don't use a spoon; mix it with your hands.

"It cooks better in a Dutch oven, but if you ain't got one you can use a stove oven. Better git you a Dutch oven 'cause it'll lift the lid offen one. But if you got to use a stove, get it plenty hot.

"And shove 'er in."

————

Slim Ellison of Globe, Ariz., was another good cowboy in his younger days, and took to cookin' for cow outfits when he got too stove-up to ride anymore. Slim was a good cook and helped us out on several occasions at shipping time.

After Slim was in his seventies he wrote a fine book that is published by the University of Arizona Press, called *Cowboys Under the Mogollon Rim*. This book sure carries the flavor of rough-country cowboying.

When I was compiling recipes for my book *Chuck Wagon Cookin'*, I wrote to Slim asking for some of his favorite recipes. Here's Slim's letter.

"Howdy you ol' cowgal! I ketched yer little smoke signal asking for some receeps for cowboy cookin'.

"Well, Stel, when I cooked for the cowboys, they was pack-mule spreads, an' anything besides beef, beans, spuds, and dried fruit was as scarce as grass on Broad Street. Sech as flavors an' spices . . . only had cinnamon, vanilla extract, an' sugar. We nearly always had raisins, dried apples, an' prunes.

"Well, furst I'll tell U how I made 'Taller

Puddin'. I prefer gut fat, chop it fine 'bout like beans, mix dough, not too stiff. Put in a lot of raisins an' some salt, an' cinnamon, an' sugar to taste, stir in taller to scatter it around. Dump it in a salt sack in a big pot of boiling water an' boil hell out of it 'til U think the taller an' dough is done. Better cook raisins furst an' use juice a little . . . we called it a Boy In A Bag, an' the damn fools et it an' called it good. Then make a white sauce with cornstarch an' vanilla flavor; sometimes only flavorin' I'd have was lemon extract, an' I'd use that.

"I reckon the only reason they et this stuff was we had no variety of sweets. I used to make a bread puddin' they liked. Take eight to ten sourdough biscuits . . . 2 to 4 days old . . . break up, stir them soft, put in cooked raisins or prunes or cooked dried apples, sweeten heavy . . . can use some condensed milk . . . don't cook too dry . . . just gooey, an' top it off with white sauce. Cook in slow Dutch oven.

"Another puddin' I used to make was one I called 'Coyote-ite'. It was made with white sauce, colored an' flavored with scorched sugar, dumped in fruit cocktail . . . heavily spiced with allspice or cinnamon. This was a floatin' island puddin'. They said it was good . . . but hungry, hard-workin' cowboys liked most anything.

"These modern models don't even like steak for breakfast! An' my style of puddin's they ignore. They want prepared puddin' and corn flakes and fruit juice. Hell, Stel, they won't even eat gravy an' biscuits for breakfast! Trouble with them, they don't get to bulldog enough calves for appetizers.

"I watched a rancher buyin' chuck for the roundup tuther day. He got 5 pounds of weeners, a gut of baloney, some sliced bacon, six big boxes cornflakes, a dozen loaves boughten bread, a ham, six dozen eggs, a bunch of cake mix, a pile of Kool-aid, an' a case of Cokes. Big deal for these modern cowboys! (Signed) *Ol' Heathen Slim*, Glenn R. Ellison.

"Today, folks, we're going to show you how to whip up a real cow-camp stew!"

3 CAMPFIRES AND DUTCH OVENS

Successful Dutch-oven cooking is accomplished by using hot coals and not by an inferno.

When I first started using Dutch ovens in a camp, I burned everything to a crisp. It wasn't much consolation to find most amateur camp cooks have done the same. After ruining countless dollars' worth of grub in the form of charred biscuits, scorched roasts, cremated steaks, incinerated bacon, and petrified eggs with lovely brown ruffles, it finally dawned on me that successful cooking in Dutch ovens is accomplished by using hot coals and not by an inferno.

My first trial-by-fire may have been less traumatic if I'd had a competent teacher, or any teacher at all. Mack, my husband of one month, while riding out of camp with the other cowboys, tossed this remark over his shoulder: "There's plenty of wood and everything you need to cook with. We won't be in 'til dark, so you have all day."

I surveyed the stack of black Dutch ovens, ranging from a tiny 8-incher to a large 16-inch one that would hold enough biscuits for 10 men. There was a once-white enamel bean pot, a 5-gallon can for hot water, and a 2-gallon coffeepot. A stout work table and a well-stocked chuck box, all under a huge canvas fly stretched over the work area, completed my kitchen.

Fine. That "you've got all day" remark lurked in the back of my mind when I

started an overly ambitious project in the form of an apricot pie. It's a durned good thing I had all day because I spent most of it burying my failures and praying Mack's cow dogs wouldn't dig them up. Just in the nick of time, after hours of burning first one thing then another, I turned out a supper of fried potatoes with corn beef and onions (I picked out the burned potatoes) and a Dutch oven of biscuits, with the burned bottoms carefully trimmed off and thrown into the surrounding brush. The coffee turned out fine. I hoped no one noticed how much flour had been used from the 20-pound lard can. The next day I started afresh, having learned by some of my mistakes.

When I first started camp cooking, it was a good thing that I was unaware of how much I didn't know. One great advantage I had was an abundance of fine oak wood, which is surpassed only (this is debatable) by mesquite or hickory.

If there's anything that's almost impossible to do, it's baking a decent biscuit *without* heat-holding, hardwood coals. It seems to be the nature of things that there are more unsuitable kinds of wood available than the correct kind. Poplar, cottonwood, cedar, juniper, pine, spruce, fir, and pinon are fine for "bull" fires, but they do not make practical, long-lasting coals for baking in Dutch ovens.

Yet, one of the finest roundup cooks I ever knew had to do all his camp cooking with cedar wood. He simply explained to me he did the best he could with whatever fuel was available, but admitted he preferred well-seasoned oak.

I've had only one experience in using hickory wood and it made me a lifetime disciple of this wonderful hardwood. Hickory burns down to a bed of hot coals that keeps an even, generous heat for hours. The coals can be deceiving, because when they turn gray and benign-looking they are at their best.

My introduction to hickory came about when I was invited to participate in the Folklife Festival in Washington, D.C., back in 1976. I was to demonstrate Dutch-oven cooking on the National Mall for a week in August. They wanted my old-time chuck wagon, Dutch ovens, and all necessary equipment. Fine, I could do that. But my first concern was proper firewood. I wrote the committee I'd need several cords of hardwood and told them

Stacked Dutch ovens save coals and allow you to cook several different items in a small space.

my preference was mesquite or oak. They wrote back telling me they'd supply all the northern hickory I'd need and assured me hickory was superior to either mesquite or oak. I snorted and slung my head. What did these Potomac couch-potatoes know about proper wood for cow-camp cookin'? Yet, I had to go along with their plans and, after arriving at the Mall and building my first fire in preparation to baking several hundred Dutch-oven biscuits, I became a convert to hickory wood for Dutch-oven cooking.

Don Holm, in his *Old-Fashioned Dutch Oven Cookbook*, lists several hardwoods he claims are suitable for Dutch-oven cooking. Among ones I can vouch for are oak, hickory, maple, and mesquite. But Mister Holm also includes *aspen* and *poplar* as being hardwoods. Even your most citified, backyard chef knows aspen and poplar are closer kin than kissing-cousins to cottonwood. Even when used as fireplace fuel, aspen and poplar fall somewhere between mediocre and downright poor.

Another book lists hardwoods found in the New England states and all the way down to Georgia and Texas. Ones not already mentioned are chestnut, beech, birch, elm, locust, wild cherry, ash, and, here we go again—poplar and willow. Even though I wouldn't recognize most of the woods mentioned if I met them in the middle of the road, I do know I'd not waste my precious time chopping either poplar or willow for Dutch-oven cooking or grilling my favorite steak. Now, I'm not talking about a brisk fire for boiling a pot of coffee or frying a skillet of bacon. You could do that with unaristocratic buffalo chips.

Oscar Blair, cowboss to a big outfit, told me about the time he hired a hobo to cook for one day while they were shipping cattle at the stockpens on the railroad at Geronimo, Arizona. The regular cook had been thrown in the hoosegow the night before, and Oscar found himself between a slick spot and a hard place, so in a rash moment he hired a hobo who was camped in a mesquite thicket nearby.

The hobo assured Oscar he was an old hand at camp cooking, and Oscar left him busily at work and returned to the stockpens some distance away. Late in the afternoon, the train loaded and gone, the crew descended on the camp, hungry as timber wolves, and found the cook had turned

Warm Dutch oven— do not get too hot. Add grease and crowd biscuits in until bottom of oven is covered. A 16-inch Dutch oven will hold 32 to 35 biscuits.

totally black. It was a puzzling transformation, because earlier that morning they'd have sworn the boss hired a white man. And, just as strange, everything else in camp had turned black. The once-white tarp spread over the cooking area was a deep slate-gray and festooned with long black streamers of soot. Oscar saw at once the dumb cook had burned a stack of new railroad ties that oozed creosote by the gallons. The hobo had completely ignored the fine mesquite wood piled nearby for his convenience.

The first cowboy, his throat as raspy as sandpaper, poured himself a cup of coffee and with the first sip he spewed it out with a whoosh, and swore. It was so strongly flavored with creosote it was undrinkable. None of the food was edible and even the biscuits were liberally smudged. The would-be cook was soon hoofing it down the railroad tracks, his bundle slung over his shoulder.

Although all camp cooks agree hardwoods are desirable for Dutch-oven cooking, many differ in their preference to building their fire pits. Almost without

Pre-heat lid so that it is evenly hot, but not red-hot.

exception, the old-time trail-driving cooks dug long, shallow pits for their fires. Many omitted digging *any* kind of trench, but all used a potrack, or crossbar, held between iron rods driven into the ground at each end of the fire. Pothooks hung from the crossbar and from these the cook suspended his Dutch ovens, pots, and pails. Cooking meals this way must have proven a real winner, because more than a hundred years later you'll find modern ranchers using an identical setup.

Camp cooks on roundup in northern states are more often supplied with a boxlike stove especially designed for use in a tent. It has handles on both sides so that it can be picked up and placed where needed. When camp is moved, the stove has its own cart, or trailer, which is towed

Set oven on level bed of coals (live and red). Pile up along sides of oven, then put on hot lid and fill to rim with hot coals.

behind the chuck wagon.

When we first moved to eastern Arizona in 1944, I found the San Carlos Apaches with a style mostly their own. They dug a long trench, sometimes as deep as 2 feet, sloped toward the back so coals could be removed with a long-handled shovel. Across the full length of this pit the Apaches place two galvanized pipes, usually 2 inches in diameter. These are spaced exactly far enough apart to hold their Dutch ovens, coffeepots, and kettles.

When peekin', be careful not to spill ashes on biscuits. Rotate lid.

The Apaches are past masters at using hot coals for cooking in Dutch ovens. Mighty little cooking is done on the fire, but instead shovelfuls of coals are placed off to one side and pots and Dutch ovens are placed on these. When roasting meat or baking bread, they dig a shallow hole slightly larger than the Dutch oven, place hot coals in the hole, place the oven on the coals, cover with lid, and pile more hot coals over all. If the wind is blowing, they tone down the hot coals by adding ashes.

I copy the Apache methods in my camp cooking and have for the last 45 years. I abhor potracks and swinging pothooks. The few times I've used them, I caught my apron on fire and ended up with eyebrows as hairless as marbles and my bangs looking like a Fiji Islander. Which pretty well explains why there are so few women roundup cooks.

Lift entire Dutch oven and rotate by quarter turns to assure even cooking.

I was asked to be a judge at a camp-fire Dutch-oven cookoff a few years ago and I traveled across three states to attend the event. I was surprised at some of the fire pits contestants considered proper for Dutch-oven cooking. Most merely dug shallow trenches—some square, some round, and some long—and threw in their

If biscuits brown faster on top, remove lid, dump coals, put lid back on oven. If biscuits brown too fast on bottom, remove oven from coals; biscuits will finish baking in hot oven.

A 16-inch Dutch oven, used for baking, should be only 4½ inches deep. Ovens 6 or 7 inches deep are called meat ovens, and are best suited for roasts or stews.

wood. Nothing wrong with that as long as it suited their needs. However, one team went to a great deal of trouble to build a real Rube Goldberg contraption. First, they dug a shallow, round pit and encased it with slabs of sandstone rocks standing on end. It was impossible for the cook to scoop shovelfuls of coals from this pit to use in baking with Dutch ovens. He got around this problem by waiting until the fire burned down, then he placed his Dutch ovens directly in the fire pit. Space was limited to two Dutch ovens at one time.

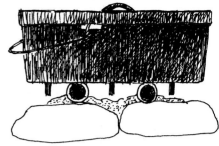

The pipes, usually 2 inches in diameter, should be placed far enough apart (about 4 inches) to hold Dutch ovens, coffeepots, and kettles. Set the pipes on rocks across the length of the fire pit. Cover with dirt to hold the pipes in place.

Ground level.   *Dirt.*   *2 iron pipes.*   *Rocks.*

The fire pit should be sloped toward the back so coals can be removed with a long-handled shovel. I usually make the pit 4 to 5 feet in length and 1½ to 2 feet deep.

← Trench for coals.

As if this fire pit were not problem enough, this monstrosity was surrounded with a cedar-pole "corral," open at two ends. Four cedar posts were set in the ground standing about 3½ feet high. Two more posts ran across the top as crossmembers, sticking out at both ends. Then, four short cedar poles were used as outside braces to the posts. An iron rod was placed across the top with several horseshoes welded to it for hanging pots. The rod was far too high above the coals to cook anything, so the designer hung varied lengths of chains with hooks on the ends. You had to be a professional juggler to remove a Dutch oven from these swinging chains without turning them over.

When running this obstacle course the cooks should have been required to wear shin-guards, crash helmets, face masks, and breast armor. If they failed to keep their eyes peeled at all times, those braces, set at the precise height to catch them exactly below the knees, would send them sprawling. When bending over to check the food, the crossbeams conked them right between the eyes—the sharpened end-poles protruded exactly far enough to stab a hip to the marrow or perforate the stomach, whichever came first. Any unlucky person stumbling into this booby trap after dark could have been maimed for life.

Fortunately, the hardy crew came out

alive, and because they were truly good showmen, wore authentic clothing, had an excellent old-time chuck wagon, and cooked good food in spite of the handicaps, they garnered third prize in their class. I personally loved the zany crew, but I sure kept a wary eye on their fire pit and never ventured too close, and then only during daylight hours.

Lots of people believe the Dutch oven originated in Holland, but after delving into the history of this peculiar pot, we find it originated in England. However, the Hollanders exported so many of the versatile pots to the Americas, it was only natural to call them Dutch ovens. Whatever its name, you can't come within a country mile of telling all its wonderful uses. And, no matter what innovations are tried (even aluminum, for heaven's sake), it's still the best cooking device ever invented, and I'll tell you why.

First of all, it's made of cast iron that is practically indestructible if handled with even a minimum of care. Some ovens have been used continuously for five generations, with possibly a new bail being added once or twice during that time. There are just no other moving parts to wear out or lose. So, an oven purchased by a pioneering family for $3, and used for 75 years, must have been one of the best bargains of all time.

A Dutch oven eliminates the need for a

stove, because it is made for cooking over an open fire or with hot coals. When the electricity fails and there is no natural gas, gasoline, or kerosene, the Dutch oven is brought out and used for frying, searing, and braising everything from fish to fowl to steaks and chops. Pies, cakes, biscuits, buns, puddings, or cookies—all can be baked to golden brown and delectable perfection. And whether it's boiled, stewed, or roasted, any meat is made tender as a grandmother's heart, because Dutch ovens are self-basting. They're perfect for deep-frying doughnuts, spuds, mountain oysters, or chicken. Buried in a pit or bed of hot coals, Dutch-oven meals can be delayed 12 hours or more, or cooked overnight.

The slightly domed lid can be inverted and used as a frying pan for eggs, bacon, or hot cakes, or even for making stove-top toast. The lid can also be heated and used as a warmer to keep food hot. Placing foil-wrapped sweet rolls on a warm lid for 10 to 15 minutes makes them as fresh as just baked.

The Dutch oven can be filled with hot coals with the lid on, and taken to a cold tent to be used as a foot warmer. The oven will remain hot for hours.

A Dutch oven is seldom, if ever, set on direct flames. Instead, it should be hung on hooks suspended from an iron bar, 12 to 18 inches above the flames. Another method involves scooping hot coals from the fire pit, placing them off to one side. Each pile of hot coals creates separate "little stoves," not only for Dutch ovens but for bean pots, coffeepots, and skillets. Slinging pots and ovens on hooks with fire irons was, and still is, a favorite method for roundup cooks—thus the name "pot slingers."

Modern hardware and sporting goods stores offer Dutch ovens for sale in sizes ranging from 8 to 16 inches. The size is designated in raised numerals on top of the oven lid. Eighteen-inch ovens have been made in the past, but in later years, they're hard to find.

I certainly don't want to cook on an 18-incher. As it is, I can barely maneuver a full 16-inch oven without a possible hernia. Slinging Dutch ovens isn't a passive sport, and it makes for Herculean muscles after a few years.

Unfortunately, there are other iron pots on the market called Dutch ovens that are not at all suitable for baking with coals. If the oven is not flat-bottomed with three stubby legs, and if it doesn't have a lid of the same heavy metal with a 2-inch flange for holding coals, it is not a camp oven and is useless for camp cooking. The so-called Dutch ovens sold in many modern houseware departments, without legs and with glass lids, are just peachy for indoor cooking, but there should be a law preventing them from being called Dutch ovens!

With normal care and use, a good Dutch oven lasts for years. You hear old wives' tales of "never, never, wash a Dutch oven in soap; instead wipe clean with a cloth." After baking a super-sticky cherry cobbler, you're not going to be able to wipe it clean, nor are you going to get out of using a soft scouring pad. Filling the oven with water and bringing to a boil for a few moments helps loosen food stuck to the pot. I feed and care for my Dutch ovens exactly like I do cast-iron skillets used in my kitchen. When storing Dutch ovens for any length of time, I make sure they are bone dry, greased with oil, and stored where they'll not get wet.

A Dutch oven can be damaged by pouring cold water into it while it's hot, or by careless packing while traveling. Legs can be broken, chunks of flange on the lid can get broken, or it can be ruined by rust or corrosion.

You can't cook with Dutch ovens without a pothook. The pothook, or goncho, as it is called in the Southwest, is the camp cook's badge of office. He couldn't cook a meal without one, no more than you could guide a wagon without a tongue. I've seen gonchos made of almost every conceivable material. In a pinch, a green oak limb, cut with a stub of a fork at the bottom, works fine until a good metal one can be found. Gonchos made from twisted telephone wire or barbed wire with the prongs removed, are not very desirable, but are better than nothing. The best ones are made from strap iron, steel rods, or even tying steel.

Regular fireplace pokers aren't made for slinging Dutch ovens. And kitchen tongs, pliers, or coat hangers are worthless when used as a goncho. A good camp cook has several gonchos hanging in convenient places around his cooking area, and woe betide any dummy who snitches a cook's goncho or moves one from its accustomed place.

Goncho, gonch hooks, or pothooks.

Tying steel *Twisted wire*

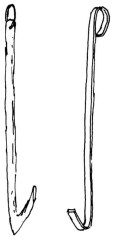

Green oak *Strap iron*

4 DAY'S A-BREAKIN'

Breakfast is the most important meal of the day—particularly for a working cowboy.

Biscuits An' Gravy

A typical breakfast on any roundup, be it a hundred years ago or today, would include biscuits—sourdough or baking powder—fried steaks, and canned milk gravy. Although the chuck wagons might have been very shy on eggs, they nearly always had canned milk. Hard-working cowhands dearly love to sop their biscuits in good milk gravy.

Don't be surprised when traveling in Texas and other parts of the South to see restaurants named simply "Biscuits an' Gravy." Besides the usual ham and eggs, the specialty is, like the name says, biscuits an' gravy.

The cowboy or mountain man may have originated our modern prepared biscuit mixes. Most of the time when traveling light, he prepared his flour, baking powder (or in the early days, saleratus), and salt in a sack before leaving home. When he camped, all he had to do was add water and shortening, and then bake. When canned milk became available, he used that instead of water, resulting in a much lighter and tastier bread. The shortening was either bacon drippings or lard.

Almost all the old-time cooks I ever knew mixed their biscuit dough in a dishpan of flour. Making a well in the middle of the flour, they poured in starter (if making sourdough bread), additional water, sugar, and salt, and began mixing by turning in small handfuls of flour as they spun the pan around. They wouldn't have known how to get a good "scald" on their bread mixing it any other way.

Other bread makers would mix their dough right in the top of the flour sack, by first rolling the sack down to flour level, making a shallow well, and pouring in the liquid. They would then pinch off biscuits and crowd them into a Dutch oven. No mixing bowl, no breadboard, no rolling pin. It looks easy, but it sure isn't.

Ever wonder just how these cooks knew how many biscuits would result from such a haphazard method? They knew that the number of biscuits in a batch was determined by the amount of water or milk used. So much water or milk takes up just so much flour. So when you're using flour that is not pre-mixed, the proportions to follow for each cup of water are approximately 1/4 cup shortening, 1 teaspoon salt, and 1 tablespoon baking powder.

Mack, when he was manager of the tribal herd for the Apaches, once hired a cook who was most untalented in bread making. He was known as Pie, and after sampling his poor excuse for biscuits, I shudder to think how he received his nickname. Anyhow, that year while the crew was camped at Maggie Jones Corral, the

Salt Pork Gravy

1/2 to 3/4 pound salt pork	1/2 pint milk (canned or fresh)
2 tablespoons flour	dash of MSG (optional)

PARBOIL slices of salt pork for 10 minutes. This can be done the night before, or you can soak the salt pork overnight to remove some of the salty taste, but do not omit parboiling. Drain well, then cut pork into bite-sized pieces and fry. Remove pork, set aside. Add flour to fat and brown slightly. Slowly add milk and stir until thickened. Season to taste with MSG. Be sure not to add salt until sampling. Add the fried pork and serve over hot biscuits.

Jerky Gravy

1 quart jerky	2 or 3 tablespoons flour
2 or 3 tablespoons bacon drippings or lard	milk

TAKE a quart of jerky and pound each piece into flakes and powder. An anvil or old-time sad iron makes a good pounding base. Use a heavy wooden mallet or hammer. Remove any dry fiber or rancid fat. Put pounded meat in hot Dutch oven with the bacon drippings or lard. When mixed well, stir in flour and let brown. Pour in milk slowly, stirring constantly so there will be no lumps, until desired consistency is achieved. This gravy will probably not need seasoning as jerky will have retained its salt and pepper. Serve on hot Dutch oven biscuits, or on plain boiled potatoes with jackets. Jerky gravy is also good on boiled rice, macaroni, or mashed potatoes.

weather turned foul and it rained for 5 straight days. The cook, working under adverse conditions, began turning out bread even worse than usual.

As was the custom when cooks baked inedible biscuits, the cowboys were wont to simply break off the crusty top and bottom and toss the rest of the doughy mass to the coyotes. However, Pie now turned out biscuits so heavy the cowboys threw the entire missile into the brush when the cook wasn't looking.

Mack told me later that even after 5 days of rain, the rain failed to disintegrate any of Pie's biscuits.

There is a secret to making light biscuits and that's to simply make your dough just soft enough to handle, pour out on a well-floured board, and pat to the thickness desired. Do not knead: Handle as little as possible. This is something Pie never learned. I watched him on one occasion (while I bit my tongue) knead his biscuit dough for 20 minutes, all the while adding more and more flour until he had a mass as tough as a Navajo saddle blanket. The results were leaden missiles he could have patented for ballast.

Some cooks are always asking just how much flour and milk is needed to make good gravy, because it's almost impossible to find a recipe giving amounts. Here's a good rule of thumb: 2 level tablespoons of fat and 2 level tablespoons of flour will thicken half a pint of liquid. Seasonings vary, with some cooks adding a smidgen of garlic or onion flakes. Drippings from ham, pork or lamb chops, chicken, spare ribs, sausage, bacon, or hamburger all make the foundation for a good gravy.

Milk Gravy

Drippings from fried ham, pork or lamb chops, sausage, bacon, and hamburger all make the foundation for a good gravy. I prefer using canned milk.

2 tablespoons drippings	1 cup milk (approximately)
2 tablespoons flour	salt and pepper to taste

PUT drippings in a saucepan over medium heat. Stirring constantly, add flour to fat and brown slightly. Continue stirring, to prevent scorching, while slowing adding enough milk to thin mixture to a desired gravy consistency. Season to taste.

Eggs

There are all kinds of legends about eggs. The Chinese believed the Supreme Being dropped an egg from the sky and man hatched from it. The early Phoenicians spread the rumor that an egg split in half, forming heaven and earth. The Egyptians had several legends involving an egg in the earth's formation. Even American Indians held the belief of the Great Spirit having hatched from an egg.

I once asked an Apache friend of mine if he'd ever been told of the earth being formed from an egg.

"Naw," he answered slowly, his kind old eyes twinkling, "I don't tink so. Apaches like eggs and I tink they'd eat da egg before it hatched an 'ert." Then he roared with laughter.

The old Indian had a point. At any rate, he was right about the Apaches liking eggs. Mack used to buy them by the case—30 dozen at a whack—for the roundups on the San Carlos Reservation.

One year on our way to market with a herd of 1,500 head of cattle, we camped

29

Eggs Northern Ranch Style

1	corn tortilla	1	tomato from a solid-pack can
2	eggs	1	4-ounce can green chilies
2	tablespoons lard		pinch sage
	salt to taste		pinch coriander
1	medium onion, chopped		

LAY the tortilla on a breakfast plate and place it in an oven at about 200 degrees.

Fry the eggs in the hot lard, salt to taste. Carefully remove them with a slotted pancake turner, place on the tortilla and return plate to oven. Fry the onion until clear, add the tomato and mash with a wooden spoon. Add the green chilies and seasonings. Stir until mixture thickens a little; pour over the eggs and serve. Makes 1 serving.

To test eggs for freshness: Place egg in a deep bowl of cold water. A fresh egg will sink to the bottom.

for the night at a very unpopular place called Beef Corral Draw. Our camp was pitched below the tank dike and was surrounded by large, old willow trees. It was late by the time the cowboys had their tents up and their beds rolled out. However, this night they might just as well as stayed up. Soon after dark, the owls started in. The extremely superstitious Apache can't stand the hoot of an owl. The cowboys milled around in their tents most of the night, flashlights blinked off and on, and there was a great deal of muttering. Some even got up and sat around the smoldering fire.

The next morning at breakfast the cook's flunky informed Mack we were out of eggs. Mack's big strawboss, Marco Davis, was about as superstitious as any Apache, but hotly denied it, claiming he'd

been around the whites so long he no longer thought like an Apache. We knew better, but that morning he was standing by the fire with shoulders humped from the chill, eyes bloodshot from lack of sleep, and he asked in mock seriousness, "And what's wrong with using some of them owl eggs?" Now that it was daylight the rest of the Apaches thought this query hilarious.

There was one time when the Apaches got their fill of eggs. It happened on a fall roundup when Mack hired a cook who wasn't too energetic, or he was simply uninspired; the lunch he'd make for the cowboys consisted of meat and lots of boiled eggs. This meal was delivered to the branding grounds on a snow-white pack mule, called Rosie O'Grady, led by the flunky. Well, after several weeks of boiled eggs for lunch, the cowboys' enthusiasm for eggs palled somewhat. When they'd sight the flunky leading Rosie, they'd growl, "Here comes Eggs." Soon the little mule's name was changed, and when she died many years later she was still known as Eggs.

Our good Mexican neighbors call poultry *aves de corral*, meaning fenced or yard birds. *Pollo* (pronounced poy'o) plays a big part in the life of Spanish-speaking Americans in the Southwest, and any household with any backyard at all manages to raise a number of broilers each spring. They raise enough laying hens to produce eggs for the family, and to enable the housewife to sell a few to less-fortunate neighbors.

Border Style Ranch Eggs

3	tablespoons cooking oil	1	clove garlic, crushed or minced
1	corn tortilla	1/2	cup tomato sauce
2	eggs	1	tablespoon tomato paste
2	tablespoons coarse-ground red chili	1	teaspoon oregano

HEAT the oil in a skillet; spread the tortilla in the hot oil and leave it there until it blisters. Lift the tortilla with a slotted pancake turner and let the oil drain back into the skillet. Slide the tortilla onto a plate and place in a 200 degree oven.

Fry the eggs on one side, and carefully place them on the tortilla. The eggs should be underdone as they will continue to cook in the warming oven while the sauce is made.

Put the red chili and garlic in the hot oil, and as soon as the garlic starts to brown, add the tomato sauce. Stir, as the sauce heats up, and then slowly add the tomato paste and oregano. Simmer sauce a few minutes, pour over the eggs, and serve. Makes 1 serving.

The best-known Mexican or southwestern egg dish is the breakfast plate called *huevos rancheros*, rancher's eggs. They are cooked differently in the North than in the South.

The southwesterner likes omelets warm with chilies, red or green, fresh or canned. Variations call for cheese, any kind, shredded and sprinkled over the omelet before folding. Crumbled crisp bacon, diced tomato, minced onion, and green pepper, lightly browned and sprinkled over the omelet before folding, is sometimes called Spanish or Denver omelet.

Breakfast Meats

Contrary to most accounts, bacon wasn't always one of the staples among the contents of old-time chuck boxes. Salt pork, yes. No self-respecting cook would be caught without his salt pork to flavor his beans. Salt pork was used as a seasoning in other foods as well; often thin strips would be added to a Dutch oven of fried spuds and onions. Small pieces of salt pork, fried and added to a pot of macaroni and tomatoes nearly always improved the flavor. Thick slabs of salt pork, parboiled and fried for breakfast, was the usual when beef was low. But day in and day out, breakfast meant round steaks, pounded, floured, and fried in a Dutch oven. When it was served with biscuits and gravy, the cowboys were satisfied— and no one dreamed of having eggs. Eggs weren't even plentiful at the home ranch, as it would have taken a large flock of good layers to have kept a bunch of cowboys' bellies full.

Outfits raising and butchering their own hogs would have a ready supply of home-cured bacon and hams for breakfast on roundups, but those outfits having to buy costly bacon at the mercantile in town simply did without.

Mack, a regular hand on the Hashknife from 1922 until the mid-1930s, says he never saw bacon fried for breakfast on the roundups. Once in a while they'd have fried salt pork and cornmeal mush, but the usual breakfast for all the years he rode for this outfit was fried steaks, biscuits, and gravy. If the cook was out of canned milk, he'd make water gravy. Sometimes the cook made hot cakes and served them

with the steaks instead of biscuits. Fried potatoes and canned cream corn were served on occasion.

Mack says it was a different story when he rode for the old J F outfit in the Superstition Mountains in southern Arizona. This outfit raised their own hogs and, in the fall before roundup started, they'd have a hog butcherin'. At least 30 hogs were hung up, and the bacon and hams were cured and smoked. Naturally, the J F cowboys feasted on bacon and ham for breakfast. In fact, so much so, some simply got "burned out" on ham and swore it made them break out in painful boils.

The boss tried to vary the cowboys' diet with beef, but when it gets hot (and in that part of southern Arizona it gets HOT) the cook depended on his cured ham and salt pork for meat. When they did butcher a beef in the summer time, it was a great rush to get it cut in strips, salted, and hung on the jerky lines.

Oven Omelet

6 slices lean bacon, cut into 1-inch pieces	salt to taste
¼ cup minced onion	pinch of mace
8 eggs	2 tablespoons minced parsley
½ cup cream	1 cup grated sharp cheese
	diced green chilies (to taste)

FRY bacon in iron skillet until just crisp. Remove and drain well. Reserve 1 tablespoon of drippings. Add onions and cook until clear or transparent. Keep warm. Beat eggs, cream, salt, and mace with fork, just to blend. Fold in parsley, cheese, and chilies. Pour mixture into warm skillet over bacon. Bake 15 minutes in oven preheated to 350 degrees. Cut into pie wedges and serve. Serves 5 or 6.

Rancher's Omelet

6 slices bacon, diced	pepper to taste
2 tablespoons finely chopped onion	dash of tabasco
1 cup grated potato	2 tablespoons minced parsley
6 large eggs, slightly beaten	(optional)
½ teaspoon salt	

FRY bacon until crisp. Remove from pan and drain. Leave at least 2 tablespoons of bacon grease. Add onion and saute over low heat until soft. Add grated potatoes and cook until light brown. Mix together eggs, salt, pepper, and tabasco; pour into pan. As omelet cooks, lift up edges with spatula to let egg mixture slide under. When firm, sprinkle omelet with crumbled crisp bacon and parsley. Fold over and serve. Serves 6.

Snow, for unknown reasons, has the same effect on pancake batter as eggs. Two tablespoons of snow equal 1 egg.

Mack said on the J F outfit, they did all the hog butchering at the Reavis Ranch, which was in the pine country on top of the Superstition Mountains. Here, they had scalding vats, scraping platforms, and long work tables, and they went about their yearly butchering in a professional manner. Any cowboy not needed elsewhere was drafted in this hated work. Generally, the boss hired extra help to cure and smoke the bacon and hams. Several women rendered hundreds of gallons of lard, ground sausage, made headcheese, scrapple, and pickled pigs feet. All of this bounty was hung in the smokehouse that stayed wonderfully cool all summer long.

One year, the women rendering lard had a grease fire, and burned the historic old log house to the ground. Mack said his brother Jim, working on a fence crew not far away, had left a brand-new 30-30 rifle on the porch of the house. One of the women grabbed it and began firing as a signal for help. Then, to Jim's disgust, she dropped the rifle on the spot and it burned with the house. Jim took a very dim view of any woman with a new rifle in her hands who wouldn't think to save it.

The cracklin's made from lard were used in a dozen ways by the cook in seasonings. He'd add them to a pot of beans and his cracklin' cornbread was something to write home about. The boss had cans of cracked corn cooked with a generous amount of cracklin's added to make dog food for the dozen hounds kept to hunt mountain lions that preyed on the ranch's prime beef. Some of the cowboys liked to take the crisp cracklin's, salt them, and eat them as snacks.

Corned Beef Hash

1	can corned beef	2	large white onions, chopped
2	large boiled potatoes, peeled and not too soft	3	tablespoons oil or lard
		7	fresh eggs

CHOP the corned beef and potatoes into pieces. In an iron skillet, fry onions in oil or lard until tender. Add the meat and potatoes, stirring hard. Press everything down into the cooking oil with a spatula, and wait a couple of minutes.

When the edge of the bottom is browned, add an egg and again stir hard; press down, and wait until the bottom is again browned. Repeat with the second and third egg.

Now make 4 nests in the top of the hash and carefully break an egg into each. Place 4 inches under the broiler and allow the eggs to cook until done. Serves 4.

Pancakes

What are flapjacks? A simple answer would be, "A thin batter made of flour and fried in the form of little, round, thin cakes on a hot griddle and served with butter and syrup."

On the face of it, that would seem to cover the subject. Well, it doesn't come within a country mile of telling even a fraction of the pancake story. Why, just consider the few regional names for the little flat cakes: hot cakes, pancakes, flapjacks, griddle cakes, and flannel cakes, not to mention the fancy name of crepes.

Cornmeal Mush and Fried Mush

3	cups hot water	1	teaspoon salt
1	cup cornmeal	2	tablespoons butter

FILL bottom of double boiler with water and bring to boil. Then put 3 cups of water in top of double boiler and bring to boil over direct heat. Add cornmeal gradually, then salt. Place over the bottom of double boiler. Cook gently until thickened, stirring frequently, for 20 minutes. Stir in butter. Serve hot with cream and brown sugar for breakfast.

Fried mush:

Spread the hot cereal on a buttered platter and chill. When cold, cut into squares and fry quickly until brown on both sides. Serve fried mush with maple syrup or spread with honey or jam. Serves 4.

Then you'll find batter cakes, breakfast cakes, slappers, gems, and drops. Mountain men called them "splatter dabs," while cowboys called large, tough pancakes "saddle blankets." Loggers liked to call them simply "flats." Trappers were wont to call wheat pancakes "gordos."

Pancakes can be made from a dozen kinds of flour or you can use rice, oatmeal, potatoes, grits, or bread crumbs. They can be made with baking powder, soda, cream of tartar, sourdough, sour milk, buttermilk, yeast, eggs, or snow.

Snow? That caught my attention, too, the first time I saw the recipe. Instead of eggs in your recipe, use 4 tablespoons of fresh snow. Snow, for unknown reasons (to me, at least), has the same effect on batter as eggs have—2 tablespoons of snow equaling one egg. The batter is made rather thick, and the snow is mixed with the batter just before pouring on the hot griddle.

Ol' long, tall Frank Banks started out as a cowhand at the C O Bar in northern Arizona when he was a smooth-faced 15-year-old back in 1925. The owners knew the makin's of a good cowboss when they saw one, and in a few years Frank did become wagon boss, eventually staying for over 30 years.

Frank is a storehouse of good yarns and I like the one he tells about a lazy cook. Frank tells it a lot better than me, so I'll turn him loose on it.

"The C O Bar manager didn't have a lot of talent in pickin' roundup cooks," Frank laughs. "One spring we had three cooks sling the pots, and each one was a little worse than the last. The boss would no sooner send one cook out when I'd have to fire him and for a while they were coming and going so fast we barely had enough time to learn their first names.

"But this one I'm telling about was the worst of the lot. The boss dumped this yahoo out at our camp, and I couldn't believe my eyes. He didn't look like any cook I'd ever seen on the range. For one thing, he wore a derby hat and a black serge suit. The pants were so short they rode 6 inches above the tops of his low-cut oxfords, and he was pink and plump and well fed, and he sure looked like a city dude to me.

"Well, it was just before noon when the boss and this new cook arrived. The boss told me the man said he was a chef, and a good one. I should have known then we were in deep trouble.

"An hour later, with no signs of dinner cooking, I quit the herd and rode to camp to see what was going on. I looked all over and couldn't even *see* the cook. The fire had gone plumb out, and not a thing was cooking. Even the coals under the coffeepot were cold.

If buttermilk is not available, it can be substituted with a mixture of: 1 teaspoon sugar, ½ teaspoon salt, and 3 tablespoons vinegar to 1 cup of milk. Canned milk works best. Blend well.

Crummy Pancakes

Grate or roll dry bread crumbs. Any kind will do, but do not use leftover baking powder biscuits.

2 cups fine bread crumbs	2 eggs, beaten
2 teaspoons baking powder	1 tablespoon honey or molasses
salt to taste	2 tablespoons butter, melted
1 cup milk	

COMBINE bread crumbs, baking powder, and salt; add milk and let soak about 5 minutes; then whip with an egg beater. Add eggs, sweetener, butter, and whip some more. If too thin, add a few more bread crumbs. Coat medium-hot griddle with grease, fry until bubbles surface, turn and fry until golden brown. Makes about 2 dozen pancakes.

Buttermilk Pancakes

3 eggs, beaten	1½ teaspoons baking soda
3 cups buttermilk	1½ teaspoons baking powder
¼ cup butter, melted	½ teaspoon salt
1½ cups flour	

MIX together eggs, buttermilk, and melted butter. Then add dry ingredients and beat until smooth. Coat medium-hot griddle with grease, fry until bubbles surface, turn and fry until golden brown. Make them small. Serves 5 or 6 people.

Dick Spencer
Colorado Springs, Colo.

Cowboy Hot Cakes

2½ cups flour	2 eggs, beaten
1 tablespoon baking powder	4 tablespoons oil or shortening,
1 teaspoon salt	melted
¼ cup sugar	1½ cups milk (approximately)

MIX ingredients in order given. Add enough milk to make a fairly thin batter that pours with ease. Coat medium-hot griddle with grease, fry until bubbles surface, turn and fry until golden brown. Makes about 2 dozen hot cakes.

"Finally, I sighted our chef sitting under some trees. I trotted down there and asked him real polite when we could expect dinner. I told him I had a bunch of men that had been working since daylight, and they were getting lean and hungry. This yahoo stood up and puffed out his pudgy cheeks and stretched.

"He said he was sorry, but he hadn't understood he was to prepare *lunch* and that he'd planned to have *dinner* about dark that evening. I told him he'd better plan on having an early supper as the boys were in the habit of going to bed by dark. The man seemed amiable enough, and sauntered towards the chuck wagon, saying he'd see what he could do. I hurried back to the herd because we still had a slew of calves to brand.

"It was close to sundown when we finished, and I saw at a glance that supper was far from being ready. The cook was sitting on a water keg peeling spuds, then tossing them into a pot full of cold water. He had built a fire but nothing was cooking. The first thing he asked me was where we kept the bread. He said he'd not had time to make up bread dough and was hoping we had some on hand.

"Well, I told him he was expected to make biscuits for the crew and usually two 16-inch Dutch ovens-full was about right. He seemed agreeable enough and said he'd see what he could do. Meanwhile, I exchanged looks with the boss and he saw I was upset and getting pretty mad, so he motioned me off to the front of the wagon. 'Good gosh-amighty, Frank,' he says, 'give the man a chance. Don't say anything or he'll quit.'

"I calmed down and assigned one of the boys to put on the coffeepot while I dug out the meat, which had been wrapped in a big tarp and stowed under the wagon. I did ask our new chef what he'd planned for supper, and he said Swiss steaks. Fine and dandy with me, the sooner the better, and I cut off enough round steaks to feed an army.

"Even with us helping it seemed to take half the night to get supper ready. It must have been 9 o'clock before the last cowboy tossed his empty plate into the tub provided for dirty dishes.

"When we were ready to turn in, Chef asked what we'd like for breakfast. We were all speechless for a minute; no

Johnnycake

1½ cups stone-ground white	1 teaspoon sugar (optional)
cornmeal	1½ cups boiling water
salt to taste	2 teaspoons butter, melted

MIX dry ingredients. Add the boiling water while stirring constantly. Be sure water is boiling (just hot water won't do). Stir in melted butter. Let batter stand a few moments, covered. If too thick to drop off of a spoon easily, add a small amount of milk. Batter should be thicker than hot cake batter.

Drop by tablespoonfuls onto hot well-greased griddle. Then turn the heat down and fry cakes for 5 to 7 minutes on each side until golden brown.

roundup cook had ever asked the hands what they wanted to eat. The cowboys ate whatever the cook served and called it good. Anyhow, they now exchanged looks and agreed hot cakes suited them fine and we bedded down for what was left of the night.

"I must have gone right to sleep because I didn't know until the next morning that Chef hadn't washed the dishes, but had just filled the tub with water. I went to rouse the cook; it was already late, and ordinarily breakfast would have been over.

"I found Chef still asleep, and when I yelled 'roll out!' he seemed really surprised and blinked at me like an owl. But he did get up. Meanwhile the boss sliced the bacon and put on the coffee. I told the boss I'd be damned if I was going to make the hot cakes. He kept whisperin' at me to take it easy or the cook would quit and he'd have to go back to town to find another.

"Well, I don't mind telling you I was fit to be tied, but I held my tongue. The sun was high and the men had been standing around for an hour before Chef served his hot cakes. I will say this, they weren't the worst I'd ever eaten and there was more than enough. In fact, he had a big batch left over, and when the boss and I left camp Chef was laying the hot cakes on a flat rock near the stock tank, and the two old wagon mules were gobbling them up.

"Those two old wagon mules were way past their prime, but as they were fat and healthy, we'd neglected retirin' them. They were both pets and terrible camp robbers to boot, but we hated giving them up. A new set of wagon mules, that never cause trouble, are hard to come by. Besides, the owners said it was high time we became mechanized, and the next chuck wagon was going to be a truck. So in order to stay progress, we'd hung on to this old team several years

---

Whole Wheat Pancakes

2	eggs, beaten	1	teaspoon salt
2	cups buttermilk or sour milk	1	teaspoon baking powder
1/3	cup shortening, melted	1	teaspoon baking soda
1	cup white flour	1	tablespoon sugar
3/4	cup whole wheat flour		

BEAT eggs in bowl, stir in milk and shortening. Sift dry ingredients together and mix into liquids; beat until smooth. Coat medium-hot griddle with grease, fry until bubbles surface, turn and fry until golden brown. Makes about 3 dozen pancakes.

---

longer than we should have.

"We came off the morning drive about 11 o'clock. I looked towards camp and the first thing I saw was that one of the mules had died. It looked like to me the old boy had just fallen over, maybe from a heart attack. Not too great of a shock as we figured the mules to be over 30 years old.

"From where we sat on our horses I could see the cook sitting in the shade of the wagon, and I couldn't see smoke from the cooking fire. I started getting hot under the collar, so I let out a loud laugh and called to one of the boys riding up, 'By Gawd, it's a shame those hot cakes were so bad they'd kill a mule.' The boss was tryin' to hush me up, sayin' the cook would quit, but I only yelled louder about what the cook's hot cakes had done to our best mule. About that time I could see Chef on his feet and untyin' his flour sack apron. The boss was whimperin', but I wouldn't shut up. I wanted to be sure Chef was really goin' to quit before I quit my hoorahin'.

"Well, he quit all right, and the boss was forced to take him to town that afternoon. We boys made out okay until he came back the next mornin' with one of the old-timers that had slung the ovens for us before. He was a good cook, but no chef, and we boys were glad of it."

5 DOUGHGODS AND OTHER BREADS

**DOUGHGODS:
A cowboy's name
for biscuits; a
logger's name for
camp bread.**

Indian Fry Bread

One of the best and most eagerly attended events at the Navajo Tribal Fair in Window Rock, Ariz., each September is the hotly contested fried bread contest.

Each Navajo woman entrant is supplied with flour, baking powder, shortening, and salt, along with a frying pan and other utensils. A plentiful supply of cedar wood is cut and ready, and the women build their own fires under small grills similar to ones found in many campgrounds. Then the mixing begins with the kneading and patting of the dough, followed by pinching off small lumps that are flopped from palm to palm until just the right thickness, and fried in an iron skillet.

The contestants are judged not only on the texture and flavor of their finished product, but the size of the fire, whether the shortening is too hot or not hot enough, cleanliness, and skill.

Most of the Indians refer to their camp breads as squaw bread. Outsiders call it Indian fry bread. But no matter what it is called, it's delicious to eat.

One October, while I attended the Arizona State Fair in Phoenix, the Papago Indians had a large concession booth where fry bread was made by the tons, and eager buyers ate it with gusto. Advertising, or hawkers, were not needed, for just one heady whiff of the delicious frying bread brought buyers in droves. The aroma was so potent it overwhelmed even the cow barns that were within rock-throwing distance.

Indians do not have a corner on the market for fried bread. It has always been a fast method of making bread in camp, be it sheepherders, cowboys, mountain men, or just weekend campers. From the time you build your fire and mix your dough, until it comes from the skillet—golden brown and ready for butter and honey—hardly a half-hour has elapsed.

What is Indian fry bread? It's one heck of a big, flat biscuit, fried in hot fat. You can make any size you like, but 9 inches across is about right to handle with a spatula in a 10-inch skillet. Some like to make small triangles of the dough and drop them in deep fat, but the Indians stick to their traditionally round, flat version. The 9-inchers fill the skillet and fit perfectly on a tin plate.

There are as many recipes for fried bread as there are Indian tribes. Basically, however, all-purpose flour, baking powder, milk or water, shortening, and salt are used. Some recipes call for non-fat dry milk and a few call for adding sugar. All dough is patted out thin, but not as thin as a tortilla. A small hole is made in the mid-

---

Indian Fry Bread

2	cups unsifted flour	1	tablespoon shortening
2	rounded teaspoons baking powder	1½	cups canned milk
1	tablespoon sugar		salt to taste (or about 1 teaspoon)

MIX all dry ingredients in bowl. Add shortening and work with hands until crumbly. Add milk and mix. Turn out on floured board and knead lightly. Avoid using too much flour. Pinch off a ball of dough large enough to make a 9-inch cake. Pat out with hands until dough is round and flat, about ¼ inch thick. Poke a hole in the middle, and fry in deep fat that is hot, but not smoking. Turn only once, frying about 1½ minutes on each side. Drain on paper towels.

dle for grease to bubble up, avoiding a doughy center. Some cooks use only an inch of hot fat, and others call for a "deep" fat frying. Some tribes call their bread "Indian popovers," but the recipe has the same ingredients as regular fried bread.

If you like, you can make your fried bread by using your favorite yeast dough, and frying in a heavy skillet or Dutch oven. The bread can be eaten with the meal, or served as a dessert with coffee afterwards. Maple frosting, made with powdered sugar, ensures a winner in any circle.

Ready-mix biscuit flour, such as Bisquick, can be used, but it is not successful unless mixed at least half and half with all-purpose flour. Bisquick alone is too rich, and the fry bread will crumble and fall apart before it can be lifted from the hot fat. Nothing else needs to be changed. Proceed as though making regular biscuits, except knead the dough into flat, round disks with a hole in the center.

Old-Time Navajo Fry Bread

3	cups all-purpose flour	1	tablespoon baking powder
1	teaspoon salt	1¼	cups canned milk (approximately)

COMBINE flour, salt, and baking powder. Add enough milk to make a soft dough. Turn out on floured board and knead. Pinch off a ball of dough big enough to pat out to a 9-inch flat cake. Heat lard or mutton tallow in heavy iron skillet and test temperature by dropping in tiny pieces of dough. If pieces rise to top at once, and begin to brown, the fat is ready. Fry dough until brown, then turn, and brown other side.

Applesauce Nut Bread

2	cups all-purpose flour	1	cup chopped nuts
¾	cup sugar	1	egg, beaten
1	tablespoon baking powder	1	cup thick applesauce
1	teaspoon salt	2	tablespoons shortening, melted
½	teaspoon baking soda		
½	teaspoon cinnamon		

SIFT together dry ingredients; add nuts. Next, mix together egg, applesauce, and shortening. Add dry ingredients. Stir just to blend. Pour into a greased loaf pan. Bake at 350 degrees for 1 hour. Cool on rack.

Mrs. Judd Bishop
Windmill Ranch
Kingman, Arizona

Holiday Eggnog Bread

3	cups sifted flour	1½	cups dairy eggnog
¾	cup sugar	1	egg, beaten
1	tablespoon baking powder	¼	cup butter, melted
1	teaspoon salt	¾	cup chopped walnuts
½	teaspoon nutmeg	¾	cup chopped candied fruit

IN a large bowl, sift together flour, sugar, baking powder, salt, and nutmeg. Combine eggnog, egg, and butter; add to dry ingredients and stir until blended. Stir in nuts and fruit. Turn into buttered 9 by 5 by 2¾-inch loaf pan. Bake at 350 degrees for 1 hour, 10 minutes. Cool.

Indian fry bread.

Blueberry Muffins

¼	cup butter	½	teaspoon salt
½	cup sugar	½	cup milk
1	egg, beaten	1	cup fresh blueberries or ¾
1½	cups flour		cup canned blueberries (well
1	tablespoon baking powder		drained)

CREAM butter and sugar; add egg and beat well. Sift together dry ingredients and add to butter mixture alternately with milk. (Muffins will be tough if the batter is mixed too much now.) Fold in blueberries. Fill well-greased muffin tins about ⅔ full. Bake at 450 degrees for 20 to 25 minutes. Makes 12 muffins.

Mrs. Frances Willis
T Triangle Ranch
Duncan, Arizona

All-Season Bread

Ever wish you had *one* good recipe for nut bread in which you could substitute a different fruit or vegetable? With this recipe for All-Season Bread, the flavors change as the seasons do. Try it with fall apples or sweet potatoes, carrots, or zucchini. Start with the basic recipe and follow specific instructions for each fruit or vegetable.

3 cups all-purpose flour	3 eggs, beaten
2 cups sugar	2 teaspoons vanilla
2 teaspoons baking soda	1 8-ounce can crushed pineapple, drain and reserve juice*
1/2 teaspoon baking powder	
1 teaspoon salt	2 cups prepared fruit or vegetable
1 1/2 teaspoons cinnamon	3/4 cup finely chopped walnuts or pecans
3/4 cup vegetable oil	

* Reserve drained pineapple juice for use in the sweet potato, carrot, and zucchini breads listed below.

Apple: Peel, core, and shred enough apples to make 2 cups total.

Sweet Potato: Peel and shred enough sweet potatoes to make 2 cups total. Stir in 1 tablespoon reserved pineapple juice.

Carrot: Peel and shred enough carrots to make 2 cups total. Stir in 1 tablespoon reserved pineapple juice.

Zucchini: Shred enough zucchini to make 2 cups total. Stir in 1 tablespoon reserved pineapple juice.

MIX oil, eggs, vanilla, crushed pineapple, and prepared fruit in a large bowl. Sift dry ingredients together and blend into fruit mixture; stir in nuts.

Divide batter into two 6-cup Bundt pans and bake about 45 minutes. Or you can divide batter into two 3-pound shortening cans and bake 1 hour, 15 minutes.

"They are not burned. They're Cajun blackened biscuits."

Quick Pumpkin Bread

1 3/4 cups flour	1/2 teaspoon nutmeg
1 1/2 cups sugar	1/2 cup vegetable oil
1/2 teaspoon baking powder	2 eggs, beaten
3/4 teaspoon salt	1 cup canned pumpkin
1/4 teaspoon cinnamon	1/2 cup chopped nuts
1/2 teaspoon cloves	1 cup raisins

MIX all ingredients together and pour into greased and floured loaf pan. Bake at 350 degrees for about 1 hour. Bread is done if a toothpick inserted in the center of the loaf comes out clean. Do not overcook.

Buttermilk Biscuits

Animal fat makes a much softer biscuit than vegetable shortening, and biscuits shortened with clear, strained bacon drippings or rendered pork fat are really out of this world.

2 cups flour	1 teaspoon salt
2 teaspoons baking powder	1 cup buttermilk (approximately)
1/4 teaspoon baking soda	2 tablespoons lard

SIFT dry ingredients together, then cut in lard. Add enough buttermilk to make a soft dough. Roll out to 1/2 inch in thickness; cut out with biscuit cutter. Place in biscuit pan or baking sheet and bake at 350 degrees about 10 minutes, or until desired shade of brown. Makes 16.

Make a milk gravy with 1 cup diced ham, or plain milk gravy, but be sure it is made from bacon drippings. See Milk Gravy recipe.

Cornbread

There's an old saying, "Whatever will satisfy hunger is good food." Now, just think about that for a moment. I'll wager the meal you remember best was very simple fare. Right?

The meal I'll never forget was prepared in camp, years ago, after a day of riding the rugged Salt River Canyon country in Arizona. Spring, that year, had settled in like a nervous bride, and April saw chill winds howling down the canyon. After we spent 10 hours in the saddle, a cold mashed potato sandwich would have tasted like pure ambrosia.

Instead, we warmed up leftover pinto beans, fried a skillet full of potatoes and onions, and made a Dutch oven of cornbread. The steaming bread, browned to a golden hue on top with a crunchy crust on the bottom, made a perfect "pusher" to round up the last tender beans on our plates.

It was like an old Mexican *cocinero* once said, "When I'm hungry, I'm pretty damn

Sourdough Starters

METHOD #1. Take 4 cups water in which potatoes have been boiled. Add 4 cups flour, 2 teaspoons salt, and 2 teaspoons sugar. Mix well and put in crock or enamel bowl, cover. Let stand several days in warm place until fermenting begins.

Method #2. In 2 cups warm water dissolve 1 cake yeast or 1 package of dry yeast. Mix in 2 cups flour. Let stand in covered crock in warm place for 24 hours to ferment.

Method #3. Take 2½ cups flour, 2 teaspoons salt, and 2 teaspoons sugar. Mix together 1 cup milk and 2 teaspoons vegetable oil and bring to boil. Cool to 105-115 degrees, and stir in 1 package dry yeast. Blend in dry ingredients. Cover and let stand 24 hours or until fermented.

The secret to making light biscuits is to handle the dough as little as possible. Do not knead.

good cook. When I'm not hungry, I'm not ver-ee good cook."

Cornmeal is unique to the Americas, and corn should be a symbol of our country. Meal made from ground corn was called Indian meal or Injun corn. Different parts of our country have synonyms for just plain cornbread. There's hoecake, ashcake, johnnycake, corndodger, corn pone, spoonbread, Indian slapjacks, and corn fritters. There are a lot more, such as hush puppies, Hopi *piki,* and the Mexican *masa,* used mostly for making corn tortillas.

New England, the Midwest, the Deep South, the Wild West, and the Southwest all have their regional favorite breads made of cornmeal.

Cowboys traveling light could cook up a batch of corndodgers which, besides being highly nutritious, were a good

Sourdough Biscuits

½	cup starter	1	tablespoon sugar
1	cup milk	1	teaspoon baking powder
2½	cups flour	½	teaspoon baking soda
¾	teaspoon salt		bacon grease

MIX starter, milk, and 1 cup of the flour in a large bowl the night before. Cover and keep in a warm place. Next morning turn sourdough out onto breadboard with 1 cup flour. Combine salt, sugar, baking powder, and baking soda with remaining ½ cup flour; sift over top of dough. With hands, mix dry ingredients into dough, kneading lightly. Roll out 1 inch thick. Cut biscuits with cutter, dip in warm bacon grease, and place close together in pan. Let rise in warm place about ½ hour. Bake at 375 to 400 degrees for 30 minutes.

Baking Powder Biscuits

2	cups flour	1	tablespoon sugar
4	teaspoons baking powder	2	tablespoons shortening (not oil)
1	teaspoon salt	¾	cup to 1 cup milk

SIFT flour, baking powder, salt, and sugar together. Cut in shortening or blend with fingers; pour in milk gradually to make a soft dough. Roll out on floured board to about ¾ inch thick. Do not knead. Cut with a biscuit cutter or juice can and place on a greased baking sheet or pan. Grease should be warm. Bake at 450 degrees for 15 to 18 minutes.

Mexican Cornbread

1	cup yellow cornmeal	1	cup cream-style or whole corn (drained)
1	cup flour		
1	tablespoon baking powder	¼	cup chopped onion
1	teaspoon salt	1	8-ounce can chopped green chilies
1	egg, beaten	2	tablespoons chopped pimiento
1	cup milk	¼	cup butter
		¾	cup shredded Cheddar cheese

COMBINE dry ingredients in bowl. Mix egg, milk, and corn together. Saute onion, chilies, and pimiento in butter until onion is tender. Add milk mixture, onion mixture, and cheese to dry ingredients. Stir until just mixed. Pour into well-buttered 8-inch square pan. Bake at 400 degrees for 35 to 40 minutes or until center springs back from touch. Goes well with *frijoles* (pinto beans).

Southern-Style Buttermilk Cornbread

Below the Mason-Dixon line, it is generally believed that white corn is for folks and yellow corn for critters. I don't care, I like yellow cornmeal for this recipe.

1	cup cornmeal	½	cup milk
½	cup all-purpose flour	1	cup buttermilk
1	tablespoon sugar (optional)	2	eggs, beaten
½	teaspoon salt	2	tablespoons butter, melted
½	teaspoon baking soda		

BLEND all dry ingredients in a bowl. Add milk and eggs; beat well. Add hot butter; mix and pour into well-greased 8-inch square pan. Bake at 450 degrees about 25 minutes.

Cracklin' Cornbread

A substitute for the cracklings is well-chopped suet with molasses or sugar added. Or buttermilk may be used in place of sweet milk, with baking soda replacing the baking powder. Your favorite recipe for cornbread may be used, omitting the shortening and adding cracklings instead.

2	cups cornmeal	2	eggs, beaten
½	cup white flour	2	cups milk
2	teaspoons baking powder	1	cup cracklings, broken into pieces
	salt to taste		

MIX cornmeal, flour, baking powder, and salt together. Mix eggs, milk, and cracklings; add to dry ingredients. Beat well; pour into a well-greased 8-inch square pan or Dutch oven. Bake in 400-degree oven for 35 to 40 minutes or until golden brown top and bottom. Cracklings must be crisp and well rendered, without skins being tough or scorched.

packer. These were also called corn pone or hoecake and were simple to make. Basically, the idea is to mix boiling water with whole ground cornmeal, with salt and bacon grease added. Balls of the stiff batter were baked in Dutch ovens until brown. The results were hard as rocks and a sure tooth-breaker, but they were a high-energy food, and a person could subsist on them, along with beef jerky and coffee, for days on end.

When the corndodgers became too hard to chew, they could be made into mush, and when they finally became too stale to eat, could be fed to the horses.

Cornbread can be whipped up in a jiffy when time is short, but no matter how fast it wasn't swift enough for Uncle Fred Haught of Young, Arizona. Uncle Fred had an odd way of talking, repeating parts of a sentence, which was a form of stuttering. Uncle Fred owned some cattle, hunted predators with his pack of hounds, and was energetic and fast moving. One time in camp he had a good cook hired, but the cook was awfully slow. This particular time the cook was making corn-

Old-Fashioned Potato Bread

2	packages dry yeast	½	cup butter or margarine, softened
2	cups very warm water (105-115 degrees)	7¾	cups unsifted all-purpose flour
¼	cup sugar	2	tablespoons butter, melted, for brushing tops of loaves
1	tablespoon salt		
1	cup mashed potatoes, without butter and seasonings		

IN large bowl, dissolve sugar in warm water. Sprinkle in yeast and salt, and stir until dissolved. Add mashed potatoes, butter, and 3½ cups flour. Beat until smooth (2 minutes). Gradually add 4 cups flour, mixing with hands until smooth and stiff enough to leave bowl. Add remaining ¼ cup of flour, if needed.

Turn out dough onto lightly floured board. Knead until smooth and elastic (10 minutes). Place in large greased bowl; turn over. Cover with towel; let rise in warm place (85 degrees) until double, about 1 hour. Turn out dough on lightly floured board. Divide in half. Roll each half into loaf and place into two greased 9 by 5 by 3-inch loaf pans. Brush surface lightly with melted butter. Let loaves rise one more time in warm place, until tops are rounded, about 1 hour.

Set oven rack at lowest level and preheat to 400 degrees. Bake 30 to 40 minutes, or until deep golden brown and loaves sound hollow when tapped. If crust becomes too brown, cover with brown paper. Turn loaves onto wire racks; brush tops with remaining butter.

bread and had just poured the batter into his Dutch oven and set it on a bed of coals, and only time would have turned it to a golden brown.

Uncle Fred rode into camp, in a great rush as always, lifted the lid on the oven, and saw the bread had barely started to bake. "Too slow, too slow. We'll have mush, we will, we will," and the old man reached over to a kettle of boiling water, poured a dipper full on the baking bread, and stirred the mass vigorously. Almost any other cook in the world would have bowed up and quit the outfit then and there, but this one was used to Uncle Fred, and partook of cornmeal mush along with him.

Honey Wheat Bread

4	to 5 cups white flour	1	8-ounce carton cream-style
2	teaspoons salt		cottage cheese
2	packages dry yeast	2	eggs, beaten
1	cup water	1	cup whole wheat flour
½	cup honey	½	cup rolled oats
¼	cup margarine or butter	1	cup chopped nuts

IN large bowl, combine 2 cups white flour, salt, and yeast; blend well. In medium saucepan, heat water, honey, margarine, and cottage cheese until very warm (120 to 130 degrees, margarine does not need to completely melt). Add warm mixture and eggs to flour mixture. Beat until moistened. Then beat hard about 3 minutes. Stir in whole wheat flour, oats, and nuts, plus enough white flour to form soft dough. On floured surface, knead dough about 10 minutes or until dough is smooth and elastic. Place dough in greased bowl, cover loosely with towel, and let rise in warm place until dough is light and doubled in size, about 1 hour. Then punch down and divide into 2 loaves. Place into 2 greased 8 by 4-inch loaf pans, cover, and let rise in warm place until dough is light and doubled in size. Preheat oven to 375 degrees and bake 35 to 40 minutes. Remove from pans immediately; cool on wire racks. For soft crusts, brush tops of loaves with melted butter.

Sweet Dough

(For cinnamon rolls or coffee cake)

2	packages dry yeast	½	cup sugar
¼	cup lukewarm water	1	teaspoon salt
1	cup milk	2	eggs, beaten
¼	cup shortening	4	or 5 cups all-purpose flour

SOFTEN yeast in lukewarm water. Scald milk; add shortening, sugar, and salt. Cool to lukewarm. Add the softened yeast, eggs, and as much flour as it takes to make dough stiff enough to leave sides of bowl. Knead on floured board using any remaining flour. Place in greased bowl, cover, and let rise until doubled in bulk. Punch down and form into rolls or coffee cake.

Filling:

2	tablespoons margarine or butter, softened	1	teaspoon cinnamon nuts or candied fruit (optional)
¼	cup sugar		

For cinnamon rolls—knead dough and roll out on floured board into a 15 by 12-inch rectangle. To fill, spread margarine over dough, combine sugar and cinnamon, and sprinkle evenly over dough. (Nuts or candied fruit may be added.) Starting with longer side of dough, roll up tightly, and seal edges. Cut into 17 slices. Arrange in greased pan with cut-side down.

For coffee cake—knead dough and roll into a ball; place in a 13 by 9-inch baking pan, and flatten dough to fit shape of pan. To fill, spread margarine over dough, combine sugar and cinnamon, and sprinkle evenly on top.

Place rolls *or* coffee cake in a warm place and let rise until doubled in size. Bake in preheated oven; cinnamon rolls, 350 degrees for 20 to 30 minutes; coffee cake, 375 degrees for 15-20 minutes.

Glaze:

1	cup powdered sugar	2	tablespoons milk

Blend all ingredients until smooth.
When rolls or coffee cake are almost cool, drizzle with glaze.

Large loaf of sourdough bread—often called "Sheepherder's bread."

6 SALADS AND STUFF

The ingredients in these salads should be easy to find.

I no longer subscribe to women's magazines published east of the Mississippi. And, for good reason, as you'll see. The two magazines I do receive are published in our western states and they've been preaching, loud and clear, that the trend seems to be "back to basics meals." This was good news to me—maybe I'd be able to whip up something for supper that didn't first require a trip to the deli, a salad bar, liquor store, fish market, or a health food store.

Magazines published mostly for farm and ranch women seem to practice what they preach, listing wonderful ways of making batter bread, frying chicken, and how to tenderize cheaper cuts of meat. Their pages are filled with no-nonsense old-fashioned recipes for fresh fruit or cream pies, luscious cakes made without benefit of a "ready-mix," sensible stews, soups and gumbos, methods for preserving garden produce, and tried-and-true recipes for wild game the hunter deposits on your doorstep (wanted or not).

I decided to see if the magazines published east of the Big Muddy had caught on yet. I spent a small fortune at the newsstand and left with an armload of glossy magazines, most published in New York City.

The first page of the food section of the May '87 issue of the slickest and thickest of the magazines gave a shopping list for Derby Day Buffet. Part of the list called for Boston lettuce, Belgian endive, chicory, fresh mint, fresh ginger root, fresh cilantro, hoisin sauce, water chestnuts, jicama, kiwi fruit, champagne, ginger ale, orange-flavored liqueur, mozzarella cheese, fresh rhubarb, and frozen blueberries. All of this, mind you, before buying the ham or gallons of bourbon for the juleps.

Almost all the recipes called for some kind of alcoholic beverage. Even the cake was loaded. The recipes that required no whiskey used rum instead. What fun. By the time the crowd would roar, "They're off!" half the spectators would be "out."

I took a hasty inventory of my cupboards and refrigerator to see if, by chance, I had some of the ingredients for even one of the Derby Day dishes. The closest thing I had to orange-flavored liqueur was a can of diet orange pop. The last bottle of champagne seen in my house

---

Taco Salad Deluxe

This recipe is from *How To Feed A Starving Artist Cookbook* and is from Mimi Jungbluth of Ruidoso, New Mexico. Mimi says nothing is really needed with this salad since it provides meat, veggies, and a starch in one dish. However, along with iced tea, the salad is complemented by a light, tart dessert such as lime sherbet or lemon souffle.

1	pound ground round steak	1	medium-size bag of small corn chips, crushed
1/4	teaspoon oregano		
1	15-ounce can kidney beans, drained	1/2	pound sharp Cheddar cheese, shredded
3	medium tomatoes, chopped	1	8-ounce bottle French or Thousand Island dressing
1	medium onion, diced		
1	medium head of lettuce, shredded	1	8-ounce bottle taco sauce

BROWN ground round steak and season with oregano, to taste. Add kidney beans to meat; set aside. Combine tomatoes, onion, and lettuce; set aside. Combine corn chips and cheese; set aside. Combine dressing and taco sauce; set aside. In a large bowl, arrange above ingredients in this order: meat and bean mixture; lettuce, tomato, and onion mixture; and combined dressing and taco sauce. Just before serving, top with shredded cheese and corn chips.

"Dear, I am trying something new for lunch: A salad made of Belgian endive, fresh cilantro, radicchio, carambola, and nasturtium blossoms—and a cup of parsley soup."

Illustration by Sandy Dean

was back in 1963 when my mare had a colt, after producing three fillies in a row. All the shelves in the fridge door did contain bottles, lots of bottles. There was Flu-Vac, Terramycin, Blackleg vaccine, Combiotic, Procaine penicillin, liquid vitamins, tranquilizers, and a bunch of what-zits (bottles minus labels). All medications for horses, cows, hogs, dogs, cats, and poultry, taking up more room than food for humans. I slammed the door and picked up another magazine.

This one had three pages for *Spring Recipes.* The first one called for a cup of marinated cucumber salad. The editors advised, "If you don't have time to stop by the deli, make your own." I skipped on to a special Italian dish. The first ingredients called for extra-virgin olive oil, Italian parsley, fresh rosemary, hoisin sauce, clam juice, and mussels. (It advised to scrub and remove beards. Was this meant for the chef or the mussels?) Well, no matter, for I not only never owned a bottle of extra-virgin olive oil but I wouldn't have recognized a mussel, clean-shaven or otherwise,

Crunchy Chicken-Cabbage Salad

2 or 3 chicken breasts or 1 whole chicken	1 4-ounce package blanched almonds
2 tablespoons sesame seeds	1 small head cabbage, shredded
	2 or 3 green onions, chopped

BOIL chicken until done. Cool, remove meat from bones and shred; set aside. Toast sesame seeds and almonds in oven at 350 degrees until golden brown. Next, stir together the shredded cabbage and onions; mix together with chicken, sesame seeds, and almonds.

Dressing:

4 tablespoons sugar	1 teaspoon pepper
2 teaspoons MSG	2 teaspoons salt
6 tablespoons wine vinegar	small can fried chow mein noodles
1 cup salad oil	

MIX together all ingredients in a jar except the noodles. Shake well and pour over chicken mixture; toss lightly. Just before serving, add noodles.

**Drain salad
ingredients well
so you don't
dilute the
dressing.**

Fresh Spinach and Mushroom Salad

1	pound of fresh spinach	2	tablespoons sesame seeds, toasted
½	pound fresh mushrooms, sliced		
½	medium red onion, sliced	6	slices bacon, cooked crisp

WASH spinach in cold water and drain. Remove stems and heavy veins from spinach. Combine with mushrooms and onion in a large salad bowl. Pour half of dressing over salad and toss. Add more dressing as needed to thoroughly coat spinach without drowning it. Add sesame seeds and toss again. Top with bacon and serve.

Dressing:

1	cup salad oil	½	teaspoon dry mustard
4	tablespoons sour cream	2	tablespoons sugar
5	tablespoons wine vinegar	2	teaspoons minced parsley
½	teaspoon salt	2	garlic cloves, mashed

Blend oil into sour cream. Gradually mix in vinegar. Combine with remaining ingredients in a pint jar. Shake well and refrigerate several hours. Serves 4 to 6.

Indian Spinach Salad

Salad:

	torn spinach	½	cup chopped nuts
1½	cups diced apple (or dried apples)	⅓	cup sunflower seeds
½	cup raisins	3	tablespoons chopped green onions

MIX all ingredients in a salad bowl.

Dressing:

¼	cup white wine vinegar	2	tablespoons apple juice concentrate
¼	cup salad oil		
2	tablespoons chopped chutney	1½	teaspoons curry powder
		1	teaspoon dry mustard

Mix all ingredients in a jar, shake well, and pour on salad.

Monticello Salad Dressing

1	small clove garlic, crushed	⅓	cup olive oil
1	teaspoon salt	⅓	cup vegetable oil
½	teaspoon freshly ground black pepper	⅓	cup tarragon or wine vinegar

PLACE all ingredients in jar, cover tightly, and shake well. Serve with mixed greens.

if I met one in the middle of the road. Nor did I have the faintest idea what hoisin sauce was, although I have since learned it's a sauce used in Chinese cooking. So I picked up another highly-touted women's magazine and it had three gorgeously full-color illustrated pages of *Glorious Salads*. It first advised, wisely, a "trip to the produce section of your favorite supermarket." Recipe number one was called savory and radicchio chicken salad. The ingredients list was headed by savory *or* napa cabbage and one head of radicchio. Radicchio was a rank stranger to me but I learned it was a member of the chicory family and that it adds a mild bitterness to salads. That, alone, was enough to prompt me to turn the page, not to mention I'd have to drive over 200 miles to Phoenix to find a produce stand that might have some for sale.

Sour Cream Salad Dressing

½	cup vinegar	½	teaspoon dry mustard
¼	teaspoon salt	2	whole eggs or 3 yolks, lightly beaten
⅛	teaspoon pepper		
1	tablespoon sugar	1	cup sour cream

HEAT vinegar and spices to boiling in top of double boiler. Mix together eggs and sour cream, then add to vinegar mixture. Cook until thick, stirring constantly, but do not overcook as this will cause curdling. This is a very old recipe and especially good for vegetable salads.

Mrs. W. A. Nunn
V7 Ranch
Chino Valley, Arizona

French Dressing #1

½ cup sugar	¼ cup vinegar
2 tablespoons lemon juice	⅓ cup ketchup
½ teaspoon salt	1 small onion, grated
1 teaspoon paprika	½ cup salad oil

IN a bowl mix together sugar, lemon juice, salt, paprika, vinegar, ketchup, and onion. Beat well with egg beater, then beat in salad oil. Keep in a pint jar and shake well before using.

Mrs. Claude Aiken
Bar H Ranch
Chino Valley, Arizona

Using fresh-ground pepper instead of pre-ground pepper gives food better flavor. The same holds true with all herbs and spices.

So on to another glorious salad. This one said to garnish with edible flowers and warned to choose only pesticide-free flowers grown especially for eating. (All the flowers I grow are highly edible—grasshoppers eat them with gusto.) The flower list called for rosemary, chamomile, arugula, orchid, and red and gold nasturtiums. Then came a list of varietal peppers and it said these taste similar to green peppers, but have a subtle sweetness, and advised the shopper to look for purple peppers too. The author says savory is also known as flowering kale, and that it comes mostly in green and has a cabbage-like flavor, but can be found in purple, pink, green, and creamy white varieties. It didn't say leftovers could be used for Easter decorations, but it's an idea. Oak leaf lettuce, it's explained in all seriousness, is named for its oak leaf shape and comes in colors of red *or* green (more ideas for holiday decor).

Next was a recipe for Caribbean shrimp and papaya salad. This recipe was relatively simple if you had fresh papayas, had just returned from the Caribbean Islands

French Dressing #2

1 can tomato soup	dash pepper
1 cup packed light brown sugar	1 teaspoon Worcestershire sauce
¾ cup vinegar	1 cup salad oil
1 teaspoon salt	2 cloves garlic, minced (optional)

PUT all ingredients into quart jar or bottle. Shake thoroughly. Store in refrigerator.

Mrs. Anna Hill
Pump House Ranch
Chino Valley, Arizona

Low-Cal Thousand Island Salad Dressing

As you can see, with this recipe you have plenty of options. You can play around with this low-cal dressing recipe and perhaps mix a winner just to your taste.

1 pint low-calorie mayonnaise	1 tablespoon prepared mustard (optional)
1 can tomato sauce	1 tablespoon finely minced onion (optional)
2 tablespoons fresh lemon juice or vinegar	2 packages artificial sweetener
2 tablespoons pickle relish or chopped pickles (optional)	

MIX mayonnaise, tomato sauce, and lemon juice. Add pickle relish, mustard, and onion. Season to taste with sweetener. Store in refrigerator in covered container.

Dressing For Coleslaw

2 eggs	¼ cup cider vinegar
1½ teaspoons sugar	½ cup heavy cream
2 tablespoons butter, melted	salt and pepper to taste
1 teaspoon dry mustard	

IN the top of double boiler, away from heat, beat eggs and sugar until thick. Then beat in butter, mustard, and vinegar. Place over the hot water in bottom of double boiler and cook, stirring constantly, until very thick. Remove from heat, strain into small bowl. Stir in cream, and add salt and pepper to taste. While still hot, pour over shredded cabbage, toss, and chill several hours before serving. Makes about 1 cup.

Autumn Slaw

1	medium-sized head cabbage	3	cups sliced celery
1	teaspoon salt	½	cup sliced green onions
1¼	cup sugar	1	large red or green pepper, sliced
1¼	cup water	1	teaspoon celery seed
1	cup vinegar	1	teaspoon mustard seed

SHRED cabbage, sprinkle with salt, and let stand 2 hours in refrigerator. Combine sugar, water, and vinegar in saucepan and boil 2 minutes; cool at room temperature. Pour off any liquid from cabbage and add celery, onions, bell pepper, celery seed, and mustard seed. Add vinegar solution and let chill 24 hours. Will last about a week in refrigerator. About 4 servings.

with lots of fresh shrimp, and had a supply of tangy carambola (star fruit), sweet coconut, and peppery nasturtium blossoms for garnishing. I had to chuckle, visualizing the scenario if I were to serve this salad to my favorite old-time cowboy.

Another recipe was roasted-pepper pepperoni salad. This one was quite simple if you had on hand large green peppers, red *or* purple peppers, yellow *or* orange sweet peppers, garbanzo beans, red wine vinegar, 6 cups of arugula leaves, curly endive, oak leaf lettuce, and a package of sliced pepperoni, along with

Carrot Salad

6	cups sliced carrots	¼	teaspoon prepared mustard
1	can tomato soup	1	teaspoon salt
½	cup salad oil		dash pepper
½	cup white vinegar	3	small onions, sliced
¾	cup sugar	1	green pepper, sliced

COOK carrots until just tender. Do not overcook; set aside. Mix remaining ingredients and bring to a boil. Add to cooked carrots; stir and refrigerate.

Sauerkraut Salad

1	16-ounce can of sauerkraut	1	bell pepper, chopped
3	green onions, chopped	1	small jar pimientos, chopped

WASH sauerkraut in cold water and drain. Add onions, bell pepper, and pimiento; toss lightly.

Dressing:

½	cup salad oil	1	teaspoon salt
½	cup wine vinegar		pepper to taste
2	tablespoons sugar		

Combine ingredients in a jar and shake until well blended. Serve on-the-side with sauerkraut salad. Serves 6 to 8.

Deaf Smith County Corn Salad

Recipe taken from *Tastes & Tales from Texas* by Peg Hein.

¾	cup vinegar	1	cup chopped celery
¾	cup corn oil	¼	cup chopped green onions and tops
¾	cup sugar		
1	teaspoon salt	1	16-ounce can shoepeg corn
¼	teaspoon pepper	1	8-ounce can small peas
1	cup chopped green pepper	1	2-ounce jar pimientos, diced

COMBINE vinegar, oil, sugar, salt, and pepper in a saucepan and bring to a boil. Set aside to cool. Place green pepper, celery, and onions in a large bowl. Drain corn, peas, and pimientos, and combine with vegetables. Pour vinegar and oil mixture over the vegetables and mix; refrigerate for several hours. Serves 8-10.

black Greek olives, and yellow Italian plum tomatoes. Thank goodness it says the arugula flowers are optional. Tried to buy fresh arugula flowers at your corner grocer lately?

All these luscious, exotic salads prompted me to check out the makin's in my crisper (a loose term if I ever heard one when it refers to the lower bins of my 35-year-old gas refrigerator). I found a somewhat road-weary jicama, limp carrots that had begun to grow, a month-old head of cabbage with an outer layer of bone-dry leaves, and a tomato that exploded when I pinched it for freshness.

About the most exotic veggies I can find in the company-owned store in the mining town where I shop are avocados, mushrooms, and jicama (Spanish; *hee-ca-ma.* My Okie accent sounds more like hick-a-ma). Jicama is a big, flattish, light-brown root vegetable from Mexico that grows best in semitropical climates. You peel it (skin is tougher than potatoes), cut it into finger-shaped pieces, and serve raw with a dip, or cut it into pieces to include in a tossed salad. It's very crisp and has a pleasant mild flavor, a little on the sweetish side. I like to use it to add "crunch" to my salads. If I've not been to the market for several weeks, the salad makin's in my crisper need resurrecting and the crunchy jicama does just that.

Three-Bean Salad

2 cups canned green beans	1/2 cup cider vinegar
1 can yellow wax beans	3/4 cup sugar
1 can red kidney beans	1 teaspoon salt
1/2 cup minced onion	pepper to taste
1/2 cup salad oil	

DRAIN beans, add onion. Mix oil, vinegar, sugar, salt, and pepper; add to beans. Let set overnight or at least 6 hours before serving. Serves 5 or 6.

Sweet and Sour Carrots

1 pound carrots, diagonally sliced	1/2 teaspoon salt
1 medium green pepper, chopped	1 8-ounce can pineapple chunks
1/3 cup sugar	2 teaspoons vinegar
1 teaspoon cornstarch	2 teaspoons soy sauce

COOK carrots, covered, in a small amount of salted boiling water, until tender. Add green pepper and cook 3 minutes, drain. Combine sugar, cornstarch, and salt in a medium-sized saucepan. Drain pineapple and reserve juice. Add enough water to reserved pineapple juice to make 1/3 cup, stir into sugar mixture. Next add the vinegar and soy sauce; cook over low heat until bubbly, stirring constantly. Stir in vegetables and pineapple; cook until thoroughly heated. Yields 6 to 8 servings.

German Potato Salad

8 medium potatoes	1 1/2 cups water
3 medium white onions, sliced thin	2 rounded tablespoons flour
salt and pepper	1 teaspoon dry mustard
celery salt	1 rounded tablespoon prepared mustard
8 slices bacon	1/2 cup evaporated milk
2 tablespoons sugar	2 hard-cooked eggs
1 cup cider vinegar	

BOIL potatoes in their jackets until tender. Do not overcook. When done, peel and slice evenly. Arrange potatoes and onions in alternate layers in a bowl while potatoes are still hot. Sprinkle each layer of potatoes with salt, pepper, and celery salt; set aside.

To prepare the dressing; dice bacon and fry crisp in a saucepan. Skim out bacon and drain on paper toweling. To the drippings add sugar, cider vinegar, and all but 1/4 cup of the water; blend. Add the remaining water to flour and stir to paste consistency. Stir in dry and prepared mustard, and evaporated milk. Stir into vinegar mixture and cook over low heat, stirring constantly, until smooth and thickened. While hot, pour over potatoes, moistening thoroughly. Serve warm or cold sprinkled with chopped hard-cooked eggs and crisp bacon. Serves 6 to 8.

Pickled Green Beans

Preserve your bountiful bean harvest using this recipe from H.J. Heinz Company. They're crisply sweet-sour.

2	pounds fresh green or yellow beans	1	tablespoon mustard seed
1¾	cups white vinegar	1	tablespoon whole black pepper
1½	cups water	1	3-inch cinnamon stick
¾	cup sugar	2	cloves garlic, split
4	teaspoons salt	3	medium onions, sliced or chopped
		3	pint jars and lids

WASH, trim, and cut beans into 2-inch diagonal pieces. Cook covered in boiling salted water until tender. Do not overcook. Drain beans.

In a saucepan combine vinegar, water, sugar, and salt. Next add spices and garlic tied in a cheesecloth bag; heat to boiling. Add onions and beans to vinegar solution, bring to boil, simmer 15 minutes. Remove spice bag. Continue simmering while packing one jar at a time. Fill to within ½-inch of top, making sure solution covers beans. Cap at once. Process 5 minutes or longer, depending upon altitude, in boiling water bath. High altitude, over 4,000 feet, should be processed 8 to 10 minutes. Yields 3 pints.

When you finish a jar of pickles, save the juice. Drain a can of beets and dump into the juice. Heat and serve immediately, or let stand in refrigerator overnight. If you are using dill pickle juice, add a little sugar.

Pickled Okra

4	to 4½ pounds small 2½- to 3-inch fresh tender okra pods with tops (do not remove tops or slice okra, leave a little stem for a handle)	7	hot peppers
		7	teaspoons dill seed
		1	quart vinegar
		1	cup water
7	cloves garlic	½	cup pickling salt
		7	pint jars with lids

WASH okra well; drain and set aside. Place 1 clove garlic and 1 hot pepper into each of 7 hot, sterilized pint jars. Pack jars firmly with okra, leaving ½ inch headspace; add 1 teaspoon dill seed to each. Combine vinegar, water, and salt in large saucepan; bring to boil and pour over okra. Screw metal bands on tightly; process 10 minutes or longer, depending upon altitude, in a boiling water bath. Let okra stand at least 5 weeks before opening. Makes 7 pints.

Pickled Eggs

12	hard-cooked eggs, shelled	2	tablespoons sugar
1	can pickled beets (tiny whole beets serve best)	½	teaspoon salt
		1	clove garlic, minced
1	cup tarragon vinegar	2	bay leaves
1	cup water	2	large onions, sliced

PUT eggs in a large jar or bowl. Combine vinegar, water, sugar, salt, garlic, and bay leaves in saucepan and simmer for 20 to 30 minutes. Cool, pour over eggs, add pickled beets and sliced onion. Cover and refrigerate at least overnight. Try to use soon, eggs have a tendency to become rubbery if left in the vinegar solution too long. Goes good with beer.

I wonder how many American house-wives, still in possession of all their marbles, dashed out to the supermarket and purchased even part of these exotic fixin's to serve to their hard-working husband when he bellied up to the table that night? Just how ridiculous can food editors get? How many produce markets in small cities and towns would even have a fraction of the vegetables and fruits called for in the recipes?

Good common sense still tells house-wives that a salad made of ordinary lettuce, found in *all* produce sections of even the most remote country stores, combined with garden-ripe tomatoes, crisp cucumber slices, green onions, and possibly avocado wedges, is still a winner anywhere, whether it's Boston or Battle Mountain, Miami or Missoula.

Coleslaw, to Americans, means a shredded cabbage salad combined with other ingredients—onions, green peppers, celery, whatever—and served with a sweet or sour dressing. There are dozens of coleslaw recipes combining vegetables and fruit. One coleslaw recipe using a can of chunk pineapple, diced tart apples with skins intact, shredded carrots, and a tangy dressing made from fresh lemon juice is a slaw that's hard to beat. Another good slaw uses shredded carrots added to the cabbage with lots of raisins and crushed pineapple (well drained), chopped celery, and served with a vinegar, sugar, and sour cream dressing.

Recently, I attended a luncheon where we were told the chef had been a cook for some of the finest restaurants in San Francisco, and that the most discriminating gourmets considered him the best in the business. A man from Montana sat across from me and asked, "What is a gourmet?"

I told him I'd always thought of a gourmet, or gourmand, as a person who likes and is a judge of fine foods and drinks, or a person who has a great liking for good food. We both agreed the latter takes in just about all of us. I told him I didn't believe a gourmet's food should cost a mint, contain mind-bogglingly strange foods, or require a botanist to determine if the ingredients are edible or not.

My new friend's eyes lit up and he said he guessed he was a true gourmet, because he derned sure liked T-bone steaks, grilled just right, served with a big baked potato slathered with real butter, along with slabs

of hot sourdough bread, and polished off with homemade apple pie topped with a couple giant scoops of vanilla ice cream.

"What about salad?" I asked.

"Not on your life!" he replied. "If I have to eat vegetables, I'll just take corn-on-the-cob and fresh tomatoes."

A few years ago I read where the Army had made a survey of food preferences of its servicemen. Topping the list were steaks, and then came hamburgers and fried chicken. First on the dessert list was apple pie, then cherry, and pumpkin, with lemon meringue placing fourth. Ice cream was a big favorite as was chocolate cake. Vegetables got short shrift, but corn-on-the-cob headed the list. I've forgotten all the results of the survey but none of it came as a surprise. Nor was it strange to me that not one said they preferred their food garnished with flowers.

I wonder who the New York food editors surveyed?

Festive Lime Jello Salad

As long as my children can remember, I made this lime gelatin salad for Christmas, and usually, Thanksgiving dinner. When the children were little, they referred to this salad as "that green stuff."

1 large box lime gelatin	1 cup diced celery
1 pint cottage cheese	1 cup diced nuts (pecans or walnuts)
2 cups crushed pineapple, drain and reserve juice	1 tablespoon lemon juice
	2 or 3 drops green food color

PREPARE gelatin according to directions, using reserved pineapple juice as part of the 2 cups of water. Put in 2-quart dish or 9 by 13-inch cake pan. Mix all other ingredients and add to slightly cooled gelatin. When gelatin has set, you can spread 1 package sour cream over the top. I seldom do this. Gelatin salad, served on lettuce leaf, is delicious as is! Yields 6 to 8 servings.

Cinnamon Jello

1/2 cup cinnamon candies (red-hots)	2 cups cold water
2 cups boiling water	1 can fruit cocktail, drained
1 large package strawberry gelatin	1 cup sour cream

MELT red-hots in 1/2 cup hot water in small pan on low heat. Remove from stove; add remaining water and gelatin. Stir well until gelatin is dissolved; add the cold water and fruit cocktail. In bottom of large dish, distribute sour cream by small teaspoonfuls, then pour gelatin mixture carefully over sour cream. Do not stir. Place in refrigerator until firm.

7 ALL BUT THE HIDE AND HORNS

Beef was one of the main staples in a cowboy's diet.

Meat, Fish, and Fowl

The wagonboss, while on roundup, usually selected beef for camp, often butchering a big calf or short yearling heifer that was a line-back or cut-back. The younger the beef, the better, since grass-fat animals usually aren't as tender as grain-fed ones. Besides, all the meat available was pan-fried by the cook. Grilled steaks weren't even thought of, and any part of the beef that could be sliced was pounded, floured, and fried in a deep Dutch oven. And cooked done! No cowboy wanted his meat oozing red; if served a rare steak, he might remark, "I've seen cows hurt worsen this an' get well!"

J. Frank Dobie in his book, *Cow People,* tells of an early trail driver who, after delivering his herd to a Kansas buyer, treated his young crew of Texans to a sumptuous meal at the swankiest hotel in town.

The youthful trail drivers, spruced up to the nth degree, ill at ease, sat poker-stiff in their chairs, waiting for their boss to order. When the boss told the waiter

Illustration by
Dick Spencer

he'd have quail on toast, every last one of the cowboys said they guessed they'd prefer the same.

Later, back home in the brush country of Texas, one of the cowboys was heard to say, "That quail on toast wern't nothin' but a lil' ol' partridge on a piece of scorched light bread. There wasn't no meat, an' not a thing was fried."

Any cowman who was stingy with his beef might be known as being "a little near." A New Mexico rancher named Bill Smith was called "very near," for he had a way of forgetting to butcher a beef for months on end. He provided nothing but frijoles and cornbread made of water, salt, and meal—no shortening of any kind. This was the fare three times a day. One morning a cowboy seemed to be shredding his throat in a terrible cough.

"What's the matter with you?" asked Mr. Smith.

"Oh, nothin' much," the hand replied. "I've just got the cornbread heaves."

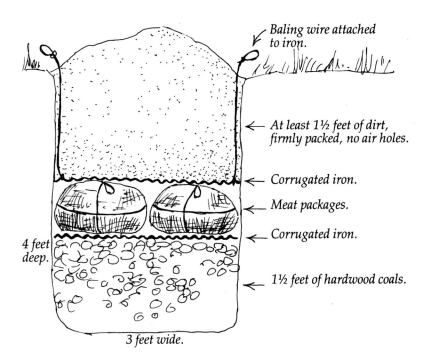

Baling wire attached to iron.

← *At least 1½ feet of dirt, firmly packed, no air holes.*

← *Corrugated iron.*

← *Meat packages.*

← *Corrugated iron.*

4 feet deep.

← *1½ feet of hardwood coals.*

3 feet wide.

Barbecue

Wire loop for easy handling.

Meat is ready for the pit. It has been wrapped in foil, then cheesecloth, then a wet burlap sack, and tied with wire.

A friend once said of me, "The trouble with Stella's recipes is that they all start with, 'First butcher a beef!'" I deny that. However, it's not a bad idea if you're planning an outdoor feast for several hundred people.

Each summer for the past 25 years, my husband Mack and I have helped "put on" the barbecue for the Greenlee County Cattle Growers annual meeting in late August. Three hundred members and their guests attend. Preparing meat for that many requires community effort. Where we live on Eagle Creek (over 40 miles to the nearest town), there is a group of closely knit ranchers who believe in the good-neighbor policy, and all pitch in and help.

We barbecue deep-pit style, so you don't need a lot of expensive equipment or unnecessary gadgets. Nor do you need to spend a lot of money on constructing elaborate outdoor grills or ovens. All you need is space, some shovels, and the manpower to dig a pit. The one we use was dug years ago, in good hard clay. The pit is 4 feet deep, 4 feet wide, and 8 feet long, and has neither rocks nor cement on the bottom. Nothing could be simpler or less costly.

The coals and ashes from the previous year remain in the pit until just before we use it again. If it has been an unusually wet summer, it may be cleaned out a few days earlier and allowed to dry.

Usually it takes close to a cord of dry oak (or mesquite) cut in 4- to 6-foot lengths, with none larger than a man's thigh. The afternoon before, Mack starts the fire in the pit and feeds it continuously for 6 to 8 hours, or until there is a bed of red-hot coals at least 2 feet deep. During this time, ranchers gather to swap lies, discuss the rainfall or cuss the lack of it, swig cold beer kept in coolers, or drink scalding coffee from tin cups. It's a time to catch up on visiting. Soon, fall roundup will start and no one will have time to wile away a lazy afternoon just gossiping.

When barbecuing deep-pit style, it is best to use a hardwood such as oak, mesquite, or hickory. It burns down to a bed of hot coals that keeps an even, generous heat.

While the fire is dying down to glowing coals, the ranch women have been preparing the meat—seasoning the meat.

Deep-Pit Barbecue

This is something you'll want to make for a crowd. Use about 3/4 pound of meat (including bone) per person. Generally, 10- to 12-pound roasts work best. Use as many as needed to make up the total weight.

10- to 12-pound bone-in beef roasts, thawed	Accent (optional) dash liquid smoke (optional)
1 large onion, sliced	aluminum foil
1 clove garlic, sliced	cheesecloth, muslin
salt	toweling, or stockinet
pepper	baling wire
1 bay leaf	gunny sacks

PLACE roast on a sheet of heavy aluminum foil large enough to wrap it in. Sprinkle generously with Accent, salt, pepper, and a dash of liquid smoke. Add onion, garlic, and a bay leaf; wrap tightly. Then wrap in cheesecloth, muslin toweling, or stockinet supplied by your butcher. Next wrap roast in a wet gunny sack. Now wrap each "package" with baling wire (or any stout wire), and form a loop at the top, so you'll have a handle to carry the meat.

The pit should be about 4 feet by 8 feet, and 4 feet deep (depending upon how much meat is to be cooked). Make sure the oak or mesquite firewood is dry, and that the dirt used to cover the meat is also dry. The wood should burn for 6 to 7 hours, or until there are at least 18 inches of bright red coals. Lay corrugated iron strips on top of the coals, and put the meat on immediately. Cover with more layers of corrugated iron strips and cover quickly with dirt (at least 1 1/2 feet). Make sure no steam escapes from any holes.

The meat is done in about 7 1/2 hours. It can be left in overnight and until almost noon the next day—it will be very done, of course—but it's still delicious. Serve with barbecue sauce and beans, cabbage or potato salad. Use one package of meat at a time while the others stay hot and juicy until they are needed.

While the fire is dying down to glowing coals, the ranch women have been preparing the meat: seasoning the roasts with slices of onions, slivers of garlic, salt, pepper, and dashes of liquid smoke. Some years the cattlemen butcher donated beef, and 10- to 15-pound roasts are cut from the front and hindquarters; even the ribs are used, with T-bones reserved for outdoor grilling later. Some years, meat is purchased in rolled, boneless roasts, wrapped in netting. Much time and labor is saved this way and the meat is delicious.

After seasoning, each roast (weighing not over 20 pounds) is wrapped in heavy foil. Then the bundles of foil-wrapped meat are put into wet burlap sacks; each is folded into a tight bundle and tied securely with baling wire, leaving a loop in the center of the bundle for handling.

When the coals are just right (no flames or large burning chunks), sheets of corrugated iron are laid directly on the hot coals, slightly overlapping. We put the bundles of meat in quickly, arranging them a few inches apart or just barely touching. We never pile them on top of each other. Two more sheets of corrugated iron are placed directly on top of the bundles of meat, making sure all are covered. Shovelers begin throwing in the dirt, and we make sure all the air pockets are eliminated. If a wisp of smoke is escaping from one corner, we add more dirt and tamp it down. Usually, 18 inches deep is enough.

Now that the burying is over, we can celebrate, unless it looks like rain; then we can worry. One good precaution is to have trenches dug around the covered pit, and plastic sheets spread all over. A few prayers wouldn't hurt. It would be a catastrophe to have the pit fill with water while the meat is cooking. Locating the pit in a well-drained area in the first place is a must.

The resurrection of the meat does not take place until serving time just before noon the next day.

Eagle Creek has giant sycamores lining its banks, and the cattlemen's barbecue is held in a secluded spot surrounded by these lovely, white-barked shade trees. Long tables made of planks placed on 50-gallon barrels are used for serving. Members of the cattlemen's group bring salads of every description: green tossed, bowls of luscious gelatin and fruit concoctions, and potato and macaroni salads, lavished with slices of boiled eggs and ripe olives. Those women who pride themselves in making desserts bring their prize-winning apple pies, chocolate cakes dripping with coconut icing, rich puddings weighed down with crushed nuts and cherries, and even iced melon salads that are a chore to keep fresh and cold. No matter, once the meat is sliced, the long line of hungry people soon make the lovely array of dainty dishes look like a Texas tornado has struck. After the meal, members hold their business meeting while the kids run amok, and locusts whir away.

William Allen White wrote about the barbecue: "At best it is a fat steer, and it must be eaten within the hour of when it is cooked, its flavor vanishes like Cinderella's silks, and it becomes cold baked beef . . . staler in the chill dawn than illicit love."

Well, Mister White is full of hooey! We freeze leftover barbecue in foil for months at a time, and it makes about the best leftover meat dishes you ever flipped a lip over.

Leftover barbecue, flaked or shredded, can be used in a dozen different ways. The one I like best uses fluffy rice, dotted with butter, lining a baking dish. Filled to the edge of the rice is hot, leftover barbecue, made rich with packaged or canned beef gravy. You can use beef stock and hot tomato sauce or picante sauce, if you prefer.

Barbecued beef, run through a meat grinder and added to a Dutch oven of fried potatoes and onions, sticks to the ribs and makes a good "one shot" pot when cooking in camp.

Stella Hughes shown with chuck-wagon display at Arizona State Fair, 1969.

Stew

Back in the mid-'30s, I was fortunate to know well one of the last old-time range cooks, Clair Haight. His kind eyes, blue as Arizona's summer skies, soft voice seldom raised in anger, patience, and ability to do anything endeared him to all who were fortunate to be his friends. Honest and loyal to the outfit he worked for, Clair personified all a roundup cook should be.

When I first met Clair, he was in his early 60s, and was still hiring out as a roundup cook for the larger outfits out of Winslow, Arizona. He most often worked for the Hashknife outfit, but was known to take on cooking jobs for various other enterprises, such as slinging the pots and pans for a team of photographers filming the Rainbow Bridge area in Utah.

Clair lived at Chevelon Butte, 35 miles south of Winslow. He was a bachelor all his life and kept his little homestead in spic-and-span order. His house was built in the shape of a Navajo hogan with a lean-to kitchen; the arrangement was just large enough to allow his huge wood-burning stove, cupboards on one side, and a narrow alley down the middle. He said he built his kitchen so as to discourage anyone from trying to help him in his cooking chores.

Of all the gourmet dishes Clair was known for cooking in camp, he probably excelled best at making the cowboys' favorite: son-of-a-gun stew. In polite circles, or when women were around, it was referred to as S.O.B. Sometimes it might be called a "Forest Ranger" or "Range Boss," or "County Attorney," or anyone else who might be in disfavor at the time. The possibilities for names were endless. For a time during the period of World War I, it went by the name of "Kaiser." At the height of the Great Depression in the 1930s, it was termed a "Hoover."

One day at the Hashknife wagon, Clair was busily dicing heart, liver, sweetbreads, kidneys, and marrow guts in preparing supper for a dozen cowboys. One of the men rode in early. Viewing Clair's activities, the cowboy beamed and said, "Well, I see we can expect a son-of-a-gun for supper." Clair never batted an eye, and replied, "Yep, I expect about 12 of 'em."

Clair's Son-of-a-Gun Stew

To be made the eve of butchering or the next day.

	lard or bacon drippings	garlic (several cloves), minced
	organs from young beef	water
1	pound butcher steak (neck meat or flank will do)	1 pound diced potatoes (optional)
2	large onions, minced	chili powder (optional)

PUT enough lard or bacon drippings in hot Dutch oven to cover the bottom about ½-inch deep. Cut up all marrow gut from 1 young beef into 1-inch pieces. Put in hot fat and brown all over, stirring frequently. This takes at least ½ hour. Meanwhile, you'll be busy dicing the heart; discard fat and muscle. Dice all the sweetbreads, both kidneys, and about a pound of butcher steak. Now, add all this to the marrow gut. Let cook for another ½ hour, then add about ¼ of the liver, diced into very small pieces. Add the onion and garlic to the mixture. Don't be afraid to use plenty of garlic; after what all has gone in, a little garlic can't hurt. Salt and pepper to taste.

By this time the whole mess might become too brown, or stick, so it's time to add water. Be sure the water is boiling and pour in enough to cover meat. Then cook, and cook, and cook some more. It will take most of a day, simmering slowly. Add more hot water if needed. Stew must be very done or marrow guts will be tough and rubbery.

This stew is very rich and most cooks add a pound or so of diced potatoes about ½ hour before serving. Some south-of-the-border cooks also like to throw in a handful of chili powder.

Prairie Stew

It is not what is in the stew but how it is made. It should be against the law to use canned vegetables.

3	pounds cubed beef	broccoli, chopped
2	medium cans tomatoes	whole corn (mostly for color)
1	large can tomato juice	cabbage, chopped
	celery, chopped	peas
	onions, chopped	butter to taste
	parsley, chopped	Worcestershire sauce to taste
	carrots, chopped	ketchup to taste
	potatoes, chopped	salt and pepper to taste

BRAISE meat until well done. Add tomatoes, tomato juice, celery, and onions. Simmer for 21 minutes. Add remaining vegetables, as desired, starting with those which require the longest cooking time (potatoes and carrots). Stir occasionally as the stew cooks.

Adding butter, Worcestershire sauce, ketchup, plus salt and pepper, to taste, is all the kick it needs. Stew is better overcooked than undercooked. Serves 15.

Tom Hatch

A respite from the usual fare of beef and beans was always welcome.

Turkey

Some 40 years ago, an old cowboy, Pete Cobb, told me about the time he had a little joke on a couple of Apaches. This was during the time the Double Circle Cattle Company had a permit to run thousands of cattle on the San Carlos Reservation in eastern Arizona. The owners often hired a few Apaches to work during the roundups. This particular time there were two old-timers—one the horse wrangler and the other the salt packer.

Pete told me their camp at Dry Lake was one of the most unpopular with the Apaches because numerous owls hooted and carried on there at night. Now, the Apaches are more superstitious of owls than they are of bears and snakes, and that is a lot. Understandably, they were highly upset when, one morning, the cook shot an owl out of a nearby pine tree. The Apaches shook their heads and said the cook hadn't ought to have done that. They predicted only evil would come of the deed, and were glad to ride off with the rest of the crew for the usual day's work.

Later in the morning, the boss drove up from the headquarters ranch on Eagle Creek, and handed the cook a fine young gobbler he'd shot earlier. The cook was delighted and, being talented in this line,

Blackie's Oxtail Stew

4	pounds of oxtails, cut in pieces	¾	cup vinegar
4	cups hot water	⅛	teaspoon allspice
	small amount of chopped onion and garlic	⅛	teaspoon cloves
		¾	cup all-purpose flour
			salt and pepper to taste

SEAR the oxtails with a little grease in Dutch oven. Turn frequently until brown on all sides. Remove from heat and slowly add hot water, vinegar, onions, and other seasonings. Cover and simmer about 2 hours.

Meanwhile, prepare browned flour by heating flour in skillet on medium heat. Stir constantly until the flour is evenly tanned. This will take about 10 minutes. Do not scorch.

After oxtails have cooked for 2 hours, remove the lid and cook for 30 minutes more. Just before serving, scoop about a cup of hot broth into a bowl and make a smooth paste by stirring in the browned flour. Stir this paste into the meat in the Dutch oven and let boil for a minute or so. Sometimes, instead of gravy, Blackie made dumplings.

made a cornbread dressing and roasted the bird in a 16-inch Dutch oven.

When the crew rode in that evening, they were assailed with the heady aroma of roasting turkey. A respite from the usual fare of beef and beans was always welcome, and the cowboys hastened to line up at the pots.

Pete, having a morbid sense of humor, slipped around and whispered to the

French-Canadian All-Meat Stuffing

(for a 15-pound turkey)

1 large loaf white bread, plus 5 or 6 slices.	1 large onion, minced
5 cups water	2 tablespoons salt (less if sausage is salty)
2 pounds lean ground round beef	1 scant tablespoon poultry seasoning
1 pound sausage	3 tablespoons Accent (optional)

TOAST bread in large pan; turn occasionally. Cut into 1/3-inch pieces, set aside.

Mix everything together, except the bread cubes, in a 5- or 6-quart kettle. Cook at medium heat for 25 to 30 minutes. Then turn fire as low as possible, and let simmer as you add bread cubes, stirring constantly until softened. Cool thoroughly; overnight is best. Store in refrigerator until time to stuff turkey. Then roast turkey your favorite way.

It's not generally known that southwestern tribes of American Indians raised turkeys over 1,000 years ago.

Cornbread Dressing for Turkey

(for a 12- to 14-pound turkey)

1 quart diced celery	2 cups bread cubes
1 cup minced onion	2 cups coarsely crumbled cornbread
1 cup butter	
1 tablespoon salt	1/2 teaspoon pepper
2 teaspoons poultry seasoning	1 1/2 cups broth

SAUTE celery and onion in butter over low heat, stirring occasionally, until onion is tender but not browned. Mix together seasonings, bread cubes, and cornbread. Add celery, onion, and butter; toss lightly to blend. Pour broth gradually over bread mixture, tossing lightly. Stuff turkey just before roasting.

Toasted Rice/Oyster Dressing

(for a 12- to 16-pound turkey)

1 1/2 cups uncooked rice	1 1/3 quarts oysters
3 cups water	3 cups fine bread crumbs, toasted
1 1/2 teaspoons salt	
1/2 cup chopped onion	3 teaspoons poultry seasoning
1 cup chopped celery	salt and pepper to taste
3 tablespoons minced parsley	3 eggs, beaten
1/2 cup butter or margarine	

SPREAD rice in shallow baking pan. Roast in a 400-degree oven about 20 minutes until golden brown. Shake pan occasionally so rice browns evenly. Combine rice, water, and salt in a 4-quart pan. Bring to boil; lower heat. Cover and cook slowly, about 14 minutes or until rice is tender.

Saute onion, celery, and parsley in butter until soft. Add oysters and cook until the edges begin to curl. Remove from heat. Stir in bread crumbs, poultry seasoning, salt, pepper, eggs, and rice. Toss lightly with fork until combined. Spread in shallow baking pan and bake at 350 degrees for 20 minutes. Yields about 24 servings.

Apaches that the cook had roasted the owl. Without further ado, and with no explanation to the boss, the Apaches slunk out of camp and rode back to their villages. The boss was highly upset over the turn of events as he was short-handed, and the Indians were sorely needed. Pete never breathed a word of his part in the Apaches' sudden departure.

It's not generally known that southwestern tribes of American Indians raised turkeys over 1,000 years ago. Archaeologists have found, around the living quarters of the great cave dwellers, enough evidence to indicate that poultry raising was a major industry.

The first Spaniards, when they invaded the country, saw the well-tended flocks of the Zuni and were surprised to learn that turkeys provided feathers for beautiful blankets, as well as a delicious alternative to venison.

The big birds were plucked and feathers wrapped on cord warps and wefts, providing blankets that were warm and soft. Blankets made in this manner, of both feathers and rabbit skins, persisted until sheep, introduced by the Spaniards, provided wool for a more serviceable product.

Turkey and all the trimmings for Thanksgiving have become as traditional in southwestern Indian homes as that of the pale-faces. Many of our Apache friends refer to Thanksgiving as "turkey day," and although they do not raise turkeys, when the hunting season opens on wild turkey, they turn out in droves. The San Carlos and Whiteriver reservations in Arizona have some of the largest flocks of this big game bird in the state.

During the 30 years Mack was manager of the tribal herd for the San Carlos Apaches, we often found ourselves shipping cattle during Thanksgiving week. Facilities at the stockpens on the railroad between Safford and Globe were primitive, the only modern convenience being one lonely water hydrant. All cooking was done in Dutch ovens. We slept in tents, and prepared our meals under a brush arbor. The closest towns were 40 miles in either direction.

Not to be cheated of our holiday fare, I would buy a turkey at the trading post, and the night before Thanksgiving stuff it with my favorite dressing, and bury the bird in our barbecue pit. The next day at noon the bird would be resurrected, and we feasted in camp under the makeshift *jacal* to the lovely tune of bawling cattle.

The recipe I use may not be too secret, but it is well over 100 years old. It was one my great-grandmother brought from Canada to Massachusetts. Then my grandmother, Georgina Bouvier, taught my mother how to make it when my mother was a girl living on a homestead in North Dakota. Recently, my granddaughter won first prize in a 4-H cooking contest using the same recipe.

The recipe has no doubt been adapted to modern conveniences, as 100 years ago few homesteaders had a meat-mincer at their disposal, so hamburger is of a more recent vintage. Monsodium glutamate was probably added by my mother, and I suspect celery may often have been unavailable in the winter in Canada and North Dakota.

Chicken

Chicken isn't just for Sunday anymore. There was a time during the Great Depression when chicken was available to us only when we got sick or it did. In slightly better times, chicken was party fare served on special occasions such as when the preacher came to dinner, family reunions, church suppers, or wedding feasts.

Cliff Mason, an old cowboy friend of mine from down in south Texas, told me of the time his family enjoyed fried chicken plumb out of season, and in providing the fare for the table he almost got his head cut off.

"I was just a big, overgrown kid, not yet out of the eighth grade, and in tryin' to help out on our starvation spread my folks owned, I'd taken on some young horses to break for a neighboring outfit. I got five dollars a head," Cliff said in a slow Texas drawl.

"One morning I saddled a big, gray, owl-headed bronc that hadn't as yet showed much promise even in being a bucking horse, because up until that time he'd bucked with me twice and I'd ridden him real easy, sitting tall in the saddle and reefing him from stem to stern. But, this particular morning things turned out a lot different and it was all in his favor.

"After untracking the bronc, I mounted and decided to ride around the back of the house and talk to my Grandma, who was

Hawaiian Chicken

2 or 3 frying chickens	1 teaspoon dry ginger
⅔ cup soy sauce	4 tablespoons sugar
6 tablespoons cooking oil	4 tablespoons packed brown sugar
dash of salt and pepper	
1 cup pineapple juice	2 tablespoons prepared mustard

CUT up chicken and place in deep container; set aside. Next mix together remaining ingredients using an electric mixer or blender. Pour the sauce over the chicken and let stand 6 to 8 hours or overnight in the refrigerator. After marinating, remove chicken from sauce; reserve sauce for basting. Place chicken in shallow baking pan and bake at 350 degrees for about 1 hour, basting several times with sauce.

Larraine Price
Show Low, Arizona

Barbecued Chicken and Ribs

1 to 2 pounds beef short ribs	2 tablespoons oil
1 to 2 pounds country-style pork ribs	2 onions, chopped
	2 cups water
2 whole chickens, skinned and cut up	1 cup vinegar
	4 cups ketchup
salt and pepper to taste	1 cup packed brown sugar

TRIM any excess fat from beef and pork ribs. Season ribs and chicken to taste with salt and pepper. Heat oil in 12-inch Dutch oven placed on evenly distributed hot coals. Add onions and saute until transparent but not browned. Stir in water, vinegar, ketchup, and brown sugar. Cook, stirring often, until mixture thickens, about 1 hour.

Add ribs to sauce, stirring to coat well. Continue cooking, stirring often and replacing coals as needed, about 1 hour.

Add chicken pieces, stir to coat well, and continue cooking until ribs and chicken are very tender, about 1 hour longer. Dutch oven may or may not be covered. Sauce is thicker if Dutch oven is not covered. Makes about 10 servings.

For conventional range cooking, use an 8-quart pot and cook on range top according to previous directions.

Chicken With Sausage

1	3- to 4-pound broiler-fryer chicken, cut up
1	tablespoon vegetable or olive oil
1	pound hot sausage, sliced (Mexican chorizo may be used)
2	cups chopped bell pepper (sweet pepper)
1	cup chopped onion
1	clove garlic, minced
2	tablespoons all-purpose flour
1	cup chicken broth
2	cups chopped stewed tomatoes
1	cup pitted black olives

BROWN chicken in oil in a large skillet or Dutch oven (a tight-fitting lid is needed). Remove chicken.

Cook sausage in same skillet until lightly browned. With slotted spoon remove to paper towel to drain.

Drain all but 1 tablespoon fat from skillet. Add green pepper, onion, and garlic, and cook 5 minutes or until tender. Stir in flour. Gradually add broth, stirring constantly.

Add sausage, tomatoes, olives, and chicken. Cover pan tightly; cook over low heat for 45 minutes until chicken is tender. Serve with cornbread or rice.

feeding her chickens. They were a bunch of Rhode Island Red fryers she was fattening up to do some trading with at the general store in town. She had a bucket of shelled corn and when I rode up she'd just gathered the flock around her in a circle and was tossin' them the grain.

"Suddenly one of the fryers jumped and let out a silly squawk that spooked my bronc. He bogged his head and jerked the reins through my hands so fast it set them on fire. He headed for the corner of the house and ran under the clothesline. The wire caught on the saddle horn and both cross beams were jerked from the posts; they came together in a wad, dragging 20 feet behind us. Then the bronc bucked in a tight circle and ran over the washpot. It

Oven-Crispy Fried Chicken

1	2- to 3-pound broiler-fryer chicken, cut up
1	cup coarsely ground herb seasoned stuffing
1/4	cup grated parmesan cheese
1	teaspoon paprika
1/2	teaspoon salt
	dash of pepper
6	tablespoons butter, melted
1	egg, beaten
3	tablespoons milk

COMBINE stuffing, parmesan cheese, and seasonings in one bowl. Combine egg and milk in another small bowl. Dip chicken in milk/egg mixture, then coat with stuffing mixture. Place in a buttered 13 by 9-inch baking pan, not crowding the chicken pieces. May have to use 2 baking pans if it's a large fryer. Then drizzle the melted butter over the chicken. Bake in a 400-degree oven for 45 minutes, or until tender. Makes about 4 servings.

was a good thing it wasn't Monday or there would have been a fire under it. By this time I had a half-hitch of wire around my neck and I was clawing for air. Faintly I could hear Granny yelling, 'Jump off, Cliffy, jump off!'

"Jump off, hell! To have gotten off that horse would have taken wire cutters and a parachute. Besides, I wasn't raised to bail out when the going got rough and I wasn't about to start now. But, if I'd known what was about to happen next, I might have taken Granny's advice, because that bronc stampeded through her bunch of chickens scattering them squawking in every direction.

"Granny was a yellin' and shooing her apron at the bronc, who was pawing his head and stomping chickens to death. Maybe anyone watching would have thought it a great circus, but not to me. The next thing I knew I had a chicken plastered to my face, clawing and fighting and it wouldn't let go. Another landed in front of the saddle with me, and through it all, made a better ride than I did.

"Feathers were a flying like a tornado had hit, and I had a mouthful of them that nearly choked me to death. Then the bronc got tangled in a backlash of clothesline and spraddled out on top of the wood pile. I still don't know how I came out of this wreck alive, because I now had a feather down my throat and was gagging to death. I was barely able to see the bronc get to his feet and run off with my saddle.

"Granny was concerned about me, but not so much that she didn't first take time to wring the necks of three of the mortally wounded fryers. I'd turned blue by the time she fed me some dry biscuits to try to force the feather down my throat. I guess we wore the danged thing out, because I had to eat a half-dozen biscuits before I got my windpipe clear enough to stop gagging.

"I'd come out a loser along with the dead chickens, because I had a wire burn thick as your finger clear around my neck, chicken claw marks all over my face, a good school shirt half ripped from my back, claw marks up both sides of my ribs, and a runaway bronc packing my saddle.

"I was late for school that morning, but that wonderful fried chicken Granny served that evening salved my wounds a little, and it was probably the first time we'd ever had fried chicken when no company was coming or it wasn't Sunday."

58

Fajitas

I don't know why this big fuss all of a sudden over fajitas. Lately, every time I pick up a magazine and turn to the food section, I see brazen type with exclamation marks and a "new" Mexican food, called fajitas, being featured. One national women's magazine, so slick you have to read it with sunglasses, proclaimed fajitas as a sensational new Tex-Mex dish that is sweeping the country. Another says, "Fajitas . . . meat-filled tortillas . . . have taken off like a Texas wildfire! From humble roots with Mexican cowboys in Texas, fajitas are now a restaurant hit."

I get a kick out of the "slicks" discovering fajitas (pronounced *fah*-HEE-*tas*). This simple Mexican dish has been around the Southwest ever since the first Indian cave wife discovered that ground corn, made into a moist paste, flattened and cooked on a hot stone, made a wonderful

Fajitas

¾	cup lime juice	½	teaspoon salt
½	cup cooking oil	1	onion, thinly sliced
1	4-ounce can chopped green chilies	1	1½- to 2½-pound beef skirt or flank steak
½	cup Worcestershire sauce dash hot sauce		8-inch flour tortillas

MIX together lime juice, oil, green chilies, Worcestershire sauce, hot sauce, salt, and onion. Place steak in a shallow dish, pour marinade over it, and cover. Refrigerate overnight or 8 to 10 hours. Turn it several times.

When ready to grill, remove the steak from marinade; reserve marinade. Pat steak dry with paper towels. With a slotted spoon remove the onion and chilies from marinade and wrap them in foil. Put the chilies and onion on to cook the same time you do the steak. Grill the steak over medium heat for 9 to 10 minutes. Turn steak and continue grilling until done to taste. Brush steak occasionally with reserved marinade during grilling.

To serve, bias-slice steak into thin strips or bite-size pieces. Place some steak strips, onion, and chilies on each warmed tortilla. Top with any number of condiments: avocado slices, guacamole, sour cream, grated cheese, chopped tomato, green onions, and chopped ripe olives. Let your conscience be your guide.

Menudo (Tripe) Con Posole

1	pound tripe, cut in 1-inch squares		pinch of coriander (cilantro)
2	quarts water	2	cups canned white hominy, drained
1	large white onion, thinly sliced		salt to taste
2	teaspoons oregano		chili powder (optional)
1	teaspoon fresh-ground pepper pinch of cumin		chiltepins (optional)

PUT the tripe in 2 quarts of water, bring to a boil, and skim. Reduce to a simmer, and add the onion, oregano, cumin seed, and coriander leaves. Cook tripe 5 to 7 hours, or until it is tender enough to cut with a salad fork. Add the hominy, bring to a quick boil, and serve at once. Most cooks add a generous amount of red chili powder or small amount of crumbled chiltepins. Serves 4 to 6.

Fajita is Spanish for "little belt or sash" and the piece of meat involved resembles a cummerbund.

wrapper for meat.

Fajita is Spanish for "little belt or sash," and the piece of meat involved resembles a cummerbund. Fajitas are derived from the diaphragm muscle on the interior of the beef forequarter, or from the interior portion of the flank in the beef hindquarter. There are only four skirts per carcass—one in each short plate and one in each flank region.

Traditionally, the beef skirts were ground into hamburger, coarse-ground for chili, or cut into stew meat. At one time this was a very cheap cut of meat, and during the Great Depression sold for as little as 15 to 20 cents per pound. Recently I noticed in our local meat market "skirt steaks" marked at $2.69 per pound. One of the main reasons for the high price of skirt steak is that Japan is now buying 90 percent of all beef skirts produced in America. Because beef skirts are classified as variety cuts, they do not fall under quotas set by Japan on American beef.

The Texas Agricultural Extension Service has printed a fine 6-page pamphlet giving the history of fajitas, hints for preparation, recipes, and nutritional value. It says fajitas originated in the area bordered by Mexico to the south and west, the

Beef Steak

(Mexican Style)

6- to 8-ounce boneless steaks	1 teaspoon minced garlic
Mexican chili powder	2 cups thick tomato sauce
cornmeal	2 cups hot water
bacon fat	salt
1 cup minced onions	

POUND about 1 teaspoon of the Mexican chili powder into each steak. Season with salt and roll in cornmeal, pressing the meal into the beaten steaks. Put bacon fat into a large frying pan or Dutch oven and heat. Place steaks into pan and fry until done.

Then mix together the onions, garlic, tomato sauce, hot water, and salt to taste. Pour over steaks and simmer until onions are done. Serve steaks with sauce. Goes well with rice and tortillas.

"Chili" Pepper
V Cross T Ranch
Magdalena, New Mexico

Nueces River to the north, and King Ranch (near Kingsville) to the east. However, it points out fajitas have been cooked and served for a very long time, but not always called by that name.

Hispanics in south Texas have been eating fajitas since the 1930s. Often, beef skirts, along with the variety meats and by-products such as head, intestine, and hide, were used as partial payment for services rendered by the workers involved in trading or slaughtering livestock.

Whenever a day of slaughtering was planned, workers built a mesquite fire early in the morning. Mesquite is a hardwood and imparts a wonderfully sweet flavor to grilled meats. On ranches, the fajitas were placed directly on the coals.

Fajitas are placed directly on the coals because there is a skin-like membrane on both sides of the meat. After a few moments, the meat is turned. When done to satisfaction, the meat is taken off the fire and the membranes are removed by peeling. The membranes keep the juices in the meat and prevent it from drying out. The fajitas are wrapped in flour tortillas and are called *taco de fajita,* or just plain fajitas.

The San Carlos Apaches know all about fajitas, only they don't call them by that name. The moment a beef is butchered, they cut off the inside beef skirt (they call this butcher steak and claim it is the most tender part of the beef). The Apaches use either white oak or mesquite for their cooking fires. Often they fashion a grill by taking the metal rims, or hoops, from wooden horseshoe kegs, and crisscross the frame with baling wire to form a mesh. Flavored only with salt, the strips of meat are quickly seared on both sides.

With sharp pocket knives, the Apaches cut thin strips of the cooked meat and eat it on the spot. If flour tortillas (they are the only kind the Apache make) are handy, they wrap the tender morsels in the tortillas. Often a can of hot chili sauce is on hand and they pour generous amounts into each taco. More often than not, though, they simply spear the meat with the tip of their knives and relish it unadorned.

At the 1986 Cowboy Artists of America show in Phoenix, part of a luncheon buffet was fajitas. I dearly love fajitas and piled strips of the tender meat on a warm flour tortilla. I added enough guacamole to choke a cow, and then discovered the meat flavor was completely overpowered with garlic. The chef had used *lots* of garlic. Unless you really like garlic, I suggest you grill fajitas with nothing for seasoning except the lingering juices of the marinade. All the wonderful condiments piled atop the fajitas, such as chopped tomato and green onions, guacamole or slices of avocado, grated cheese, sour cream, chili peppers, or picante sauce, are flavoring enough.

Keeping Meat Cool

In these days of insulated ice chests, deluxe campers with gas or electric refrigerators, and ice available in every small hamlet, we forget the old ways of preserving meat and perishables. Before refrigerators, ranchers and homesteaders in the hot Southwest could keep meat for days, even in the summertime. Nights being cool, beef was hung in a tree just at dark, where it would receive all the cool air available.

In the morning, long before sunup and pesty flies began buzzing around, the meat was taken down, wrapped in canvas, and stored in a cool place. Under the bed was a favorite spot, or under the porch—anyplace cool and out of the sun is okay.

Care had to be taken that the meat was not rained on. If wet, beef sours quickly. Then, to avoid losing the meat, it had to be cooked at once. If it was boiled, all the broth had to be drained off when it was done. This way, the meat would keep several days longer. When all else failed, the meat was salted and dried as jerky.

Southwesterners knew all about the simple but efficient desert cooler. This was a wooden frame from 3 to 4 feet square, most often covered with chicken wire, with the wire covered with burlap.

This box frame could have from one to two shelves made of the chicken wire to allow the best circulation possible. The door would also be covered with wire and burlap.

The cooler was mounted on legs about 3 feet high, and each leg was set in a tomato can of water, to prevent ants and bugs from using the legs as a freeway to the food. On top of the cooler was placed a 5-gallon can, or perhaps a larger container, of water. Small holes were punched in the bottom of the can and, as the water slowly dripped onto the burlap, the warm breezes acted as an evaporator.

In 1939, as a young bride, I lived on the remote Navajo Indian reservation 35 miles north of Winslow, Arizona. We had such a desert cooler placed in the ell of the old frame ranch house where it was always shady. The raging dust storms would cement the wet burlap with dirt, sealing it as permanently as plaster. We had to replace the gunny-sack covering frequently.

In this cooler I kept gelatin desserts, as well as milk, cool and fresh for several days. I also kept our butter, bacon, and

An artist's rendition of a desert cooler made out of wire and burlap.

eggs (when we had such luxuries), along with a jug of lemonade (the only way a person could drink the alkali water from the windmill). Fresh fruit and vegetables kept fresh for approximately as long as those of city dwellers with their iceboxes and daily ice delivery.

During the summer, without this cooler, everything melted. Ever try to reunite mayonnaise once it's gotten hot and separated? Salt pork, left in the hot kitchen, became as limp as a greasy dishrag, and eggs cooked in the shell.

Temperatures in northern Arizona run to extremes. A fresh beef hung in the saddle room in January would freeze so solid it had to be quartered with a crosscut saw. Once I hung a chunk of beef in the spare bedroom and it was mid-March before I could cut it with a knife. We had to keep fresh vegetables beside the living room stove all winter, and even these had to be covered with a quilt, for after the fire went out, they would freeze.

When researching the history of these simple coolers, I was amazed at the lack of information to be found. One homesteading handbook fails to mention evaporating coolers, even when instructing farmers in Mexico on the proper method of keeping fresh meat and produce during the hot months. The authors assumed *anybody* would naturally have access to "spring houses, root cellars, and basements."

Backpackers, bikers, and horseback vacationers, on a weekend trip into the wilds, might remember some tips on keeping fresh meat for several days without ice. Pork or poultry needs to be used the first day. If this isn't possible, sprinkle it liberally with plain table salt, keep in a cool place unwrapped, and, before cooking, rinse well to remove the excess salt. Remember that salt draws the juices, and meat will become dry in a few hours.

Beef usually keeps twice as long as other fresh meat (but hamburger does not keep long at all and must be cooked the first day without fail). Steaks or roasts,

kept overnight, need to be unwrapped and placed where cool night air can circulate around them. Steaks dry out, so should be used as soon as possible.

If you doubt that meat is good, use your nose! It's easy to tell when meat is beginning to sour. Or feel it; if it is becoming slightly sticky, wipe with a cloth dipped in vinegar, and cook at once. Or meat can be placed in a pan of cool water with 1 teaspoon of baking soda and ½ cup of vinegar. Let marinate 5 to 10 minutes, drain, wipe dry, and cook. It's amazing how vinegar and baking soda tenderize a tough steak. It sure doesn't hurt a pot roast, either. Meat must be well done; rare meat, in camp, is dangerous.

When you make camp for several days, butter and fresh vegetables can be kept by wrapping them loosely in a dishtowel and placing them in a container, which in turn rests in a shallow pan of water. The cloth should touch the water at all times; the food is cooled by evaporation. The shallow pan of water also keeps ants off food.

Illustration by Keith Walters

The Spanish word for dried beef is *charqui;* **we call it jerky.**

How To Make Jerky

The Spanish word for dried beef is *charqui;* we call it jerky.

beef	pepper
salt	chili powder (optional)

TO dry beef, cut lean meat in strips as long as 6 to 14 inches. No wider than 1 inch is best so the meat will dry quickly. Do not leave fat on meat as it becomes rancid in a short time. Cut against grain when possible. Sprinkle each piece with salt and pepper; some prefer adding a small amount of chili powder.

Hang strips of meat in a dry place. Full sun is not necessary, but is best. A shed or barn loft will do. Cellars and basements are not at all suitable as they are usually too damp. Hang on wires or clothesline. Do not worry about flies as the salt and pepper repels them. In very hot weather, meat will be jerked in a few days or a week. In cold weather, the meat will take a week or more. Do not let meat get wet. When meat looks and feels like old shoe leather, remove from drying wires and store in flour sacks in a cool place. Hanging from rafters by thin wires keeps weevils, mice, and other pests away. *Clair Haight*
Winslow, Arizona

Beef Sausage

Hamburger can be made into sausage for camping trips. Now, don't panic; *anyone* can make beef sausage, and you don't need to butcher a pig, build a smoke house, or buy a sausage stuffer and meat grinder.

Buy 2 pounds of hamburger and 2 pounds of the best ground beef, or you can buy 4 pounds of ground round beef. I don't advise using all cheap hamburger, as it tends to shrink too much. You can purchase curing salt at most meat markets and you need 1/4 cup for this amount of meat. I find it on most grocery shelves near the spice racks. Morton Tender Quick is easy to use and contains the finest quality salt and a combination of meat curing ingredients. Be sure to use garlic *powder*, not garlic salt (about 1 teaspoon).

A tablespoon of Wright's Bar-B-Q Liquid Smoke will give your sausage a real hickory flavor. You can use 1½ teaspoons coarse ground pepper or whole peppers. Sometimes I slightly crush whole peppers with a rolling pin. There are several variations in making beef sausage, such as adding crushed red chili pods. I like to add a teaspoon of oregano for flavor. However, try it this way once, then branch out by experimenting with other seasonings.

Mix all ingredients into hamburger with your hands, then put in large bowl and chill 24 hours. This is necessary for the curing salt to do its work and the flavoring to "set."

After it is chilled, divide meat into four equal portions. Have ready four squares of toweling, or cheesecloth, about 15 inches wide. Pat each portion of meat into a firm, smooth roll with your hands. Try to press out all air pockets and shape up nicely.

Wrap each roll separately in cloth, tucking ends under. Place on oven rack, with tucked ends on the bottom. Place a drip pan under sausage rolls, and bake at 225 degrees for 4 hours.

When it's done, remove toweling and let cool. It will be a light mahogany color and very firm. You can start eating it right away or store in your refrigerator. For long keeping, it is best to freeze. However, this sausage keeps very well without refrigeration for several days. It's a dandy way to prepare meat for snacks on pack trips. It goes great with cheese and crackers, and isn't a bit out of place on a snack tray at the swankiest cocktail parties.

Shape sausage into four equal rolls.

Pat each roll to remove any air bubbles.

Wrap each roll in squares of toweling; bake at 225 degrees for 4 hours.

Anyone **can make beef sausage, and you don't need to butcher a pig, build a smoke house, or buy a sausage stuffer and meat grinder.**

Rib Roast in Rock Salt

SOME cooks, when using the rock salt method, like to use a great deal more salt, as much as 5 pounds, using a layer of salt 1 inch deep in bottom of roaster. Others like to marinate meat for as long as 10 hours before cooking. If nothing else, applying Worchestershire sauce to the entire surface of the roast, rubbing it in well, gives the meat a wonderful flavor.

You won't be able to make gravy. All the juices are still in the delicious, mouth-watering beef.

1	10-pound standing rib roast	1/2	cup water
3	cups rock salt		

LET the rib roast stand at room temperature at least 8 hours. Place rock salt in a bowl, moisten it with the water.

Place rib roast, rib side down, into a large roaster which has a cover. Pack the moistened rock salt over top and sides of the roast. Cover roaster and place in preheated 500-degree oven for 1 hour. Reduce temperature to 350 degrees for 1 hour more, then turn oven off, allowing roast to remain in the oven for another hour. *Do Not Open* your roaster at any time during the 3 hours. Remove from oven and allow to cool 15 to 20 minutes. Crack off salt, slice roast, and serve. Roast will be done on the outside and rare to medium-rare on the inside.

John Hampton

Stuffed Beef Tenderloin

6	slices bacon, cut in half	1/2	cup sliced green onion
1	2- to 4-pound beef tenderloin	1/2	cup butter or margarine
4	ounces cooked frozen crab meat	1/2	cup white grape juice
1	tablespoon butter or margarine, melted	1/8	teaspoon garlic salt
1 1/2	teaspoon lemon juice	1/2	green pepper
	garlic salt	1/2	red pepper
	freshly ground pepper		heavy string to tie meat

PLACE 14-inch Dutch oven over coals and cook bacon slices until transparent. Store bacon slices for later use. Trim excess fat from beef tenderloin. Cut tenderloin lengthwise in 2 different slits to within 1/2 inch of each end and bottom. Place frozen or thawed crab, end to end, inside tenderloin slits.

Melt 1 tablespoon butter on Dutch oven lid. Combine with lemon juice; drizzle over crab. Fold top side of tenderloin over crab. Tie tenderloin securely with heavy string at 2-inch intervals. Sprinkle outside of meat evenly with garlic salt and pepper; place in Dutch oven. Cook with coals on top and bottom of Dutch oven with a moderately high heat, 40 to 60 minutes.

While meat is cooking, saute green onions in 1/2 cup butter on a Dutch oven lid. Add white grape juice and 1/8 teaspoon garlic salt. Cut 1 large green pepper and 1 large red pepper in half crosswise. Remove seeds and discard. Pour half of butter mixture into green pepper and red pepper halves.

After the meat is cooked, arrange bacon crosswise on top of tenderloin. Put coals on lid of Dutch oven and cook for 5 minutes until bacon is crisp. For garnish, place pepper halves containing butter sauce on each side of tenderloin. Remove string, slice, and serve. Yields 8 to 10 servings. *David and Irene Johnson*

Roast Meat Gravy

3 tablespoons fat
4 tablespoons all-purpose flour
2 cups hot stock

1/2 teaspoon Kitchen Bouquet (optional)
salt and pepper to taste

POUR off fat from roast. Measure the correct amount of fat and place in a separate pan. Blend in the flour until smooth. Stir in the stock and Kitchen Bouquet. Cook and stir until gravy boils, about 1 minute. Adjust seasonings to taste.

Dutch Oven Short Ribs

4 or 5 pounds beef short ribs, cut up
2 tablespoons oil
1 onion, chopped
1 clove garlic, minced
1 cup chili sauce

1 cup ketchup
2 tablespoons vinegar
1 cup water
1/2 teaspoon celery seed or oregano

SALT and pepper ribs and brown in hot oil in Dutch oven. Add all other ingredients and simmer until done. Skim off excess fat and serve with mashed potatoes or noodles.

"Chief" Mabre
Double Circle Ranch
Clifton, Arizona

Pasties

3 pounds venison or beef, diced
2 onions, sliced

5 large potatoes, diced
butter
salt and pepper to taste

PLACE meat, onions, and potatoes in separate bowls; cover potatoes so they won't turn brown.

Crust:

5 cups all-purpose flour
1 tablespoon salt

3 cups vegetable shortening
water

Mix flour and salt into a large bowl, work the shortening into flour, one cup at a time, until the mixture is similar to small grains of rice. Then add just enough cold water to make the mixture stick together. Work the dough as little as possible, to prevent it from getting tough.

For individual pasties take some dough and roll it out on a floured board to the size of a large pie pan. Then, on half of the rolled-out dough, first spread a layer of meat, next onions, and potatoes last. Then dot with butter, salt, and pepper; fold over the other half of dough, making the pastie take on the shape of a half circle. Moisten edges and pinch together or press edges together with the tines of a fork. Make a few small slits in top of pastie to let moisture out. Place them on a large baking sheet and bake at 350 degrees for 1 hour, 15 minutes. Makes 4 or 5 pasties. Serve with a salad.

One large pastie makes a lunch for a hungry man.

Easy Meat Loaf

1 pound hamburger
1/2 pound sausage
1 egg
1/2 cup cornmeal
2 teaspoons salt

1/2 teaspoon pepper
1/2 cup chopped bell pepper
1/2 cup cream-style corn
1 1/2 cups canned tomatoes, chopped
1 onion, chopped

COMBINE all ingredients, blend well. Bake in loaf pan for 1 1/2 hours at 350 degrees.

Joyce House
Kingman, Arizona

Hamburger Chop Suey

1	pound hamburger	¼	cup soy sauce
1	cup diced celery	1	can cream of chicken soup
2	onions, diced	1	can cream of mushroom soup
	salt and pepper to taste	¾	cup uncooked rice
1½	cups water	1	can chow mein noodles

BROWN hamburger, celery, and onions in skillet. Season with salt and pepper to taste. Then add water, soy sauce, soups, and rice; stir well. Put in deep dish and bake 1 hour in a 350-degree oven. When done, stir in 1 can of chow mein noodles and serve immediately. Yields 5 or 6 servings.

Meat and Potato Cakes

2	cups cooked ground meat (can be pork, beef, or lamb)	1	small onion, minced
2	cups mashed potatoes	½	cup tomato juice or puree
2	eggs	1	teaspoon salt
			pepper to taste

COMBINE meat, mashed potatoes, eggs, onion, tomato juice, and seasonings. Shape into 8 patties, put into greased baking dish, and brush with melted butter. Bake in oven for 30 minutes at 350 degrees.

Original House Hash

1	box instant sour cream potatoes or Ranch Style instant potatoes		salt and pepper to taste
		1	4-ounce can diced green chilies
1	pound hamburger	1	4-ounce can sliced mushrooms (optional)
1	onion, minced	½	cup chopped celery
1	clove garlic, minced	1	cup grated longhorn cheese

FRY hamburger, onions, garlic, salt and pepper, chilies, mushrooms, and celery. Follow directions for mixing potatoes on box. Add to hamburger mixture. Bake in oven at 350 degrees for 10 to 15 minutes. Add cheese to casserole and return to oven until cheese is melted. Serve at once.

Joyce House
Kingman, Arizona

Rancher's Meat Pie

1	pound ground round	1	cup canned whole kernel corn, drained
1	cup chopped onions	1	tablespoon chili powder
1	15-ounce can tomato sauce	1	teaspoon salt
2	medium-sized sweet green peppers, chopped	1	teaspoon pepper

BROWN beef (just until no longer pink) and onions in Dutch oven or large kettle, breaking up meat. Stir in tomato sauce, green peppers, corn, chili powder, salt, and pepper. Bring to boil, lower heat, cover, and simmer 15 minutes. Pour meat mixture into ungreased 10-inch deep-dish pie plate.

Crust:

2	eggs	¾	cup yellow cornmeal
1	tablespoon vegetable shortening	1	tablespoon all-purpose flour
		1	teaspoon baking soda
½	cup buttermilk or sour milk	¼	teaspoon salt

Beat together eggs, shortening, and buttermilk in bowl for 1 minute. Beat in cornmeal, flour, baking soda, and salt. Spoon over top of meat; spread evenly to cover entire surface. Bake in preheated oven at 350 degrees for 20 minutes or until topping is done. Makes 6 servings.

Meat and potato cakes are an easy way to use leftovers.

Barbecued Pork Shoulder

1	3½- to 4-pound pork shoulder roast	1	tablespoon red chili powder
1	cup ketchup	6	tablespoons vinegar
½	cup packed brown sugar	2	tablespoons lemon juice
2	teaspoons salt	¼	cup Worcestershire sauce
1	teaspoon pepper	2	teaspoons prepared mustard
			hamburger buns

COVER roast with salty water in a large Dutch oven. Cover and cook for 2 to 2½ hours or until tender. Drain and thinly slice; place in shallow baking dish, at least a 2-quart size.

Combine remaining ingredients, stir well. Spoon mixture over roast, turning slices to coat. Bake at 300 degrees for 45 minutes. Serve on buns. Yields 6 servings.

The recipe for Southern Pork Chops can be doubled and tripled for a large crowd. I sometimes make enough to serve 50 to 75 people.

Stuffed Pork Chops

5	or 6 pork chops (ask the butcher to cut a pocket in chops)	1	tablespoon fresh sage
		1	tablespoon fresh thyme
½	cup chopped onion	1	cup chicken stock
½	cup chopped celery	1	can cream of celery soup
¼	cup butter	⅓	can water
½	loaf bread, broken into bread crumbs	10	small mushrooms
1	teaspoon salt		garlic (optional)

SAUTE onions and celery in butter until onions are clear. Put bread crumbs in a large bowl and sprinkle with salt, sage, and thyme. Mix in sauteed vegetables and chicken broth. Mix together and stuff into the pork chops.

Place the stuffed chops in a 12-inch Dutch oven. Mix the soup, water, mushrooms, and garlic in a bowl and pour over pork; cover with lid. Put the Dutch oven on hot coals and place more coals on the lid. Bake 90 minutes, turning a quarter turn every 20 minutes. Or bake in a conventional oven at 350 degrees.

Jake and Jeami Anderson-Jenks

Southern Pork Chops

This goes well with mashed potatoes. Recipe can be doubled and tripled for a large crowd. I sometimes make enough to serve 50 to 75 people.

6	to 8 pork chops, thick cut	1	cup milk
2	tablespoons onion flakes	1	tablespoon Worcestershire sauce
2	tablespoons peanut butter		
2	cans cream of mushroom soup	1	small can sliced mushrooms (optional)

BROWN pork chops on both sides in small amount of grease. Mix other ingredients in saucepan and heat until peanut butter melts. Place pork chops in baking pan and pour sauce over. Cover with foil and bake at 350 degrees for 1 hour. May uncover during last 15 minutes of baking.

Lorraine Price
Show Low, Arizona

Baked Ham

1	7- or 8-pound boneless precooked ham	1	teaspoon nutmeg
	whole cloves	½	teaspoon allspice
1⅛	cups packed brown sugar	1	tablespoon Accent
1	teaspoon cinnamon	1	6-ounce can pineapple juice

SCORE ham in 1-inch squares and insert clove in each corner. Place ham in a baking pan at least 2 inches deep. Mix remaining ingredients and pour over ham. Bake at 325 degrees for 3 hours. Cover with foil during the first 2 hours of baking, then remove foil and baste every 15 minutes.

Bill Price
Show Low, Arizona

Oven-Barbecued Fresh Ham

The ham is good served with candied sweet potatoes, fresh black-eyed peas, and cherry or fresh peach cobbler for dessert.

1	10- to 12-pound fresh ham	1	teaspoon mustard seed
2	cups packed brown sugar	6	whole cloves
2	cups wine vinegar	½	teaspoon celery seed
2	cups water	1	teaspoon coarsely ground
2	cups condensed consomme		black pepper
1	bay leaf		

SCORE the fat surface of the fresh ham in a crisscross pattern with cuts running down slightly into the flesh. Place ham in a large enamel pot or preserving kettle. Combine all the remaining ingredients in a saucepan and bring to a boil; simmer 5 minutes. Pour over the ham while still hot; cover and let stand in a cold place overnight, turning the ham at least twice to marinate it evenly.

Reserve marinade and place ham in an open roasting pan, fat-side up. Roast at 350 degrees for 5 hours. Baste with the marinade at 20-minute intervals, drain excess fat from the roasting pan as it accumulates.

Mountain oysters are obtained twice during the year—spring and fall—when the bull calves are castrated. Very young calves (only a few weeks old) are too small, and ones taken from older animals (1½ years) are too large and strong tasting.

Braised Lamb Chops

3	meaty lamb shanks (about 4 pounds)	2	carrots, pared and cut into 2 by ½-inch strips
⅓	cup olive oil or vegetable oil salt and pepper	2	bay leaves
3	cloves garlic, minced	½	teaspoon oregano
1	large onion, sliced	½	teaspoon thyme
		1	16-ounce can stewed tomatoes

BROWN lamb shanks in oil in a large, heavy skillet over medium-high heat for 7 to 10 minutes. Salt and pepper as desired. While shanks are browning, lightly oil bottom of Dutch oven or casserole dish large enough to hold shanks in one layer. Sprinkle bottom with garlic, onion, and carrots.

Transfer browned lamb shanks to bed of vegetables, next add bay leaves, oregano, thyme, and tomatoes with their liquid. Cover; cook over low heat for 2½ to 3 hours or until tender. Turn shanks occasionally to make sure liquid is not boiling dry. Add a little water if necessary.

With slotted spoon, transfer vegetables to large platter. Arrange shanks on top. Keep warm. Skim fat from surface of cooking liquid. Boil sauce rapidly until reduced to about a cup. Serve half a shank per person with sauce spooned over. Serves 6.

Mountain Oysters

MOUNTAIN oysters are obtained twice during the year—spring and fall roundup when the bull calves are castrated. Very young calves (only a few weeks old) are too small, and ones taken from long yearlin's are too large and strong tasting.

As soon as the pail of oysters is brought in from the branding, wash them in cold water. Then put in fresh water with 1 cup salt to soak for a while. Drain and wipe dry. Cut off tips, peel skin off, and if large enough slit lengthwise. Salt and pepper and roll in flour. Fry in hot fat as you would frying chicken. Be sure oysters are well done and crisp. Serve hot with potatoes and salad. Waldorf or cabbage salad is good with mountain oysters.

Salmon Croquettes

1	No. 2 can red salmon	2	cups cooked rice
2	tablespoons butter	1	teaspoon salt
½	cup flour		pepper to taste
1	cup milk	1	cup fine cracker crumbs
3	eggs		deep fat for frying

REMOVE bone and skin from salmon. Melt butter and blend half the flour into butter. Add milk slowly, stirring constantly, and bring to a slow boil to make a thick cream sauce.

Combine salmon, 2 well-beaten eggs, white sauce, rice, and salt and pepper. Shape into croquettes, preferably 3 inches across. Roll in remaining flour, dip into remaining beaten egg, then roll in cracker crumbs. Fry in deep, hot fat. Makes about 10 croquettes.

Catfish and Tomato Sauce

Almost every large river in the Southwest is inhabited by catfish. It's the opinion of most fishermen that catfish should be skinned before cooking. After being skinned, the fish can be cut crosswise in steaks about ¾ inch thick, or filleted.

½	pound butter	1	can tomatoes, puree or stewed
2	pounds catfish fillets		
1	cup chopped green chilies several fresh green onions or shallots, chopped	½	teaspoon oregano salt and pepper to taste

MELT about half the butter in a skillet. Put the fillets in the hot butter and brown on one side. Add all chopped vegetables to tomatoes and season. Turn the fish, and dot the cooked side with the rest of the butter. Cover each fillet with the tomato mixture, cover skillet, and cook until fish can be pierced with a fork, about 10 minutes.

Fried Trout

Of all fish, trout is always first on my list for goodness. Frying is the easiest and preferred way to cook them.

trout	lemon juice
salt and pepper to taste	oil
flour	margarine or butter
dry bread crumbs	

WHEN you have cleaned your fish, season with salt and pepper an hour or so ahead of cooking time (if you can wait that long). Mix equal amounts of flour and dry bread crumbs and roll the fish in the mixture. Heat equal amounts of oil and margarine (butter is better)—in a good-sized frying pan. When hot, fry the trout. Trout is done if, when pierced with a fork, the meat flakes. Serve with lemon juice.

Sauces that are good with fried trout are lemon butter, tartar sauce, Thousand Island dressing, mayonnaise, a relish sauce, or barbecue sauce.

8 COOKIN' THE WILD ONES

Rabbit Stew

1 large young rabbit or 2 small
   rabbits, cut in serving pieces
2 teaspoons salt
3 tablespoons butter
1 cup potatoes, cut in strips
½ cup celery, cut in strips
½ cup carrots, cut in strips
1 medium onion, sliced
   water
1 8-ounce can tomato sauce
¼ cup chopped parsley
   salt to taste

COVER rabbit with cool water and 1 teaspoon salt. Bring to boil for 10 minutes; discard water. Cover rabbit again with cool water and 1 teaspoon salt. Simmer until rabbit is tender. Remove pieces and reserve 2 cups broth. When cool, bone rabbit and cut into 1-inch pieces.

Melt butter in deep skillet and add vegetables. Cover and cook 15 minutes. Add broth and tomato sauce. Bring this mixture to boil and add rabbit pieces, parsley, and salt. Thicken with flour and water paste and cook 15 minutes. Serves 3 to 4.

Wild Game Stew

Stews have always been popular in America since the days of Indians and colonists. Even when the pioneers headed west and camped out at night, the pots were hung to cook over the fire. Long, slow cooking produces tender and moist meat. You can use our modern versions of our ancestors' iron kettle: electric slow-cookers, Dutch ovens, and cast iron pots that allow the ingredients to simmer very slowly. This type of cooking locks in the flavor of all the ingredients in your stew, but more importantly, it tenderizes game animals and birds.

Beer Camp Stew

5 pounds lean venison or other
   game meat, cut in 1-inch pieces
3 tablespoons oil
½ pound onions, cut into
   ¾-inch pieces
½ pound celery, cut into ¾-inch
   pieces
3 cloves garlic
3 ounces flour
1 quart boiling water or stock
1 pint canned tomatoes, chopped
2 12-ounce cans beer
1 teaspoon dried thyme
2 bay leaves
1 teaspoon pepper
1 teaspoon salt
½ pound carrots, cut into
   ¾-inch pieces
½ pound rutabagas, cut into
   ¾-inch pieces
½ pound potatoes, cut into
   ¾-inch pieces

BROWN meat in oil in a heavy pot; then remove and set aside, leaving oil. Add onions, celery, and garlic to pot and cook until tender. Add flour, stirring well. Gradually add boiling water or stock until thick and smooth. Add tomatoes, beer, spices, and the browned game meat. Reduce heat and simmer, uncovered, for 1½ hours, stirring occasionally. Add carrots and rutabagas and cook 30 minutes more, covered. Add potatoes and cook until they are tender. Serves 12 to 15.

Smothered Quail

6 quail
½ cup vinegar
1 gallon cold water
6 tablespoons butter
3 tablespoons flour
2 cups chicken broth
½ cup sherry
salt and pepper to taste
cooked rice

PLACE cleaned quail in water and vinegar solution. Let stand several hours; wash with cold water several times and dry thoroughly.

Brown in butter in heavy iron skillet or Dutch oven. Remove quail to baking dish. Add flour to butter in skillet and stir well. Slowly add chicken broth, sherry, salt and pepper to taste; blend well and pour over quail. Cover baking dish and bake at 350 for 1 hour. Serve with cooked rice.

Long, slow cooking produces tender and moist meat.

Roasted Quail With Mushrooms

4 quail
½ cup vinegar
1 gallon cold water
4 slices bacon
1 tablespoon butter or margarine
¼ cup lemon juice
½ cup hot water
⅓ cup chopped mushrooms

PLACE cleaned quail in water and vinegar solution. Let stand several hours; wash with cold water several times and dry thoroughly.

Wrap bacon around each quail, securing with skewers or toothpicks. Put birds into shallow buttered pan; cover and bake at 350 degrees for about 30 minutes, basting with mixture of lemon juice and water. When birds are tender, remove from oven. Add mushrooms and heat. Serve on toast or rice with gravy. Makes 4 servings.

Fried Quail

Wild game cooks will agree that dry plucking rather than skinning the birds helps conserve moisture and flavor in quail. Birds should be drawn as soon as possible if weather is warm. After the bird is drawn, the body cavity should be wiped dry. Hanging the birds in a cool place to season improves their flavor.

quail
½ cup vinegar
1 gallon cold water
salt and pepper
flour
1 cup hot water

PLACE cleaned quail in water and vinegar solution. Let stand several hours; wash with cold water several times and dry thoroughly.

Season with salt and pepper and roll in flour. Fry in deep, hot fat until well browned on all sides. Add 1 cup hot water slowly, cover, and simmer over low heat for 1 hour or until pan is dry. Increase heat; cook until quail is crisp.

Stew is made in a Dutch oven. This type of Dutch oven used is called a meat oven because it is higher on the sides. From left: Poncho Casillas, Whitman Cassadore, and Calis Lupe.

Boy Blackwell, a wrangler for the Spurs in the Texas Panhandle, dragging wood to the chuck wagon. Erwin Smith took this picture around the turn of the century.

From the Erwin Smith Collection of the Library of Congress, on deposit at the Amon Carter Museum, courtesy of the Texas and Southwestern Cattle Raisers Foundation, Fort Worth.

Cornish Game Hens With Cranberry Sauce

1 16-ounce can cranberry sauce	1 14-ounce package herb
3 tablespoons margarine	stuffing, cubed
1 6-ounce can frozen orange	1 small apple, chopped
juice concentrate, thawed	1 egg, beaten
1/4 cup light corn syrup	salt and pepper to taste
1/4 cup chopped onion	6 canning lid rings
1 cup chopped celery	3 Cornish game hens

COMBINE half of cranberry sauce, 1 tablespoon margarine, 1/3 cup orange juice concentrate, and corn syrup in small bowl. Place 14-inch Dutch oven on 10 evenly distributed hot coals. Place bowl in oven and, stirring occasionally, bring mixture to boil. Remove from oven, cover with foil, and set aside.

Line hot oven with enough foil to extend at least 5 inches up sides. Melt remaining 2 tablespoons margarine in foil-lined oven, add onions and celery, and saute until tender. Stir in cubed stuffing, apple, and egg, being careful not to pierce foil. Season to taste with salt and pepper. Stir in remaining orange juice concentrate. Fold mixture up in foil oven lining and set aside. Wipe oven out lightly with oiled rag.

Start 40 coals for Cornish hens 45 minutes before cooking time. Rinse hens and pat dry. Sprinkle cavities with salt and fill loosely with some of stuffing. Tie legs and tail together with heavy string. Place 2 canning lid rings per bird in bottom of oven and arrange stuffed birds on them. Cover birds loosely with foil; cover with lid. Place oven on 15 evenly distributed hot coals and arrange 25 coals on lid in even pattern. Cook about 45 minutes, giving oven 1/4 turn every 15 minutes. Check birds at same time and turn lid 1/4 turn in opposite direction. After 45 minutes baste hens with reserved sauce 3 or 4 times. About 20 minutes before birds are done, spoon remaining stuffing around them to heat through. Total cooking time will be about 1 hour, 15 minutes. Garnish with parsley and orange cups filled with remaining cranberry sauce, if desired. Makes 3 to 6 servings.

Note: In conventional oven, game hens can be cooked in a 10-inch roasting pan at 375 degrees for 1 hour, 15 minutes to 1 hour, 25 minutes. Cover for first 30 minutes of cooking time. Then baste and add stuffing according to previous directions. If birds begin to brown too much, cover loosely with foil.

Venison Liver

venison liver
oil or bacon drippings
onion, chopped
green pepper, chopped
celery, chopped

2 tomatoes, chopped (optional)
1 can mushrooms (optional)
1 lemon, juiced
    oregano

PUT the liver in a bucket of salted water for an hour or more. Remove, dry well, and slice about the same as you would beef liver. Fry in oil or bacon drippings until medium done; put in baking dish. Fry onion, green pepper, and celery until tender. If there is danger of the onion mixture getting too brown, add a little water. Add tomatoes and mushrooms and place the mixture on top of the liver. Add lemon juice, a little oregano, and bake for 5 to 10 minutes at 350 degrees.

Game Marinade

This marinade can be used on venison, elk, antelope, or bear.

3 onions, diced
1 cup diced carrots
1 cup chopped green onion
1 cup vinegar
5 cups dry wine

1 clove garlic, crushed
2 teaspoons salt
1 teaspoon fresh ground pepper
2 bay leaves
1 cup diced celery

COMBINE all ingredients in saucepan and cook for 5 minutes. Cool. Pour over steaks or roast; keep submerged and turn daily. Let meat marinate in cool place for 2 to 4 days.

Roast Venison

("Pride of the Ozarks" Pot Roast . . .)

½ cup vinegar
2 cloves garlic, minced
2 tablespoons salt
    cold water to cover game
1 4-pound venison roast
    salt
2 tablespoons flour

2 cloves garlic, minced
1 large onion, sliced
2 tablespoons brown sugar
1 tablespoon Worcestershire sauce
1 teaspoon mustard
¼ cup vinegar or lemon juice
1 1-pound can tomatoes

MIX vinegar, garlic, and salt in a bowl with enough water to cover game. Soak overnight.

Remove from marinade, season with salt, roll in flour, and brown in hot skillet. Place in crockpot; add remaining ingredients. Cover and cook on high for 2 hours, then turn to low for 8 to 10 hours.

Using a marinade on venison, elk, antelope, or bear gives the meat a delicious flavor and tender texture.

Wild Game Marinated Rump Roast

A wine and vegetable/herb-seasoned marinade is an excellent method to tenderize a game meat roast. Moose, elk, deer, or bighorn sheep may be used.

1 4-pound rump roast
2 cups dry red wine
1 14-ounce can clear beef broth
1¼ cups cooking oil
1 bay leaf
1 teaspoon salt

1 teaspoon pepper
1 teaspoon garlic powder
½ teaspoon dried mustard
2 onions, sliced thin
½ teaspoon grated lemon peel
3 to 4 tablespoons flour

PLACE game roast in a large plastic bag (and place in a bowl for support). Add all ingredients, except flour and ¼ cup oil. Carefully shake bag to mix ingredients. Refrigerate roast in marinade for at least 10 hours, occasionally shaking bag to coat all sides.

To cook roast, remove from marinade, reserve, and bring to room temperature. Dredge meat in flour, then brown on all sides in oil in a large Dutch oven or roasting pan. Add marinade and bring to a boil. Cover pan, reduce heat, and simmer for 1½ to 2 hours. Makes 6 to 8 servings.

Trim off all fat before cooking. The fat will give the meat a rancid taste.

Marinated Brisket

(good for game meat such as elk or venison)

1	bottle liquid smoke		celery salt to taste
1	5- to 6-pound whole brisket	2	large onions, sliced
	salt to taste		Worcestershire sauce
	garlic salt to taste	6	ounces barbecue sauce

DRIZZLE entire bottle of liquid smoke over brisket. Liberally season with salts and cover with onion. Cover and refrigerate overnight. Before cooking, drain liquid smoke (keep it for the next brisket) and douse the brisket with Worcestershire sauce. Cover and bake at 275 degrees for about 5 hours. Uncover, pour on barbecue sauce, and bake 1 hour more. Serves 6 to 8.

Elk Steaks, English-Style

Elk is more like beef than any other game meat, and it is best treated like beef. This is a good way to prepare steaks if you're sure your meat is fairly tender. The quantity of ingredients depend upon how many steaks are being prepared.

½-inch-thick elk steaks		flour
salt and pepper to taste	2	onions, sliced
Accent	1	can onion soup
paprika		

SPRINKLE steaks with salt, pepper, a little Accent, and paprika. Roll in flour. Fry just long enough to brown. Place in a flat baking dish. Fry onions slowly with a little salt and oil until clear; put over steaks. Add the onion soup. Bake covered for 1½ hours at 350 degrees. Add a little water if they become too dry.

2-Day Elk Roast

1	3- to 4-pound lean elk roast	1	tablespoon oregano
3	to 5 fresh garlic cloves, diced	½	teaspoon pepper
2	tablespoons salt	5	strips bacon, quartered
3	cups water	1	can condensed cream of
3	tablespoons white vinegar		mushroom soup
3	tablespoons red wine vinegar	1	soup can full of milk
2	tablespoons cider vinegar	½	pound fresh mushrooms
7	tablespoons chili powder		(optional)
2	teaspoons cumin		

REMOVE all fat from roast; pierce top and sides every 2 inches with sharp knife, leaving small openings to stuff the bacon in. Mix garlic with salt and set aside. In a bowl mix together water, vinegars, chili powder, cumin, oregano, and pepper. The garlic and salt should be mushy by now. Mash it to a pulp and stir into marinade. Put roast and marinade into a plastic bag. Close and refrigerate overnight, turning bag several times.

Preheat oven to 300 degrees. Place meat in a large roaster and push a small piece of bacon into each opening. Blend soup and milk and stir into marinade along with mushrooms; pour over roast. Insert a meat thermometer in a meaty portion of roast—140 degrees for rare, 160 for medium, 170 for well-done. Cover loosely with foil; roast 1½ hours or until desired doneness. The juices may be thickened and served as a gravy.

Marilyn Petrenas
Colorado Springs, Colorado

Elk Spaghetti Sauce

1	pound ground elk	2	tablespoons oregano
1	pound ground turkey	1	tablespoon rosemary
2	tablespoons olive oil	1	tablespoon marjoram
2	medium onions, sliced	2	teaspoons sweet basil
1	large green bell pepper, coarsely chopped	1	tablespoon salt
		1/2	teaspoon pepper
3	to 5 fresh garlic cloves, diced	2	30-ounce cans tomato sauce*
1/2	pound fresh mushrooms, sliced		

STIRRING often, crumble the meats together and brown in medium-hot oil until barely cooked through but still a pink color. Drain fat, if desired. Mix the onions, green pepper, and garlic with meat; cover and steam on medium heat until tender, 5 to 10 minutes. Add mushrooms, seasonings, and tomato sauce. Cover and let sauce simmer on low for at least 1 hour; stir occasionally.

*You may use canned tomato sauce or go completely homemade. If you decide on the homemade, choose 3 to 5 pounds ripe, firm sweet tomatoes. De-stem them, blanch quickly in boiling water to remove skins, and cut into quarters. Put in the cook pot and mash them down each time you stir the sauce so it becomes thick and juicy by serving time. This is my family's favorite.

Marilyn Petrenas
Colorado Springs, Colorado

Since elk has very little fat, to keep it from drying out during cooking, make sure there is at least 1/2 cup of liquid on meat at all times.

Pork and Venison Sausage

10	pounds lean pork	1/4	cup pepper
4	pounds venison	4	teaspoons cloves
5	pounds pork fat	2	teaspoons nutmeg
8	tablespoons sausage seasoning or sage	5	tablespoons salt
		1	tablespoon garlic salt

CUT meat into strips and put through grinder. Sprinkle with spices and salt; mix well. Put into pans that can be covered and place in cool place for 2 or 3 days. Make rolls of sausage to size desired for slicing and package in freezer wrap; store in freezer. In wintertime, in most parts of the country, this sausage can be kept most of the winter stored in a very cold place.

Illustration by Bill Culbertson

75

9 HOT STUFF!

Chili is the ambrosia of modern man.

"Chili mania focuses on a bowl of chili. It is a craving, a passion, an obsession for a simmered combination of meat and chili peppers whose distinctive aroma makes an indelible imprint on the senses." So begins a chapter in the book *Chili Lovers' Cook Book,* published by Golden West Publishers of Phoenix, Arizona. Authors of the book, Al and Mildred Fischer, elaborate:

"Even the word chili is exciting to a chili

Illustration by Dick Spencer

lover, for it evokes memories of a dish that warms the heart and embraces the body in an aura of sensuous satisfaction. Chili is the ambrosia of modern man."

Chili lovers fall into two groups: "If you want to make chili, make chili . . . if you want to make beans, make beans." But the chili-with-beans devotees say, "Chili tastes better with beans." So most chili cooks solve the dilemma by cooking meat with chili and serving beans on the side.

Even then, the confusion about chili and chili con carne has persisted for more than a century. To add the Spanish words *con carne* (with meat) to chili is redundant. Chili *is* meat, usually beef, flavored with ground red chili (the fruit of the capsicum), plus garlic, cumin, oregano, and sometimes other spices. Chili con carne, on the other hand, is green or red chili, and tomatoes, stewed with meat to flavor it. It is delicious, but is another dish entirely.

Whatever you call it, Americans have been eating it for generations. Although die-hard chili lovers profess to scorn canned chili, it is one of the top-selling canned goods in the country. Every major American meat packer cans it, and chili is marketed under almost every American food brand label.

Some chili brands are found only regionally, some are widely distributed. Gebhardt's is the brand most likely to be found on market shelves around the world. When William Gebhardt began canning chili in San Antonio in 1911, he first tried labeling it "carne con chili" for the sake of accuracy, but it never caught on. Now there are many other large canned chili makers, such as Hormel; Ranch Style, Incorporated, of Fort Worth; and Wold Brand, owned by The Quaker Oats Company.

Along in the 1960s "chili mix" was introduced—powdered chili ingredients to be added to meat (and beans if preferred). These range from hot to hottest and are much more pungent than the familiar chili powders found on spice shelves, which are blended to appeal to a wide market. Chili mixes are conveniently packaged in metal foil envelopes, brown paper, or clear plastic bags. They're canned in paste form, and are also sold in cellophane-wrapped bricks. More recently, liquid chili mixes in cans or glass containers have become available.

Gordon "Wick" Fowler is credited with one of the first mixes. He made up packets of special chili ingredients and gave away lots of packets to friends and chili enthusiasts. Before long, the demand got so great that it was either go into the chili business or go broke. So Fowler went into the chili business. He founded the original Caliente Chili Company on Red River Street in Austin, Tex., and began packaging his 2-Alarm Chili Mix in quantity. Wick's mix is now sold worldwide.

There are almost as many theories about how chili originated as there are one-and-only chili recipes. The only thing on which all agree is that chili, as we know it today, is as American as apple pie. It is believed that chili had its origins in the pemmican of the Southwest—jerky, fat, and native chilies pounded together to form a highly concentrated and nutritious trail ration.

Wick Fowler's Original Chili

3 pounds lean ground beef	6 or more cloves garlic, chopped
1½ cups canned tomato sauce	1 teaspoon salt
water	1 teaspoon cayenne
1 teaspoon Tabasco sauce	1 tablespoon paprika
3 heaping tablespoons chili powder	12 or more whole dried Japanese chilies (very hot)
1 teaspoon oregano	6 to 8 chiltepins (very, very hot)
1 teaspoon cumin	
2 onions, chopped	3 tablespoons flour

SEAR meat in a large skillet until gray in color. Transfer meat to chili pot, along with the tomato sauce and enough water to cover meat about ½ inch; mix well. Stir in Tabasco, chili powder, oregano, cumin, onions, garlic, salt, cayenne, and paprika. Add Japanese chilies and chiltepins; be careful not to break them open lest the hot seeds escape into the pot. Leave this for each chili eater to decide, after being served. Let simmer 1 hour, 45 minutes, gently stirring at intervals. About 30 minutes before done, skim grease off of the top. In separate bowl mix flour with enough water to make a paste. Add to chili and blend thoroughly.

Verl Miller's Plain Texas Chili

5 pounds coarse-ground chuck beef	6 tablespoons paprika
	¾ cup cumin
3 pounds coarse-ground antelope (or substitute equal amounts of beef or pork)	¼ pound fresh jalapeno peppers, minced
	¼ cup MSG
2 pounds chopped yellow onions	3 tablespoons salt
	5¾ cups whole canned tomatoes
5 ounces garlic, diced	2 10-ounce cans tomato sauce
½ cup chili powder	3 cans beer

BRAISE meat, then add all other ingredients except tomatoes, tomato sauce, and beer. Add these as needed. Simmer about 4 hours.

No Alarm Chili

1/4	cup margarine or butter	1 1/2	tablespoons cumin
5	pounds lean beef, cubed	1/2	teaspoon pepper
4	large onions, chopped	4	cups tomato sauce
1 1/2	green peppers, chopped	2	tablespoons beef bouillon
1	clove garlic	3/4	teaspoon red pepper
8	bay leaves	1/2	cup red wine vinegar with
1	tablespoon salt		garlic
2	tablespoons chili powder	1/2	tablespoon Accent
1	tablespoon paprika	1	tablespoon oregano

MELT butter and brown meat in a 14-inch Dutch oven. Add onions and green pepper. Cook until tender. Add remaining ingredients. Simmer 2 to 3 hours or until desired thickness. Garnish with hot peppers. Serves 10 to 15 people.

Val and Marie Cowley

It stands to reason that chili would originate where there was an abundant supply of its two prime ingredients: meat and chili. The meat was buffalo, venison, and later, beef, and the spice was the fiery *chilipiquin*, which still grows wild in Texas and Louisiana. Pemmican chili is about as basic as chili can get.

In wagon trains passing across the sparse wilderness of west Texas, food was eaten on the move. Jerky and pemmican were the prime fare on these on-the-trail meals. Travelers going east are certain to have carried the makings for jerky and pemmican chili, or both, and the mountain men carried them from their Texas rendezvous all over the West and Northwest.

Chili was firmly established on the Army menu sometime after the Civil War, but others argue that chili was regular fare as far back as 1830. Western history scholars claim chili originated on the Rio Grande and was created by the *lavanderas* (washerwomen) who'd come north with the Mexican armies. Some of the women stayed north of the border when the Mex-

ican army left and served the Texas militiamen who kept border watch. The tough meat available needed long cooking and the lavanderas had little seasoning except the native wild marjoram and red chili. From these scant ingredients the women created a stew, and the dish known today as chili is a lineal descendant of these stews.

Bill Bridges of Ventura, Calif., may have written the bible on chili. His book titled *The Great American Chili Book* has more than 200 pages of chili lore and almost 100 recipes for chili, if you can imagine that many variations using basically meat and peppers.

One of Bridges' recipes is LBJ's Pedernales River Chili, which Lyndon Johnson served at the White House when he was president. Johnson's recipe is fairly simple, but does call for venison instead of beef, which is surprising in that Mr. Johnson raised beef cattle.

Bridges' book has many interesting titles for chili. There's Coney Island, Green Bay Super Bowl, Ptomaine Tommy's, Laid Back, Bandito, Bite-the-Bullet, Bowl of Fire, Es Not Too Bad, Hog-Heaven, Penny Pincher's, and Working Women's Chili.

If those don't suit you, try a bowl of Buzzard's Breath Chili, or you can cook up a pot of Father Tom Warren's Oso Flaco (lean bear) Chili. The recipe says it's okay to substitute ground round if you can't find bear meat in your market. Bridges' book gives a recipe for Mountain Oyster Chili and Bridges goes on to tell that Will Rogers, the gum-chewin', rope-twirlin' cowboy-turned-actor from Oklahoma, dearly loved his Mountain Oyster (calf fries) Chili.

There are plenty of recipes for chili using venison, moose, caribou, antelope, buffalo, mutton, chicken, canned roast beef, sausage, beef kidneys, and, of course, beef. All the exotic kinds of meat aside, it's plain that good old down-home chili is made chiefly from hamburger meat or coarse ground beef. Many chili cooks prefer lean beef cut in very small pieces or diced, with suet added. The tougher (and cheaper) cuts not only suffice, they are superior in chili making.

Some claim that a 5-cent bowl of chili saved more lives in the Great Depression than any other thing. In those days, all-night chili joints not only offered warmth on a cold night, but a bowl of hot chili

Basic Chili

4	pounds chili meat (coarse-ground round steak or well-trimmed chuck)	3	tablespoons chili powder
		1 1/2	cups crushed canned tomatoes
1	large onion, chopped		salt and pepper to taste
2	cloves garlic, diced		small amount of liquid hot sauce (optional)
1	teaspoon oregano		
1	teaspoon cumin	2	cups hot water

PLACE meat, onion, and garlic in large fry pan or Dutch oven. Cook until light colored. Add remaining ingredients. Bring to boil, lower heat, and simmer about 2 hours. Serves 10.

Mountain Oyster Chili

An essential part of the cowboy mystique is the love of roasted or fried mountain oysters, or calf fries, or prairie oysters—all cowboy names for the testicles of bull calves. During spring roundup, as the annual crop of calves is branded, the bull calves are turned into meat-producing steers by castrating them.

2	pounds calf fries, washed, skinned, and minced butter or margarine	3	tablespoons chili molido or chili powder salt to taste
1	large onion, chopped		water
2	cloves garlic, minced		flour (optional)
2	tablespoons whole cumin		

IN a heavy pot, cook the calf fries in butter or margarine for a few minutes. Add onion, garlic, and cumin and continue cooking until browned. Stir in chili molido or chili powder and salt. Add enough water to cover and cook gently for 1½ to 2 hours, stirring occasionally. Water may be added, if necessary. About 10 minutes before serving make a paste by mixing a small amount of flour and water; stir into chili until desired consistency.

"My chili is so hot the crew keeps the branding irons in it."

usually carried with it the right to enough free crackers to fill in the empty corners of the stomach. As times got worse and money got scarcer, the ratio of beans to chili grew steadily higher in chili pots, both at home and in the chili joints. Straight chili lovers yearned for the good times, when they could march into a chili parlor again and order a bowl straight, and to heck with the cost, which could be as much as 25 cents.

I was attending a luncheon in October of 1987 at the downtown Hyatt Regency in Phoenix, given by the Cowboy Artists of America, when Chan Bergen, retired *Western Horseman* editor, handed me a bottle containing a bunch of bilious-green, peanut-sized berries pickled in vinegar. Chan explained that the bottle of sauce had been delivered to the magazine offices in Colorado Springs by Luther and Agnes Richardson of Fort Worth, with instructions that it be given to me. I was seated at a table with friends Jim Bob Tinsley and wife Dottie, from Ocala, Florida. I removed the cap from the bottle and took a whiff. It seared the membranes of my nostrils, but I managed to keep a straight face. I handed it to Jim Bob, suggesting he sample this "mild" chili sauce. Trustingly, Jim Bob tilted the bottle back and took a long swig.

After the fire department left and Jim Bob quit smoking, he said, "Let me have

Sweet Chili

1	pound ground beef	¼	cup packed brown sugar
1	pound bacon	1	tablespoon liquid smoke (or hickory seasoning)
2	31-ounce cans pork an' beans		
1	pound can kidney beans	3	tablespoons white vinegar
1	pound can butter lima beans	1	teaspoon salt
1	cup chopped onions		dash of pepper
1	cup ketchup		

BROWN beef and fry bacon to medium crisp, drain. Combine meats and set aside. Stir all remaining ingredients together in a large crockpot. Gently stir in meats. Cover and cook on high for 3 hours or low if cooking all day; stir occasionally. Serve hot with a tossed green salad and French bread. Serves 8 people.

Lorraine Cocroft
Woodland Park, Colorado

this a while. I want to try it on some of these *tough* guys." His fun was spoiled somewhat, because CA members were cautious and highly suspicious, most only venturing a timid smell. Some others, more daring, wet one finger in the sauce and gingerly touched it to their tongues.

Jim Bob got out of that one alive and, after returning to our table, we discussed chili and chiliheads (knowledgeable chili lovers). I told him you have to have a deep respect for the power of the chili pepper. Some even have a devout reverence and shudder to think of consuming a meal without flavoring their meat, beans, salads, or eggs with generous amounts of their favorite chili sauce. I told him chilies

Green Chili

1	pound lean pork, cut in 3/4-inch cubes	1	16-ounce can whole tomatoes, coarsely chopped
2	tablespoons flour	2	7-ounce cans diced green chilies
2	tablespoons lard	1/4	teaspoon oregano
1/2	cup chopped onions	2 1/2	teaspoons salt
1	clove garlic, minced	2	cups water

ROLL meat in flour. Melt lard in a large skillet and brown meat thoroughly. Add onion and garlic, and cook until onion is soft. Add remaining ingredients. Simmer covered for 1 to 2 hours, stirring occasionally. Remove cover and simmer until desired consistency, about 10 minutes.

aren't just a spicy seasoning and the red varieties, whether fresh, canned, or dried, are a good source of vitamin A. All fresh chilies, no matter their color, contain vitamin C.

Jim Bob snorted, "If you don't mind, I'll take my vitamin C in Florida sunshine and oranges!"

Back at the ranch, I decided I'd find out all I could on these little-bitty, great-balls-of-fire chilies. I wrote to Luther Richardson, thanking him for the sauce and asking him for all the information he had. In a short time I received his letter. He wrote:

"I can't give you a lot of information, but these grow wild in Texas and other parts. Some call it the "chili-p-teen" (chiltepin). I think they're also called Bird's Eye and Turkey Pepper. I guess they're called Turkey Pepper because in dry season down here the turkeys are short on food and they eat a lot of these little peppers. The peppers make the meat so hot, when

you eat it you'll need a sweatband, and a napkin as big as a saddle blanket to mop with.

"To make the pepper sauce, put the green peppers in a bottle with cold vinegar and let it age about three months. If you don't like food real hot, kinda tiptoe when you shake this sauce on your beans. You can add more vinegar as it gets low in the bottle. A bottle of peppers, with vinegar added once in a while, has been known to last many years.

"You can also make red salve out of it. When the peppers are red, but not dry, put them in a blender with a little vinegar and olive oil and blend until smooth like mustard or mayonnaise. When you take the top off the blender, stand back, or you will find yourself on the back forty when you get your breath and stop coughing and sneezing. This red salve is good on a sandwich, or just a small amount on the point of your knife and use it on pinto beans, soup, stew, or mulligan. Unless you are about 100 percent mean, don't lick the knife. Some salve on your lips is like sticking the wrong end of a cigarette in your mouth. You can pick these peppers off the stalk barehanded, but when you crush them, look out—they're *bad!*

"I grow chili-p-teens on the south side of my house. When they die down after the first frost, I cut them back about 4 to 6 inches from the ground and cover them with old hay. In the spring I take the hay off and they come back year after year. It takes a loose, sandy soil for them to get 3 to 4 feet tall and make a lot of peppers. It's

Chilies Rellenos

(stuffed chilies)

1	tablespoon flour	1	pound Cheddar, sliced thick
4	eggs	3	tablespoons cooking oil or lard
8	canned green chilies		

WHIP the flour and eggs to make a thin batter; a little water may be added if desired. Take as many seeds out of the chilies as needed to reduce the heat. Lay the cheese inside the chilies evenly. Drag each chili through the egg batter, first one side up, then the other. Drain any surplus batter back into dish and repeat until most of the batter is used up. Heat the oil or lard until very hot and lay the chilies in it. Turn after 5 minutes; pour any leftover batter over the chilies and fry until done. If any egg is left uncooked, tip the skillet and let the batter run down and catch in the fried batter and cheese sticking out of the chilies.

hard to get seeds to come up, but if you have a green thumb you can get them to start. There are a lot of seeds in each pod."

Luther's letter only whetted my appetite for more information, so I wrote to the real chili expert, my good friend Judy England. Judy owns and operates the Santa Cruz Chili & Spice Company of Amada and Tumacacori, in the beautiful Santa Cruz Valley north of Tucson, Arizona. Judy wrote back:

"Chiltepins grow wild on bushes and are also cultivated near Hermosillo, Mexico, and we carry them at our chili center. They are very hot and are often used in menudo. They are dried when fully ripe, and used sparingly for seasonings in meat and beans. I once saw a man at our ranch in Mexico crumble a handful on his fried eggs. He then cut up the eggs and tossed them in his mouth without a grimace. My advice, unless a person has a highly cultivated south-of-the-border taste— go easy on chiltepins."

Judy sent me a small packet containing about 35 wrinkled red peppers that are about the size of peas. Just the size of the packet should be a clue to its potency.

Naturally, the Southwest is the hotbed of chili lore. Most people north of Lapland (where Texas laps over into Oklahoma) refrain from getting into passionate arguments about chili, yet all over the world, lovers of clams, oysters, lobsters, and other seafood like chili sauce as a condiment. A tablespoon of hot chili sauce added to mayonnaise, along with a liberal squirt of lemon juice, lends character to seafood salads.

The chili belt runs roughly from south-ern California, with forays into Nevada, Utah, and Colorado, to as far south and east as Georgia. Most people are familiar with Louisiana hot sauce, and peppers grown in Louisiana are deserving of an article of their own.

I've been eating chilies for more than 50 years, and love the stuff, yet I've a good idea that Luther Richardson's chili-p-teen sauce will last a long, long time at our house.

Support groups for chili and chili making have sprung up and there are three organizations with worldwide memberships. The earliest of these is the Chili Appreciation Society International (CASI) founded in Dallas in 1939. Then there is the International Chili Society (ICS), and the International Connoisseurs of Green & Red Chili (ICG&RC). There are world championship chili cookoffs each year, and the ICS cookoff in California attracts 30,000 or more people who watch 40 state or regional champs attempt to prove that their chili is the one and only. All I can say is, if you've never attended a chili cookoff and the opportunity presents itself, run, don't walk, and get a front seat to a great show.

Make Your Own Enchilada Sauce

2	cups tomato sauce	1	teaspoon salt
2	cups water	1/2	teaspoon garlic powder
1	cup minced onion	1	teaspoon chili powder (more
2	bouillon cubes, dissolved		if you like it hot)

MIX all ingredients in saucepan and boil 5 minutes.

Joyce House
Kingman, Arizona

Hot Sauce

(salsa picante)

In Spanish, *picante* means spicy hot, and *caliente* means hot from flame.

2	medium cans tomatoes, drained	1	cup vinegar
4	tablespoons coarse-ground		salt
	red chili		pinch of oregano
1	medium onion, grated		pinch of cumin

MASH the tomatoes with a fork and stir in the chili. Marinate onion in the vinegar. Let both stand for half an hour. Mix together, then add salt and spices, stir well. Refrigerate and serve as a side dish.

This sauce will freeze, and can be prepared well in advance.

81

10 FRIJOLES

The lowly bean has been largely ignored by our affluent society, but in the Southwest, beans are considered a necessity.

There's a legend in the Southwest that says in order for a man to start a cow ranch he needs only three items: sourdough starter, jerky line, and a bean pot.

The beans for the pot are *frijoles*, a Mexican word for beans. Even when a tenderfoot calls them "fry-joles" a southwesterner knows what he means. But, any way you say it, just plain beans means only one kind, and that is the spotted brown-and-white-pinto bean.

There's a little town in the southwestern corner of Colorado called Dove Creek that loudly proclaims to be "The Pinto Bean Center of the World." Maybe so, because that area sure raises jillions of pinto beans, probably enough to blow some small countries off the map. Still, there are trainloads of beans raised in other states such as Arizona, New Mexico, Texas, and even Nebraska.

The lowly bean has been largely ignored by our affluent society, but in the Southwest, beans are considered a necessity. They take the place of the Irishman's potatoes, the Oriental's rice, the Italian's pasta. And every westerner has his or her own idea how pinto beans should be cooked, and arguments short of shooting wars have been waged over their proper preparation.

On the West Coast, some backyard chefs cook up a pot of beans, doctor them up, and call them chili beans. They put in a handful of chili powder, which in truth is about two-thirds sawdust and one-third red chili.

Arizonans and New Mexicans almost never put chili in their beans. I know this denial probably comes as a shock to many readers, but the chili is usually served as a salsa, or as a fiery hot sauce that can be dashed on the frijoles, or as a dish of canned green chili on the side. *Chili con carne* is chili and meat and is not added to the beans.

In the summer of 1976 I was invited to take part in the Bicentennial Festival of American Folklife in Washington, D.C. I had hauled my old chuck wagon from Arizona and each day cooked sourdough biscuits, chili con carne, and frijoles. I had to take a 100-pound sack of New Mexico pinto beans because I was told the D.C. area had no pinto beans for sale in their grocery stores. Thousands of tourists to the mall that week got their first sample of pinto beans. Many questions were asked: Why isn't chili in the beans? How come my chili con carne (chili and small chunks of beef) isn't made of hamburger? Why aren't the chili con carne and beans mixed together? It's hard to re-educate the general public on their idea of what chili beans should look and taste like.

Beans and bean cookery can be a passionate subject. All cooks agree, however, there are some cut-and-dried rules not even a teen-age bride would dream of breaking when it comes to cooking beans. One of them is that altitude has a lot to do with how long it takes beans to cook. At sea level, beans are done in 3 hours or less, while in the high country of anything over 6,000 feet, it might take most of the day. Also, old beans take longer to cook than new beans. Old beans (any past 2 years old) should be soaked overnight. New beans, and this means ones harvested the past fall, seldom need soaking; if they do, an hour will do the trick, after first bringing them to a boil.

Here's a cowboy crew camped by a set of stockpens (background). The cook has his chuck wagon set up, and some of the boys are eating. There's no date or ID on this photo, loaned courtesy of the Texas and Southwestern Cattle Raisers Foundation, Fort Worth.

Beans should be cooked slowly. Hard boiling makes them tough. So let them take their time, at an even simmer. An iron pot isn't suitable for cooking beans, as it turns them dark and imparts a metallic taste. Dutch ovens may be wonderful for baking sourdough bread or frying cowboy steaks, but they shouldn't be used for cooking beans. Granite or stainless steel pots work best.

Basic Frijoles

(pinto beans)

2	cups pinto beans	1	onion, diced
6	cups water	1	clove garlic (optional)
1/2	pound salt pork or 6 slices bacon, cut in small pieces	1 1/2	teaspoon salt

SOAK beans overnight. Add salt pork, onion, and garlic. Simmer until almost done, then add salt. Cooking time varies depending upon altitude.

Saturday Night Special

(pinto bean casserole)

4	cups cooked pinto beans with juice	1	cup ketchup
1	tablespoon packed brown sugar	1	teaspoon savory salt
2	tablespoons white sugar		cheese, grated or diced

COMBINE all ingredients except cheese. Pour in a 2-quart casserole dish. Sprinkle with cheese and bake 30 to 40 minutes at 375 degrees.

Pinto Bean Sandwiches

When our kids were small and in grade school, I worked, and often when it came to lunch-making time in the mornings, I found no lunch meats, cheese, or anything else that is supposed to be suitable for school lunches. The kids clamored for bean sandwiches and, even though my conscience hurt me, I complied. Later I found they traded their lowly bean sandwiches to their schoolmates, and I overheard them bragging they could get a "real baloney" sandwich in trade anytime.

Mack, on the rare times I can force a lunch on him, asks for a bean sandwich. He likes thick slices of onions on his.

pinto beans, cooked	chopped green chilies (optional)
onion, chopped	mayonnaise
sweet or dill pickle, diced	mustard

DRAIN well and mash cooked pinto beans. Add onion, pickle (sweet or dill), green chilies, and as much mayonnaise or mustard as you like. Just don't get the spread too soupy.

Beans and Short Ribs

1	pound pinto beans	2	tablespoons prepared mustard
6	cups water	2	teaspoons chili powder
2	tablespoons oil	1/2	cup packed brown sugar
4	pounds beef short ribs	1	teaspoon Worcestershire sauce
4	medium onions, chopped	2	teaspoons salt
1	8-ounce can tomato sauce	2	teaspoons liquid smoke
1	tablespoon cider vinegar		

SOAK beans overnight. Brown ribs in oil and set aside. Saute onions in pan drippings until tender. Stir remaining ingredients into undrained beans. Top with ribs; cover and simmer 4 to 5 hours, or until beans are tender.

Slow cooker method may be used. Use the 4½-quart or larger size. Soak beans as above; drain, reserving only 1 cup liquid. In cooker, combine all ingredients except ribs. Brown ribs and add to cooker. Cover and cook 7 to 8 hours or until ribs and beans are tender.

Use a granite or aluminum pot for cooking beans. A Dutch oven will turn the beans dark and imparts a metallic taste.

Another important rule is never, never add cold water to boiling beans. When adding water, it should be the same temperature as the water cooking the beans. And remember, salt is added toward the end of cooking time.

Pinto beans do not need a lot of mumbo jumbo added to make them tasty, but most cooks agree that a generous amount of diced bacon or salt pork, a big juicy onion, and salt and pepper are necessary. Old-timers called salt pork "sow-belly" or "sow-bosom" and most thought salt pork made beans taste better than bacon. They are not alone in this belief, as I much prefer salt pork as a seasoning in making beans tasty.

No one has yet found a way, luckily, to botch the lowly bean the way wheat flour and white rice have been ruined. If a person is still interested in a food that is cheap, keeps indefinitely while in the dry state, is low in fat, high in protein, and improves in flavor each time it is reheated, he'll do well to stock up on sacks of pinto beans, "Mexican strawberries" as southwesterners like to call them.

When cooking for a roundup crew, the cook never stops his bean cooking; while one batch is soaking, a second is cooking, and a third is being eaten by hungry cowboys. Seldom are any left from one meal to the next for refrying.

Mexican Beans

(refritos)

1	pound pinto beans	½	cup bacon drippings or lard
1½	quarts water		salt to taste
2	medium onions, minced		

SOAK beans in water overnight. Simmer slowly until they are very tender, 3 hours or more, depending upon altitude. Saute onion in bacon drippings until soft, but not browned. Mash beans with potato masher and add onions, drippings, and salt; mix well. Continue cooking over very low heat, stirring frequently, until beans thicken.

Never add cold water to boiling beans. Make sure it is the same temperature as the water cooking the beans.

Now, we come to refried beans, or *refritos* as they say in Spanish. Refritos are cooked beans fried once, not twice; don't argue—they're always called refried beans.

Beans to be used as refried beans are usually cooked with little or no seasoning, and salt and fat added as they are mashed. Then the beans are used for refried beans, or *refrito con queso*. This is made by melting Monterey Jack cheese, cubed, in the beans and cooking slowly until the cheese has melted. Sharp Cheddar cheese is also good.

A *tostada* is a corn tortilla fried crisp in deep fat, spread with refried beans, topped with grated cheese, and sprinkled with diced fresh tomatoes. Canned tortillas can be found in most grocery stores throughout the United States.

You often hear the complaint: "I like beans, but they don't like me." There are as many different remedies for taking the "sting" out of the volatile bean as there are ways of cooking the brutes. A teaspoon of baking soda, added while the beans are cooking, seems to be the most popular method. Others swear a diced carrot, added to the seasonings, will tame the beast; I've even heard that half a cup of castor oil can successfully remove its

Red Fire (Beans)

When serving Red Fire Beans, keep hot over candle warmer or in chafing dish with tostados or fried tortillas; or serve on small individual plates over fritos; or as a filling for split broiled hot dogs. This is also delectable over rare hamburgers.

4	cups red kidney beans	1	teaspoon juice from peppers
½	pound butter	¼	cup grated onion
½	pound mild Cheddar cheese, grated	1	large clove garlic, minced salt to taste
4	jalapeno peppers, diced		paprika (optional)

COVER beans with cold water, bring to boil, reduce heat and simmer until tender (cooking time varies depending upon altitude). Drain and puree through food sieve or mill. Place in large double boiler or saucepan over hot water; add remaining ingredients and cook until cheese is melted. Paprika may be added for a redder red.

Tostadas

12	corn tortillas	1	or 2 ripe tomatoes, diced
	oil		shredded lettuce
2	cups cooked beans		hot sauce (optional)
½	pound Cheddar cheese, grated		

FRY each tortilla in hot fat until crisp and brown. Place on paper toweling to drain.

Place cooked beans in small skillet; bring to boil and mash with potato masher until blended. Spread a generous layer of beans on each tortilla. Add cheese, while beans are still hot, lettuce, and top with tomatoes. Sprinkle on a few drops of hot sauce if you are so inclined.

Makes 12 tostadas but does not mean it will serve 12 people, or even 6. Allow at least 3 tostadas per person.

Pinto beans do not need a lot of mumbo jumbo to make them tasty.

There is no date or identification on this old photo of cowboys chowing down.

Photo courtesy Texas and Southwestern Cattle Raisers Foundation, Fort Worth.

Bean Bake

1	27-ounce can baked beans	¼	pound bacon, cut into thin strips and lightly fried
1	28-ounce can whole kernel sweet corn, drained	1	tablespoon (or more) brown sugar
1	large onion, sliced		

LAYER all ingredients in a casserole dish or bean pot and bake at 350 degrees for about 1 hour. Makes 4 to 6 servings.

Generous amounts of salt pork or diced bacon added to the beans give a wonderful flavor.

claws. Many cooks swear by another method of first soaking the beans and pouring off the water; then adding fresh water and simmering one hour. Then drain off this second water, add new water and your seasonings, and cook until done.

My dear reader: Try one, or all the remedies, and if one works, be sure to let me know.

Baked Pork an' Beans

1	large can of pork an' beans	1	tablespoon prepared mustard
½	cup packed brown sugar	6	strips sliced bacon
½	cup dark molasses		

USE a shallow baking dish and mix brown sugar, molasses, and mustard well with the pork an' beans. Lay thin strips of bacon on top and bake at 350 degrees for 1 hour or until bubbly and the bacon is crisp. This dish is good hot or cold and makes a fine addition to a picnic lunch.

Western Baked Beans

3	cups pinto beans	1	or more teaspoons red chili powder
	salt and pepper to taste	1	cup tomato sauce
2	small onions, diced	3	slices bacon or ½ cup salt pork, diced
1	clove garlic, minced		
½	cup packed brown sugar		

COVER beans with water and soak overnight. Simmer slowly for about 1 hour. Drain the beans saving the liquid. Put beans, salt, pepper, onions, and garlic into casserole dish. Sprinkle beans with brown sugar and chili powder, then cover with tomato sauce and 1 cup of reserved bean water. Arrange bacon or salt pork on top. Cover and bake in 300-degree oven for 5 hours. Add bean liquid when needed. Serves 8 to 10.

Vera's Baked Beans

½ pound bacon
1 pound lean ground beef
1 large onion, chopped
1 small green pepper, chopped
½ cup packed brown sugar
½ cup ketchup
1 16-ounce can homestyle chili sauce
2 tablespoons mustard
½ pound precooked ham, cut into ½-inch cubes
2 31-ounce cans pork an' beans

BROWN bacon and ground beef in a 12-inch Dutch oven, preheated over 9 to 10 briquets. Saute onion and green pepper until onion is clear. Drain off excess fat. Add brown sugar, ketchup, chili sauce, and mustard. Simmer for 15 minutes. Add beans and ham. Cover and add approximately 15 briquets to lid. Simmer for 2 hours. Serves 12.

Beans are low in fat, high in protein, inexpensive, and keep indefinitely in the dry form.

Barbecue Baked Beans

Barbecued beans are very similar to the so-called Ranch beans in the Southwest and, as you'd expect, they have the characteristic barbecue taste.

A generous slice of smoky bacon rind used instead of sliced bacon will give a more decidedly country flavor. You can use brown sugar to replace the molasses if you like. Some like a generous dash of hot pepper sauce.

2 cups dried navy or pinto beans
8 slices bacon, diced
½ cup chopped onion
2 tablespoons molasses
2 tablespoons chili powder
¾ cup ketchup
2 tablespoons prepared mustard
1 teaspoon salt

SOAK beans in cold water overnight. Fry bacon until crisp. Drain drippings from bacon into baking dish or bean pot. Add all remaining ingredients to fat and blend. Drain soaked beans and add to mixture. Crumble the crisp bacon over top. Add enough water just to cover beans. Cover dish or bean pot and bake at 325 degrees for 4 hours. Add more hot water if needed. Uncover beans during last 30 minutes. Serve from baking dish. Serves 6 to 8.

Barbecued Lima Beans

2 1-pound, 13-ounce cans lima beans
⅔ cup evaporated milk
5 slices bacon, diced
1 cup sweet green pepper, seeded and chopped
1 clove garlic, minced
¼ cup vinegar
¼ cup packed dark brown sugar
1 tablespoon Worcestershire sauce
1 teaspoon chili powder
1 tablespoon cornstarch
1 tablespoon prepared mustard
2 8-ounce cans tomato sauce

DRAIN lima beans and put in mixing bowl. Add milk and set aside. In skillet saute bacon until cooked but *not* crisp. Add green pepper and garlic. Cook 10 minutes over moderate heat. Add vinegar, sugar, Worcestershire sauce, chili powder, cornstarch (moistened with a little water), mustard, and tomato sauce. Blend. Cook until thickened, stirring constantly. Add salt if needed. Combine sauce with beans and milk. Turn into a 9½ by 13½-inch baking dish or casserole dish. Bake at 350 degrees for 50 minutes. Serve with beef, ham, chicken, pork, or hot dogs. Serves 6.

11 Y'ALL COME!

VEGETABLES AND CASSEROLES

Vegetables

Pat Paulsell once told me about the time he and his brother Lloyd were holding down a cow camp on their daddy's spread near Sanders, Arizona.

"We were just two big, overgrown teenagers and glad to have a summer job. Only thing we didn't like about the setup was we were batchin' and neither one of us knew how to cook. So we lived mostly out of cans, and when we ran out we had permission to go to the Indian trading post and charge whatever grub we needed.

"During the summer we had a flood, and when we went to the post we found the owners had suffered quite a bit of damage to their stock. Almost all the labels had washed off the canned stuff. We wanted peaches in the worst way, and the trader sold us a half-dozen cans, swearing he knew for sure they were peaches. But, when we got back to camp we opened a can and found, instead of slick yellow

Clair Haight, cook for the Hashknife outfit (out of Winslow, AZ) from 1916 to the late 1920s.

88

Spinach Loaf

2 cups chopped spinach, washed and drained
1 cup toasted, soft bread crumbs
1 medium onion, grated
1 clove garlic, crushed
1 medium green pepper, chopped
3 eggs, beaten
1/4 cup butter, melted
salt and pepper to taste
hard-cooked egg yolk, sieved

IN a mixing bowl combine all ingredients except egg yolk and blend thoroughly. Turn into a buttered 5 by 8-inch loaf pan. Set in a larger pan with 1 inch of warm water and bake at 325 degrees for about 1 hour. When done, let cool for a few minutes, then turn out on a heated platter. Sprinkle with egg yolk. Serve with chicken, turkey, ham, or lamb. Serves 6 to 8.

peaches, some sort of dark green stuff that looked like alfalfa."

Years later, in telling of the incident, Pat laughed, "Well, that's what we thought it was, canned alfalfa! And we threw it out. We were so ignorant . . . we'd never seen canned spinach."

We live on canned tomaters
An' soggy sourdough bread
Coffee strong as alkali
It's a wonder we ain't dead

This little verse was found in an old-time cowboy's journal. So we gather not all roundup cooks were good cooks, nor did all owners provide ample supplies. Back in the 1930s there was one ranch in southern Arizona, best left unnamed, that was more than skimpy on chuck, and this outfit was known far and wide as the Macaroni Cattle Company. Some of the cowboys working for this spread swore they were lucky if they got the "tomaters" to go with the macaroni.

Sweet Potatoes With Marshmallows and Pecans

3 cups mashed sweet potatoes
3 tablespoons honey
1 teaspoon cinnamon
3/4 teaspoon salt
3 tablespoons butter
1 package marshmallows
1/2 cup chopped pecans

BEAT potatoes until light; add honey, cinnamon, salt, and butter. Spread half of the potatoes in a buttered baking dish, add a layer of marshmallows, sprinkle with nuts. Cover with remaining potatoes and top with layer of marshmallows. Cover and bake at 375 degrees for 10 minutes. Uncover and let marshmallows brown. Serve immediately with ham, turkey, or chicken. Serves 6 to 8.

Scalloped Corn

1 can cream-style corn
1/4 cup chopped onions
1/2 cup minced celery
3/4 cup grated sharp cheese
1 egg
2 tablespoons chopped green pepper
1 cup milk
salt and pepper to taste
2 or 3 slices bacon, chopped
1 cup coarse cracker crumbs

MIX all ingredients except bacon and cracker crumbs, and pour into buttered casserole dish. Top with bacon and cracker crumbs. Bake at 325 degrees for 1 hour.

This goes well served with baked ham.

Lorraine Price
Show Low, Arizona

Scalloped Onions

4 large onions, sliced
1 can chopped green chilies
1/2 pound grated cheese
2 cups toasted bread cubes
1/2 cup margarine or butter
1/4 cup flour
2 cups milk
1 teaspoon salt
1/2 teaspoon pepper
2 eggs, beaten

COOK onions in boiling water about 10 to 15 minutes; drain. Place half in a 2-quart casserole dish. Add half of the green chilies, cheese, and bread cubes. Repeat layers.

In saucepan melt butter and blend in flour. Add milk gradually and cook, stirring constantly until thickened; add salt and pepper. Add a little of the hot mixture to eggs, gradually combining together. Pour sauce over the layers of onions and bread cubes; top with remaining bread cubes. Bake at 350 degrees for 30 minutes. Serves 6.

Tomato and Green Bean Casserole

This is a good dish served in camp, as so often you run out of fresh vegetables. Also, most of the time I fried some diced bacon or bits of salt pork and sauteed the onion in the grease.

1 16-ounce can tomatoes	¼ teaspoon salt
1 16-ounce can whole green beans, drained	⅛ teaspoon pepper
½ teaspoon dried dillweed or other herb	1 tablespoon butter or margarine
	1 tablespoon ketchup
	1 small onion, diced

SAUTE onion in butter, then combine all ingredients in a 1-quart casserole dish. Cover and bake on center rack at 350 degrees for 20 to 30 minutes. Makes 4 servings.

Tomatoes

Canned tomatoes have been around for quite a while, but probably not as long as some people think. It was between 1830 and 1840 when William Underwood first started canning tomatoes. Earlier than that, Underwood had offered to wholesalers canned or bottled pickles, sauces, mustard, preserves, and cranberries preserved without sugar in bottles. However, tomatoes were not canned until 1830, as people were convinced tomatoes were deadly

Tomato Pudding (Casserole)

For a very large roundup crew or hunting party, increase biscuits by 5 for every can of tomatoes. Bacon drippings make the best pudding.

5 or 6 leftover baking powder biscuits	1 large can tomatoes (mashed)
¼ cup butter or bacon drippings	salt and pepper to taste

IN a skillet, melt butter. Crumble biscuits into melted butter, stirring constantly until biscuits are golden brown. Add tomatoes and mix slightly. Add salt and pepper as needed. Place lid on skillet and let pudding cook on very low heat for 5 to 10 minutes. Serve with pinto beans and Dutch-oven steaks.

Mock Oysters

(taken from *Queen of the Household* cookbook, 1902)
Instead of canned tomatoes, you can use 4 large ripe tomatoes, peeled and chopped and mashed, but do not need to be cooked.

½ teaspoon salt	2 cups canned tomatoes, drained
¼ teaspoon pepper	1 cup flour
1 tablespoon sugar	1 teaspoon baking powder

ADD seasonings and sugar to tomatoes. Combine flour and baking powder to tomato mixture. Melt a small amount of bacon drippings in a skillet. Drop batter by tablespoonfuls and fry over moderate heat. Fry on both sides until browned.

poison. We know this prejudice was overcome because Underwood had tomato plants imported from England and was raising them to can. One of the old labels, of the 1835-40 era, now in the possession of the present Underwood firm, reads: "Hermetically sealed tomatoes. This bottle contains the substance of about two dozen tomatoes and will keep any length of time. It is prepared by straining the seeds and skins from tomatoes and evaporating the watery particles by slow heat."

Cow country cooks weren't long in finding that canned tomatoes were almost indispensable when it came to turning out larrupin' meals for hungry cowboys. Next to canned milk, it was probably the one item of canned goods always on the list handed to the boss headed for town to replenish supplies. Most outfits thought canned goods a horrible extravagance.

I asked my favorite old-time cowboy what he considered a convenience food. He replied, "Whatever is to the front of the icebox." I told him that wasn't exactly what I meant, so he went on to say, "Canned tomatoes." He said back in the late 1920s, one hot summer he and John

Breaded Tomatoes

This dish is best cooked in a Dutch oven or heavy iron skillet with a well-fitting lid. A very good way to use up leftover bread. Some cooks add 1 tablespoon sugar.

6 slices bacon, chopped	1 large can tomatoes
1 medium onion, diced	salt and pepper to taste
4 cups bread, cubed	grated cheese

FRY bacon and onions until just done. Leave in all bacon grease and add bread cubes. Stir to mix and let brown slightly before adding tomatoes. Season to taste. Add lid and let simmer at very low heat for 15 to 20 minutes. Top with grated cheese and let melt.

Squash and Corn Casserole

This recipe is made by guess and by gosh. The kinds of squash depend on what you have on hand. I like to use three kinds: yellow gooseneck, tender Patty Pan scallop, and a few young zucchini.

4	cups sliced squash	3	or 4 sun-ripened tomatoes, sliced
1	medium onion, sliced	1	or 2 mild chilies
1	clove of garlic, minced (optional)		salt and pepper to taste
3	to 4 cups fresh corn	1/4	cup butter or margarine
		2	cups shredded yellow cheese

COMBINE all vegetables in saucepan with about 1 cup water. Boil until about half done; drain well. Add all to casserole dish; stir in butter and top with shredded cheese. Bake in 350-degree oven for about 30 minutes. Do not overcook.

Variations: omitting cheese, topping with crisp bacon bits and dotted with butter. All chilies can be omitted. You can even leave out the tomatoes. This casserole goes well with barbecue.

"Coming into camp in the early afternoon, me and John fixed up a meal of some kind. Generally we just crumpled up some cold biscuits in a bowl and soaked them with a couple large cans of tomatoes."

Dallies were hired by the Hashknife outfit out of Winslow, Ariz., to snap out a bunch of broncs.

"Coming into camp in the early afternoon, me and John fixed up a meal of some kind. Generally we just crumpled up some cold biscuits in a bowl and soaked them with a couple large cans of tomatoes. We kept the tomatoes cool by lowering the cans into a barrel that caught our drinking water from the end of the pipe comin' from the windmill. Other times, coming in after dark, we'd fry up some pieces of salt pork and a big yellow onion in an iron skillet. We'd break up some leftover sourdough biscuits. We'd let the bread soak up the grease, then pour in a large can of tomatoes. We'd cover this with a lid and let it cook slow for a while."

Mack told me a lot of times when they'd run plumb out of dried fruit and were hungry for something sweet, they'd open a large can of tomatoes each and pour in sugar and eat it as a dessert. In fact, right to this day, Mack adds sugar to tomatoes whether fresh or canned. At times (brace yourself), he pours on a generous amount of canned milk.

Mack says he always liked the tomato pudding Clair Haight used to cook up about once a week. This was made by crumbling up leftover bread in a large Dutch oven with onions and bacon fryings and covering with canned tomatoes.

Karen Oscar of Phoenix tells me when she was a child in Canada her mother often made a casserole of leftover bread,

Eggplant Casserole

4	cups peeled and cubed eggplant	3/4	cup herb-seasoned stuffing mix
1	egg, slightly beaten	1	cup shredded Cheddar cheese
1/3	cup milk	2	tablespoons butter, melted
1/2	cup chopped onion	1/2	cup herb-seasoned stuffing mix, crushed
1	can cream of mushroom soup, undiluted		

COOK eggplant in boiling salted water about 7 minutes or until tender; drain and set aside. Combine egg, milk, onion, soup, and 3/4 cup stuffing mix; stir until blended. Stir in eggplant and spoon into greased 1 1/2-quart casserole dish. Combine remaining ingredients, sprinkle over casserole. Bake at 375 degrees for about 30 minutes. Yields about 6 servings.

Vegetables in Chicken Sauce With Dumplings

2	cups broccoli pieces	1	cup sliced red onion
2	cups cauliflower pieces	2	cans cream of chicken soup
2	cups whole small mushrooms	1	can cream of mushroom soup
3	cups whole small potatoes, seasoned	1	cup grated mild cheese
1	cup warm water	1/4	cup butter
			salt and pepper to taste

CLEAN and measure vegetables into large bowl. Heat Dutch oven and wipe clean with oil. Place vegetables in Dutch oven with warm water, steam for 15 minutes. Add soups, butter, salt, and pepper; mix well. Bring to boil, then mix in grated cheese.

Dumplings:

2	cups Bisquick	2/3	cup milk

Mix together ingredients forming a soft dough. Drop dumplings by spoonfuls into vegetables in chicken sauce. Remove Dutch oven to low bottom heat, add briquets to top of Dutch oven, and cook until dumplings are golden brown. Serves 10 to 12 people.

Lynn and Sue Packers

Hopping John

If using chiltepins as a substitute for the red peppers, only 1 little fiery devil is enough. This is not a chili dish, and I do not recommend using red chili powder as a substitute. If you have nothing else on hand, season with a small amount of cayenne pepper.

1 16-ounce package black-eyed peas
   water to cover
1 smoked ham hock or ½ pound
   smoked bacon or salt pork
1 onion, diced
1 or 2 red peppers, crushed
1 bay leaf (optional)
½ cup diced celery
   salt and pepper to taste
2 cups cooked rice

SOAK black-eyed peas in water overnight. Cook with meat, onion, peppers, bay leaf, celery, salt, and pepper. Simmer at least 2 hours, or until peas are tender and liquid is low. If cooking with ham hocks (and this is the best, by far), remove hocks, trim off meat, and discard bones. Return meat to kettle and fold in rice. Continue simmering, uncovered, until all liquid is absorbed. Or pour into casserole dish; cover and bake in 350-degree oven until liquid is absorbed.

layered with thin slices of green tomatoes and onions. She says their growing season was so short they had lots of green tomatoes in the early fall. She said her mother made green tomato pickles, sweet or sour green tomato chow-chow, baked green tomato pie, and stored green tomatoes in their root cellar, most of them ripening before Thanksgiving.

Laura Ingalls Wilder writes in her book, *Little House on the Prairie*, that when the Ingalls family had a successful garden on their Dakota farm they enjoyed tomatoes at their very best—fresh from the vine.

In those days tomatoes were quite tart and needed sugar. Turn-of-the-century scientists worked to improve sweetness,

New Peas and Potatoes

5 pounds new red potatoes
   water to cover
1 tablespoon salt
4 cups fresh or frozen peas
1 tablespoon butter or
   margarine
1 heaping tablespoon thyme
1 heaping tablespoon rosemary
1 heaping tablespoon tarragon
12 heaping tablespoons flour
8 cups milk
   salt and pepper to taste

SCRUB potatoes, leaving the skins on; cut into 1-inch pieces. Place in Dutch oven and cover with water and 1 tablespoon salt. Boil until tender. Add peas and cook 5 more minutes. Drain and set aside.

Melt butter in the Dutch oven. Add spices and saute a few minutes. Add flour and mix well. A wire whip works great. Add milk very slowly, stirring vigorously. If milk is added too quickly, the sauce will be lumpy. Stir constantly until sauce has thickened. Add potatoes and peas, serve immediately.
Serves 15 to 20.

Lynn and Tonia Hopkins

Cheesy Potatoes

8 medium potatoes
6 slices bacon, chopped
4 to 5 medium carrots, sliced
1 medium yellow onion, diced
20 mushrooms, sliced
¼ cup butter
1 pint sour cream
1 can cream of chicken soup
1½ cups sharp Cheddar cheese

WASH potatoes and put in a 12-inch Dutch oven; cover. Set oven on top of 10 evenly placed coals and place 12 coals on lid. Bake potatoes about an hour until they are baked through. Take out of oven and put potatoes in a bowl of cold water. Place bacon, carrots, onions, mushrooms, and butter in the Dutch oven. Cook until onions are clear and carrots are tender.

Peel potatoes and dice into ½-inch squares. Stir sour cream and soup into carrot mixture, then add cheese and potatoes. Place oven on 10 new coals and about 12 coals on lid. Bake 30 minutes or until cheese melts and mixture bubbles in the middle. For a conventional oven, bake at 350 degrees for 30 minutes. Serves 8 to 10.

Jake and Jeami Anderson-Jenks

hardiness, disease resistance, and yield. Now greenhouse cultivation and gas ripening have made tomatoes available the year-round. But fresh-picked, sun-ripened tomatoes are a summer specialty whose flavor simply can't be matched.

Laura Ingalls Wilder gives a recipe for tomatoes the way the Ingalls family enjoyed them in late summer: "Pick the tomatoes in the morning, before the dew is gone, taking only those that lift easily from their stems. To peel the skins easily, insert a fork in the tomato's stem end and plunge the tomato for 3 seconds in boiling water. Without removing the fork, peel off the skin with a knife. Cut tomatoes crosswise in slices about ⅜-inch thick and arrange on a platter with some greens: parsley, lettuce, or sorrel. At the table, each person adds

Sheepherder's Scalloped Potatoes

8 to 10 thick-sliced pork, ham, or lamb chops
potatoes, enough to fill half of Dutch oven

2 large onions, sliced
salt and pepper to taste
1 tablespoon flour, per layer
canned or powdered milk

MELT a little fat in the bottom of a Dutch oven. Place meat in oven and brown lightly on both sides; remove and set aside.

Slice enough raw potatoes to fill half the Dutch oven. Mix together the onions and potatoes. Leave the pork grease in the bottom of the oven and put in layers of potatoes and onions, then salt, pepper, and about 1 tablespoon of flour per layer. Place all the pork chops on top and cover with milk. Cover Dutch oven with foil and put on lid.

Dig a hole large enough to hold about 6 inches of good hardwood coals. Place oven in hole, cover with hot coals at least 6 inches deep. Cover all with dirt—6 inches or more.

Meat and potatoes will be done in 3 to 4 hours but can be left for up to 8 hours if necessary. Do not remove until ready to eat. This can be made in a covered casserole dish and baked at 350 degrees for 1 hour. Remove cover the last 15 minutes and increase heat to 375 degrees to brown meat. Allow 2 pork chops each for hungry, hard-working cowboys.

The best keeper of all vegetables, cabbage played an important part in pioneering days. No housewife would dream of planting a garden without row after row of cabbages, which were eaten summer and fall, and stored in root cellars or pits for winter.

cream and sugar to taste."

As a young girl, growing up on a river-bottom farm in Oklahoma, my mother made tomato preserves in the late summer—so many tomato preserves we never seemed to run out of them. In fact, I got burned out on tomato preserves and have *never* made them myself. However, old-timers get a faraway look in their eyes when tomato preserves are mentioned and they tell me how much they miss this long-ago sweet. They swear, when using thick slabs of warm homemade bread, slathered with fresh churned butter, and topped with generous gobs of red, red tomato preserves, it's a dessert that's unbeatable.

Cabbage

Cabbage came to the new world via Canada, and our pioneers knew a good thing when they saw it. The best keeper of all vegetables, cabbage played an important part in pioneering days. No housewife would dream of planting a garden without row after row of cabbages, which were eaten summer and fall, and stored in root cellars or pits for winter. Possibly one of the most popular ways of putting cabbage up for long periods of time was making sauerkraut.

Although we don't know what they called it (sauerkraut is a German word, meaning sour cabbage), the Chinese were

Potato Casserole

1/4 cup butter
1 can cream of chicken soup
1 pint sour cream
6 to 8 medium potatoes, boiled until done, peel and grate

1 1/2 cup grated Cheddar cheese
1/2 cup chopped green onions
2 tablespoons butter
crushed corn flakes

MELT 1/4 cup butter, add soup and sour cream, blend. Add potatoes, cheese, and chopped onions. Toss lightly to mix. Then melt 2 tablespoons butter, mix with corn flakes (enough to cover casserole), and spread over potatoes. Bake about 45 minutes at 350 degrees, uncovered.

Stuffed Cabbage Rolls

8 large cabbage leaves
boiling water, salted
1 pound lean ground beef
3/4 cup wheat germ
1/2 cup minced onion
1 teaspoon salt
1/8 teaspoon freshly-ground black pepper
1 medium clove garlic, minced

1/2 teaspoon oregano
1/4 teaspoon basil
2 eggs
1 1-pound can tomato sauce
3/4 cup water
2 tablespoons dark brown sugar
2 tablespoons vinegar
1 tablespoon cornstarch

DROP cabbage leaves into boiling water in large saucepan. Boil gently for 4 to 5 minutes. Drain.

In medium bowl, mix ground beef, wheat germ, onion, salt, pepper, garlic, oregano, basil, and eggs. Blend well. Divide beef mixture evenly into cabbage leaves. Fold sides of leaf over mixture and roll leaf around filling. Place rolls, seam side down, in a 2 1/2-quart baking dish. Blend tomato sauce, water, brown sugar, vinegar, and cornstarch smoothly. Pour over rolls. Cover with foil. Bake in preheated oven at 375 degrees for 40 to 45 minutes. Spoon sauce over rolls once or twice while baking.

93

Frankfurters-Cabbage Skillet

1	small head cabbage (about 2 pounds), shredded	1/4	teaspoon pepper
1/4	teaspoon nutmeg	2	tablespoons butter or margarine
2	large carrots, shredded		boiling water
2	large green onions with tops, sliced	1	pound frankfurters or smoked sausage, scored
3/4	teaspoon salt		

PUT cabbage in large deep skillet or Dutch oven; sprinkle with nutmeg. Add carrots, onions, salt, and pepper. Dot with butter. Pour boiling water into skillet to 1/2-inch deep. Cover tight, bring to boil over high heat, then simmer for 10 minutes, stirring once. Place frankfurters or sausage on vegetables. Cover and let simmer 10 minutes longer or until vegetables are tender and frankfurters heated through. Serve with mustard and ketchup. Good with rye or pumpernickel bread. Makes 4 servings.

In great-grandma's day, kraut was made at home in a barrel stashed in the basement or cellar, and was a thrifty use-up of all the extras from the family cabbage patch.

Chicken Enchilada Casserole

2	large fryers	1	pound longhorn or Cheddar cheese
1	onion, chopped	4	cans cream of chicken soup
1	cup chopped celery	12	ounces sour cream (optional)
1	teaspoon salt	7	ounces chopped green chilies
1/2	teaspoon pepper	2	cups chicken broth
2	dozen corn tortillas		

BOIL whole chickens or cut into pieces in large saucepan with water to cover. Add onions, celery, salt, and pepper. Cook until tender and allow to cool. Reserve liquid for broth. Pick meat off bones and shred. Discard skin and fat. If done the day before, store in refrigerator.

Fry the corn tortillas, one at a time, by briefly dipping them in hot fat until they are limp. Do not fry crisp. Grate cheese and place small amounts of cheese and chicken on tortillas, roll them, and place in baking dish.

Next mix together soup, sour cream, green chilies, broth, and leftover chicken or cheese. Cover tortillas with the mixture. Bake in 350-degree oven for 25 to 30 minutes.

This won't serve near as many people as you think! They keep coming back for seconds. And thirds.

eating it some 2,000 years ago. Later, sauerkraut was adopted in Europe. There, the Germans fell on it with joy.

That early cabbage was pickled in wine, but some thrifty German discovered that similar results could be had by fermenting the cabbage in salt; and that's the way it's been ever since.

In great-grandma's day, kraut was made at home in a barrel stashed in the basement or cellar, and was a thrifty use-up of all the extras from the family cabbage patch. In early grocery stores, the sauerkraut barrel and the dill pickle barrel stood side by side. Today, sauerkraut is sold in cans to be found in grocery stores all year-round, and as "fresh" kraut in jars in the refrigerated sections of the market.

Clair Haight was roundup cook for the Hashknife outfit back in the 1920s, and one year he lived on the old Vincent Sum-

Tamale Pie

1 1/2	pounds ground beef		salt and pepper to taste
1	onion, chopped	1	cup grated cheese (any kind of yellow cheese)
1	green pepper, chopped		
1	clove garlic, minced	2	cups cold water
1	can yellow corn, drained	3/4	cup cornmeal (yellow or white)
2	cups canned tomatoes		
1 1/2	tablespoons chili powder	3	tablespoons soft margarine

BROWN meat and remove from pan. Saute onion, green pepper, and garlic in the hamburger grease. Stir in corn, tomatoes, chili powder, salt, and pepper. Return meat to pan, mix well, and simmer about 30 minutes. Put in greased baking dish, cover with cheese.

To make batter; mix together the cornmeal, water, and margarine well. Pour over meat mixture and bake at 350 degrees for 45 minutes.

mer Ranch near the Mogollon Rim in Arizona. Here, Clair planted a fine garden and the rich, loamy soil was so conducive to growing, Clair reaped a harvest of giant potatoes, and cabbages weighing as much as ten pounds each.

That fall, as usual, Clair cooked for the Hashknives, and took along in the wagon a gunny sack full of hefty cabbages. While visiting Old Dutch Joe, who owned a ranch near where the wagon was working, Clair talked the old German out of several dozen spicy sausages. That night, Clair cooked a huge kettle of cabbage, and

slicing the sausages lengthwise, added them to the pot.

The cowboys, then as well as now, welcomed a break from the usual diet of beef and beans, and readily filled their plates with cabbage and sausages. The first one to take a bite swore and spewed the stuff from his mouth with a disgusted whoosh. Unbeknownst to Clair, the gunny sack of cabbages had been riding next to the coal oil can and some of the kerosene had sloshed onto the sack of vegetables. It's a good thing Clair was so well-liked or the cowboys would have held a lynching.

Babe McEven checking Dutch-oven biscuits during the 1983 Cowbelle Trail Ride on Eagle Creek.

12 FLUFF-DUFFS AND OTHER SWEETS

The luxury of flour and sugar on the frontier gave rise to more than one story pointing out the scarcity.

I'm always reading the accounts of our early settlers in the West and making notes of the food they ate. I have notebooks filled with short paragraphs where some old-timer took time out from warding off Indian attacks or turning stampedes to mention briefly the simple fare they had. One of J. Frank Dobie's books told this

story about John Young who lived in Texas about 1840. John, as a boy, says, "I shucked corn on Fridays and shelled enough to take next morning to the grist mill 7 miles away, to be ground into our week's supply of meal." John then goes on to tell that their principal fare was milk, corn dodgers, and salt pork. John said he

remembered well the first flour bread he ever tasted. "My grandpa and grandma made us a visit, and up where they lived on the San Saba they'd grown some wheat and had it ground into white flour. For the trip my grandma had made some biscuits, enough to last them over the journey. She gave me some and, old as them biscuits was, I thought them the best thing I had ever eaten. Sometimes to this day when I'm hungry, the taste of them comes back to me."

The luxury of flour and sugar on the frontier gave rise to more than one story pointing out the scarcity. This story took place in about 1849 in Texas. A table of a settler was set for a wedding feast and the guests had yet to arrive when along comes "a yahoo from up the creek" stopping on his way home from the mill with some freshly ground cornmeal. Of course, hospitality demanded that he be asked to dinner, though his presence at the wedding feast was not desired. Saying nothing of the impending sociable, the hostess suggested the fellow sit down and eat at once so that he not be delayed, as he lived a "fer piece" up the creek.

Losing no time the backwoodsman bellied up to the table and made free of the many good things laid before him. He particularly fell head over heels in love with a plate of thinly sliced pound cake, which was of a rich, golden color like that of cornbread made of yellow meal—a color, if not a flavor, that he was used to. He lavishly spread each piece of cake with butter and the precious cake began disappearing like ice cream at a church social. The hostess, in alarm, wanted to steer the hungry man off on cornbread but she judged that she had better be tactful. So she pressed him to have some biscuits, which ordinarily would have been a treat.

"Thank you kindly, ma'am," he said with a full mouth. "You just save them there biscuits. This here yaller bread is good enough for me."

The thoughtful guest continued to eat until he had devoured all the "yaller bread," and he stacked up a graveyard full of chicken bones next to his plate.

Baking powder did not come on the market until the early 1850s. This powder was reasonably stable, ready-powdered, ready-combined, ready to use. Before this, the only leavening agent available was saleratus, a less refined version of what we

Applesauce Fruitcake

This is a simple fruitcake that is a chewy combination of nuts, dates, raisins, and homemade applesauce. This is so simple a child can bake it.

2½	cups sifted all-purpose flour	1	cup packed brown sugar
1	tablespoon baking powder	2	eggs
½	teaspoon salt	1	cup unsweetened applesauce
1	teaspoon cinnamon	1	tablespoon brandy (optional)
½	teaspoon nutmeg	2	cups chopped dates
¼	teaspoon ground cloves	1	cup raisins
½	cup butter or margarine	1	cup chopped nuts

SIFT flour, baking powder, salt, and spices together; set aside. Cream butter or margarine and sugar. Add eggs; beat well. Stir in applesauce, brandy, dates, raisins, and nuts. Stir in flour mixture. Preheat oven to 325 degrees. Grease and line a 9 by 5 by 3-inch loaf pan with waxed paper. Pour batter in pan. Bake for 1½ hours or until cake is done. Cool on wire rack for about 5 minutes, turn out of pan, remove paper. Cool completely on wire rack right side up. Wrap in waxed paper, then in foil. Store in refrigerator.

To make homemade applesauce, peel and core about three tart apples, slice and place in saucepan with ½ cup water. Turn heat low and simmer about 15 to 20 minutes. Mash with potato masher and cool before adding to cake batter.

Gumdrop Fruitcake

This cake may sound silly and takes a bit of derring-do, plus nibbley ingredients. Better buy an extra package of gumdrops for the nibblers, or let them eat the licorice ones.

2	cups cut-up gumdrops (omit licorice)	1	teaspoon vanilla
1½	cups chopped pecans	1	teaspoon baking powder
1	15-ounce package raisins	1	teaspoon cinnamon
3½	cups flour	¼	teaspoon baking soda
1	cup butter	¼	teaspoon salt
2	cups sugar	¼	teaspoon ground cloves
2	eggs	¼	teaspoon nutmeg
		1	cup applesauce

COMBINE gumdrops, pecans, and raisins with ½ cup flour; toss to coat. Cream butter in large bowl; gradually add sugar and beat until light and fluffy. Beat in eggs, one at a time; add vanilla. Sift together remaining flour, baking powder, cinnamon, baking soda, salt, cloves, and nutmeg. Add to creamed mixture alternately with applesauce, beginning and ending with dry ingredients. Stir in gumdrop mixture. Pour into a 10 by 14-inch tube pan lined with waxed paper and bake at 275 degrees for 3½ hours. Place a pan of hot water on bottom shelf of oven so cake will have greater volume and a more moist texture. Cool in pan. Remove paper. Wrap in foil and store in a cool place.

now know as baking soda. When saleratus was used as the sole leavening agent, it was necessary for a batter to contain an acid ingredient, such as buttermilk or sour

Fast Rhubarb Dessert

4	cups cut up rhubarb	1	box white cake mix
1	cup sugar	¾	cup water
1	package strawberry gelatin	⅓	cup margarine, melted

SPREAD the rhubarb over the bottom of a greased 9 by 13-inch pan. Sprinkle sugar, package of dry gelatin, and then the cake mix over the rhubarb. Pour the water over the mixture and then drizzle with melted margarine. Bake at 350 degrees for about 1 hour. Serve with whipped cream or ice cream.

Mary Ellen's Rhubarb Duff

You may also want to try making this duff with plums, apples, peaches, or any other well-drained, cooked fruit.

1	quart or more of sweetened rhubarb	1	cup flour
¼	cup margarine	½	teaspoon salt
1	cup sugar	2	teaspoons baking powder
		1	cup milk

MELT margarine in 9 by 13-inch pan. Pour fruit in pan. Top with batter made from remaining ingredients. An egg may be added if desired. Bake about 400 degrees until top is brown.

Cheesecake

1½	cups graham cracker crumbs	¾	cup plus 2 tablespoons sugar
3	tablespoons sugar	2	teaspoons vanilla
1½	teaspoons cinnamon	¼	teaspoon salt
⅓	cup butter, melted	1	teaspoon fresh lemon juice
16	ounces cream cheese, softened	2	cups sour cream
2	eggs, well beaten	4	tablespoons sugar
		2	teaspoons vanilla

THOROUGHLY mix the first 4 ingredients to make crust. Press this mixture into the bottom of a 9 by 9-inch glass oven-proof dish. Freeze overnight. Next day, combine the next 6 ingredients and mix until creamed. Pour this mixture over the frozen crust and bake at 350 degrees for 18 minutes. Meanwhile, mix the sour cream, sugar, and vanilla. Remove the cake from the oven, pour the sour cream mixture over the baked cake, and return it to the oven to bake 5 more minutes. Chill several hours. Serve with warm cherry topping.

Cherry Topping:

¾	cup sugar		red food coloring
1	tablespoon flour	1	can pie cherries
1	egg, beaten		

Combine sugar, flour, and egg. Add to the cherries and juice. Add a few drops red food coloring. Mix well and cook down to desired thickness. Serves 6 if you're generous, 8 if you're frugal, and 10 if you're downright stingy.　　*Grant and Sue Speed*

milk, molasses, vinegar, or lemon juice. The acid combined with baking soda, releasing gas—carbon dioxide—that "raised" the batter. Such mixtures had to be hustled into the oven as soon as possible before so much gas escaped that a heavy product resulted.

There was another recourse if the cook's recipe did not call for an acid ingredient. She could add cream of tartar to the baking soda, thereby making her own baking powder. It wasn't as easy as it sounds, as both the cream of tartar and baking soda could be purchased only in solid lumps. They had to be pounded to a powder and carefully measured—2 teaspoons of cream of tartar and 1 teaspoon of baking soda for each cup of flour the recipe called for—before they could be used.

When the first baking powder came on the market in the early 1850s, it was not long until baking powder manufacturers produced cookbooks loaded with recipes using their product, some of which became kitchen bibles for generations of home bakers. Not to be outdone, flour processors put out cookbooks, too, and a whole new era of kitchen expertise was under way.

For 30 years my husband, Mack, and I ate at the roundup camps on the Apache Indian reservation, and I always spent several weeks in camp during the last of the fall gathering and the long trek to market with the cattle. As part of the supplies, Mack bought flour by the 50-pound sack, and an order would usually be for 200 pounds. Baking powder was purchased in the largest commercial size available at the trading post and baking powder biscuits were baked by all the Apache cooks. Woe betide a cook who shorted them on plenty of Dutch-oven biscuits. The Apaches are great and enthusiastic bread eaters but, if they had their druthers, would buy white bakery bread and load it on their plates, the minimum number of slices for starters being four and the maximum according to the appetite of the cowboy.

Some of the cooks had learned how to use yeast and made rolls that were greatly enjoyed by the crew lucky enough to eat at the wagon of such a gifted cook. Almost none of these cooks attempted making cakes; you can't blame them, for if you've ever attempted making a truly light cake in a Dutch oven, you know why it was rarely attempted.

Cakes

Some years we were lucky and Mack was able to hire a good cook or maybe a passable cook, but other times our luck ran out and we had to put up with an un-inspired, incompetent, and often surly cook. One such was Ernie, a middle-aged noncommittal Apache who slung the pots and pans on one of the most miserable cattle drives we ever had to endure. During the 7 days of the trip, we had snow and ice, cold rain, and high winds. We were short-handed and had hundreds of sore-footed cattle, which made them almost impossible to drive over the rocky trails. After a long day in the saddle, miserable and shivering, we arrived in camp to face a supper of fried potatoes swimming in grease, along with a pot of boiled meat with cans of hominy, string beans, and peas added. This concoction may have been filling and nutritious, but after many days it was almost nauseous to see a pot of such stew bubbling away on the coals.

Besides the bad food, Ernie did only what was strictly required of him. The cook's flunky drove the truck, unloaded the gear, set up the tent, chopped the wood, built the fire, made the coffee, cut the meat, opened the cans, peeled the spuds, and rang the triangle for meals. Then he washed the dishes, cleaned and dried the Dutch ovens, and finally wound the clock and set the alarm for 3 a.m.

Rich Golden Cake

Easy to make and very good!

1	cup margarine or butter	1	cup milk
3	eggs	1	tablespoon baking powder
1½	cups sugar	2¼	cups flour
1	teaspoon salt		

CREAM margarine or butter, add eggs, sugar, salt, milk, baking powder, and flour. Beat at low speed for 2 minutes or beat by hand about 3 minutes. Pour into a greased and floured 9 by 13-inch cake pan or 2 layer pans. Bake at 350 degrees for 30 to 40 minutes or until done.

Sourdough Carrot Cake

2	cups all-purpose flour	1	teaspoon cinnamon
2	cups sugar	2	cups shredded carrots
1	teaspoon salt	1	cup cooking oil
1	teaspoon baking powder	1	cup sourdough starter
1	teaspoon baking soda	4	eggs

IN large mixing bowl, stir together the flour, sugar, salt, baking powder, baking soda, and cinnamon. Add carrots, oil, sourdough starter, and eggs to the flour mixture. Mix until moistened, then beat for 2 minutes. Pour into greased and floured 13 by 9 by 2-inch baking pan. Bake at 325 degrees for about 55 minutes. Cool thoroughly.

Cream Cheese Frosting:

1	3-ounce package cream cheese	2	cups sifted powdered sugar
¼	cup butter or margarine	1	teaspoon vanilla
		½	cup chopped walnuts

Soften cream cheese and butter or margarine. Beat together until fluffy. Slowly beat in powdered sugar until smooth. Stir in vanilla. Frost cake and sprinkle with chopped nuts.

There-Should-Be-a-Law-Against-It Cake

(Mississippi Mud Cake)

1	cup shortening	¼	teaspoon salt
2	cups sugar	2	teaspoons vanilla
4	eggs	1	cup chopped nuts
1½	cups flour	1	large package small marshmallows
⅓	cup cocoa		

CREAM together shortening, sugar, and eggs. Sift together the flour, cocoa, and salt, and add to the shortening mixture, mixing thoroughly. Stir in the vanilla and nuts. Bake for 25 minutes at 300 degrees in a greased and floured 9 by 13-inch cake pan. Remove cake from oven and add the marshmallows to top. Return to oven and bake 10 minutes longer at 350 degrees. Remove cake from oven and cool.

Icing:

1	pound powdered sugar	¼	cup canned milk
½	cup cocoa	1	teaspoon vanilla
1	cup butter, melted	1	cup chopped nuts

Beat all ingredients (except nuts) together until smooth, then add nuts and pour on top of cake. Leave in pan and cut into squares.

Apple-Pie Cake

¼	cup butter	1	teaspoon cinnamon
¾	cup sugar	½	teaspoon nutmeg
1	egg, beaten	½	teaspoon salt
1	cup flour	1	teaspoon vanilla
1	teaspoon baking soda	2	cups peeled and chopped tart apples
⅛	teaspoon ground cloves	½	cup chopped nuts

IN large saucepan, melt butter. Remove from heat; add sugar and egg. Mix all dry ingredients together, then add to batter. Fold in apples, nuts, and vanilla. Pour batter into a greased and floured 9- or 10-inch pie pan. Bake at 350 degrees for 40 to 45 minutes. Serve warm.

Waldorf Astoria Cake

A lady from California was staying at the Waldorf Astoria Hotel in New York. This chocolate cake was served, and she asked the chef if she might have the recipe. She added that she would be glad to pay for it. After she got home, she received the recipe, also a bill for $100. We got it for nothing, and it's really a wonderful cake.

½	cup butter	2	cups cake flour
2	cups sugar	2	teaspoons baking powder
2	eggs, beaten		pinch of salt
4	squares chocolate, melted	1½	cups milk
2	teaspoons vanilla	2	cups nut meats

CREAM butter and sugar. Add eggs, melted chocolate, and vanilla. Sift together flour, baking powder, and salt. Mix dry ingredients into batter alternately with milk. Stir in nuts. Bake in a large, greased and floured loaf pan for 45 minutes at 350 degrees.

Frosting:

¼	cup butter	1	egg
2	squares chocolate, melted	1	teaspoon lemon juice
2	cups powdered sugar	1	tablespoon vanilla
	pinch of salt	1	cup nut meats

Mix all ingredients together, except nuts. Beat until smooth, add nuts, and spread on cake.

Then the crowning glory was unveiled when Ernie removed a tea towel covering a 16-inch Dutch oven disclosing a cake. A CAKE, and wonder of wonders this one proved to be edible.

Mack told me in disgust, "Ernie has quit, he just ain't left yet."

Yet the last night of the long drive when we riders came in after one of our longest days, I found Ernie had outdone himself by serving a Dutch oven of roast beef and brown gravy along with a granite pot of mashed potatoes. *Mashed* potatoes instead of the ever-lasting fried, and no stew in sight! We all feasted on the good fare, our first in days. Then the crowning glory was unveiled when Ernie removed a tea towel covering a 16-inch Dutch oven disclosing a cake. A *CAKE*, and wonder of wonders this one proved to be edible. It was baked to perfection, golden brown top and bottom, no heavier than need be, and sweetened just right. Ernie had used the correct amount of vanilla instead of adding a teacupful as was the usual custom of Apache cooks. This cake was hard to fault, and after supper I asked Ernie how come he'd never baked a cake before. He shrugged his shoulders, bringing them level with his ears and said, "I dunno."

I found it hard to ever forgive Ernie for possessing such a wonderful talent and holding out on us for so derned many days.

I'm sure many readers will wonder, "Why make a cake from scratch? Why bother, when there are all the varied cake mixes on our grocery shelves?" All I have to say is if you are a timid baker, by all means make a cake from your favorite box mix. Cowards are poor cake bakers. So follow the directions concerning measuring, beating, pan size, oven temperature, and baking time. Having faithfully

Ginger Cake

½	cup butter, softened	2	teaspoons ground cloves
1	cup sugar	1¾	cups all-purpose flour
3	eggs	1	teaspoon baking soda
1	teaspoon cinnamon	⅔	cup sour cream
1	teaspoon ginger	1½	cups applesauce

CREAM butter and sugar until light and fluffy. Add eggs and spices and beat well. Sift flour and baking soda together, then add to creamed mixture alternately with sour cream and stir until well blended. Spoon batter into 2 greased 8-inch cake pans and bake at 325 degrees for 15 minutes; reduce heat to 250 degrees and bake for 15 to 20 minutes longer, or until cakes are done. Cool. Put layers together with applesauce. Cover top with frosting or whipped cream and decorate as desired.

This is a good cake for the holiday season because you can use bits of candied fruit or crushed nuts for decorating frosting.

followed the simple instructions, you will produce a cake you have no qualms about serving to anyone. It may not be as good as a baked-from-scratch, but it certainly will be good to eat, and besides, the world is full of people who won't know the difference.

However, I feel obliged to pass on a few tips in ways to improve cakes made from mixes. Plain yellow and white mixes are mildly flavored with (usually imitation) vanilla. These mixes can be reflavored with such extracts as lemon, almond, maple, peppermint, rum, or brandy. Some lend themselves well to adding flavors such as mocha, strawberry, banana, and so forth. Cake mixes are sturdy and can take some monkeying with and not fail. But don't tamper with the proportions of liquid to dry mix. If you add orange juice, for instance, substitute it for part of the water; don't use it in addition to the amount of water called for.

In spite of the many cake mixes and the trend toward lighter desserts, there are still a great many cake bakers around, dedicated to bringing joy to their families and friends, and taking a modest pleasure in baking a magnificent, truly delectable, homemade cake. A thing of beauty, and a joy as long as it lasts, which generally isn't all that long.

Devil's Food Cake

1½	cups flour	1	teaspoon salt
1¼	cups sugar	⅔	cup vegetable shortening
½	cup cocoa	1	cup milk
1¼	teaspoons baking powder	1	teaspoon vanilla
¼	teaspoon cream of tartar	2	eggs

SIFT flour, sugar, cocoa, baking soda, cream of tartar, and salt into mixing bowl. Add shortening, ⅔ cup of milk, then vanilla, and beat 150 strokes or for 2 minutes on low speed with an electric mixer. Scrape bowl and spoon often. Add eggs and beat 250 strokes. Then add remaining milk and beat 50 strokes, or with electric mixer at low speed for 3 minutes. Divide batter into 2 greased and floured 8- or 9-inch layer pans. Preheat oven to 350 degrees and bake 35 to 40 minutes. Use favorite frosting.

Clair's Sourdough Chocolate Cake

1	cup sourdough starter	1	teaspoon cinnamon
1	cup sugar	3	squares semi-sweet chocolate, melted
½	cup shortening		
2	eggs	2	cups flour
1	cup milk	½	teaspoon salt
1	teaspoon vanilla	1½	teaspoons baking soda

PREPARE a cup of thick sourdough starter the night before. Let rise in warm spot.

Cream sugar and shortening together. Add eggs. Add sourdough starter, milk, vanilla, cinnamon, and melted chocolate. Beat well.

Mix together flour, salt, and baking soda, and add to mixture. Fold in gently but thoroughly. Pour into greased and floured cake pans. Bake at 350 degrees for 35 to 40 minutes.

Jovonne's Prune Cake

1	cup sugar	1	teaspoon salt
1¾	cups flour	2	eggs, beaten
2	teaspoons baking powder	1	cup cooking oil
¼	teaspoon cloves	2	4¾-ounce baby food jars of strained prunes
1	teaspoon cinnamon		
1	teaspoon baking soda	¾	cup pecans (optional)

SIFT all dry ingredients into a bowl. Make well in center and add eggs, oil, prunes, and pecans. Beat on low speed for 1 minute, scraping sides constantly. Then beat on medium speed for 2 minutes or until well blended. Pour into a greased and floured 9 by 13-inch pan. It won't seem like enough batter but it is. Preheat oven to 350 degrees and bake 35 to 40 minutes.

Icing:

2	cups packed brown sugar	1	teaspoon vanilla (optional)
½	cup butter		nuts (optional)
½	cup milk		

Place brown sugar, butter, and milk in saucepan and boil until soft ball stage (234 to 240 degrees on a candy thermometer). Test by dropping a spoonful of mixture into a cup of cold water. If it is at the soft ball stage, the mixture can be picked up but flattens. Beat until cool. Add vanilla and nuts (if desired). Leave cake in pan and cover with icing.

Jovonne Newby
Farmington, New Mexico

There are still a great many cake bakers around taking pleasure in baking a truly delectable, homemade cake.

Banana-Nut Loaf Cake

¾ cup butter	6 tablespoons buttermilk
2 cups plus 2 tablespoons sugar	1 teaspoon vanilla
3 eggs, beaten	½ teaspoon allspice
3 cups all-purpose flour	1 cup mashed bananas
¾ teaspoon baking soda	1 cup finely chopped pecans

CREAM butter with sugar, and beat in eggs. Sift together flour and baking soda, then add to creamed mixture alternately with the buttermilk. Blend very well. Stir in vanilla and allspice, then the bananas and chopped nuts. Turn into a greased and floured 10-inch tube pan. Bake at 325 degrees for 1 hour. Cool 10 minutes in pan when done, then turn out on a cake rack to cool completely. Frost with lemon or orange frosting or simply serve sprinkled with powdered sugar.

Easy Nut Jam Cake

(the name says it all!)

3¼ cups all-purpose flour	1 cup buttermilk
1½ cups packed brown sugar	¾ cup margarine or butter, softened
1 teaspoon cinnamon	
½ teaspoon nutmeg	3 eggs
1 cup peach jam or preserves (apricot jam goes just as well)	1 cup chopped pecans
	¼ cup granulated sugar

GREASE and flour 9 by 13-inch cake pan. In large bowl combine all ingredients except pecans and granulated sugar. Beat about 1 minute at low speed, then beat 3 minutes at high speed. Pour batter into prepared pan. Sprinkle pecans and granulated sugar over top. Preheat oven to 350 degrees and bake for 45 to 55 minutes or until done. Serve with caramel sauce. Makes 12 servings.

Caramel Sauce:

1 cup packed brown sugar	1 cup cream or half-and-half
1 cup granulated sugar	2 teaspoons vanilla
1 cup margarine	

In medium saucepan, combine all ingredients. Bring to boil, stirring constantly. Then cook over low heat, stirring occasionally, for about 10 minutes or until thickened. Serve warm over cake.

Mrs. Ashly's Crumb Coffee Cake

The old-time original recipe called this a pie. It's not a pie. It's a cake. Topping makes it a coffee cake. It's so easy to make, and part of it can be mixed the night before and left in the refrigerator until ready for use the next morning. I like to use this recipe for strawberry shortcake. Different toppings include crushed nuts sprinkled with brown sugar and added to top of cake for last 10 minutes of baking, or any kind of fresh fruits that have been mashed and sweetened to taste. Or just serve hot from the oven with coffee. Try this; it's so simple a child can bake it.

4 cups all-purpose flour	1 tablespoon cream of tartar
2 cups sugar	2 eggs
1 cup butter	1¾ cup sour milk or buttermilk
1½ teaspoons baking soda	cinnamon

MIX together flour, sugar, and butter until crumbly. Take out 1 cup crumbs for topping. Mix the baking soda, cream of tartar, eggs, and buttermilk lightly with crumbs. Pour into 2 greased and floured 9-inch pie pans. Sprinkle the reserved crumbs on top and then sprinkle lightly with cinnamon. Bake in 350-degree oven for about 30 minutes. Leave in pie pans and while it's hot put on different fruit or nut toppings or spread with melted butter and serve at once.

Pies

Somewhere, perhaps in darkest Africa or outer Siberia, there may be somebody who doesn't like pie. But pie-haters must be as scarce as grass growing on the Santa Ana Freeway in Los Angeles.

How long has it been since you've had a piece of sweet potato pie? Or a slab of raisin, winter squash, green tomato, or jelly pie? How about the old favorites made with dried apples, peaches, apricots, or prunes? Then there's buttermilk pie and oatmeal pie. All kinds of mock pie including lemon and pecan pie. Mock lemon pie is the old-timey vinegar pie and mock pecan is made from pinto beans. Honest!

The pie recipe book called *Farm Journal's Complete Pie Cookbook* has more than 700 recipes for pie. There are pies made from fresh fruits and berries, and even oddball pies, such as fudge, peanut, and brown sugar. There are meringue pies and ice cream pies, and topless and bottomless and deep-dish pies.

A national survey made by *Farm Journal* resulted in a list naming, in this order: apple, cherry, pumpkin, lemon, chocolate, pecan, and coconut—a vote that tallies with other surveys.

Pies have always been party fare, and became a part of neighborhood festivities from the start. Even now there are still pie-eating contests at county fairs, and pie suppers, or pie socials, are still being held in rural communities. I can remember, as a young girl in Oklahoma, attending pie suppers held in our one-room country school.

Mock Pecan Pie

It's fun to fool your family and friends. They never guess this delicious pie is made from the lowly *frijole*.

2	cups sugar	2	teaspoons vanilla
½	cup butter or margarine	½	teaspoon salt
4	eggs, beaten	1	cup mashed pinto beans
2	tablespoons molasses or dark corn syrup		chopped pecans or walnuts, enough to cover

CREAM sugar and butter. Add eggs, molasses, vanilla, and salt. Beat in well-mashed beans. Beans must have been cooked unseasoned and well done. Pour into unbaked pie shell and sprinkle nuts on top. Bake at 350 degrees, 40 to 45 minutes.

Rhubarb Popover Pie

You'll never find a more tasty dessert than this homey, last-minute pie. it's a good idea to finish baking the pie while everyone is enjoying the main course (put it in the oven about 10 minutes before you sit down to eat). Just before serving, make the sweet, caramel-tasting syrup that contrasts so delightfully with the crisp, hot crust and cold ice cream.

2	eggs	1½	cups fresh, cut-up rhubarb
¾	cup milk	½	cup pineapple chunks (canned), drained
¾	cup flour		brown sugar syrup
½	teaspoon salt	1	pint vanilla ice cream
¼	cup butter		

BEAT eggs and milk; add flour and salt and beat until smooth. Put butter in a 9-inch pie pan and heat in oven until it bubbles. Immediately pour in batter. Combine and drop rhubarb and pineapple in center of batter, within about 2 inches of pan edges. Bake at 425 degrees for 25 minutes, or until batter is puffed and brown.

Immediately cut in 6 wedges for serving, topping each with a spoonful of warm brown sugar syrup and a small scoop of ice cream. Serve at once.

Brown Sugar Syrup:

⅓	cup butter	1	cup packed brown sugar

Melt the butter in a saucepan. Add brown sugar and stir until a syrup.

Green Tomato Pie

One of the joys of having a garden is that you can gather green tomatoes for cooking. Spicy pies made with them have a distinctive flavor of their own. Green tomatoes can also be substituted for apples in your favorite apple pie recipe.

4 or 5	cups skinned and thinly sliced green tomatoes	½	teaspoon cinnamon
⅔	cup packed brown sugar	½	teaspoon salt
⅓	cup granulated sugar	1	tablespoon lemon juice
2 to 3	tablespoons flour	2	tablespoons butter

TO peel green tomatoes easily, place in boiling water. Let stand 3 minutes, or until skins can be slipped off.

Combine tomatoes, sugars, flour, cinnamon, lemon juice, and salt. Place in an unbaked 9-inch pie shell; dot with butter. Adjust top crust and flute edges; cut steam vents. Bake at 425 degrees, 50 to 55 minutes.

Texas Pecan Pie

4 eggs	2½ tablespoons butter, melted
1 cup sugar	1 teaspoon vanilla
pinch of salt	1¼ cups pecan halves
1½ cups dark corn syrup	

PREHEAT oven to 350 degrees. Beat eggs, but not frothy. Add sugar, salt, and corn syrup. Add melted butter and vanilla, mixing just enough to blend. Spread nuts in bottom of unbaked 9-inch pie shell. Pour in filling and place pie in oven. Reduce heat to 325 degrees at once. Bake 50 to 60 minutes.

Shoofly Pie

1½ cups sifted all-purpose flour	¾ cup molasses
½ cup sugar	½ cup hot water
½ teaspoon ground cinnamon	½ teaspoon baking soda
3 tablespoons butter or margarine	

PREHEAT oven to 350 degrees. Sift flour, sugar, and cinnamon together. Cut in butter or margarine to make a fine meal. In a separate bowl combine molasses, hot water, and baking soda; then add molasses mixture to flour-butter mixture, stir only to moisten. The bubbles that form act as a leavening agent so you must work rapidly. Over-mixing will result in a fallen or soggy pie. Pour into unbaked 9-inch pastry crust at once. Bake 40 to 45 minutes or until filling is set. Serve with whipped cream or ice cream.

Staging box socials, or pie suppers, was a good way to raise money for a needy cause. All the women and young girls baked their best pies and packed them in fancy boxes. The containers were as original as imagination could make them: stitched and ruffled crepe paper, fancy wallpaper, artificial flowers, satin ribbons. They were shaped like hearts, sunbonnets, flower baskets, butterflies, or log cabins. I remember one in the shape of a wooly lamb, a dead giveaway to the owner, a lovely young girl who helped her father raise prize-winning sheep.

The box suppers were nearly always held in conjunction with a dance. At midnight the auctioneer began selling the boxes. He used showmanship tricks and would sniff elaborately at the boxes and pretend to swoon from the heady aroma. He hinted who baked the pie, but more often its maker was kept a secret until its purchaser opened the box and found the maker's name.

Dan Webb, a cowboy from New Mexico's famous Diamond A Ranch, once told me about a pie social he attended in the 1920s. Dan said he had a terrible crush on a neighboring rancher's daughter, but had

Sweet Potato Pie

People south of the Mason-Dixon Line know all about sweet potato pie. The sweet potatoes used in southern recipes are the varieties with a light, reddish, coppery skin and a rather moist, bright, orange-yellow interior.

During harvest season this vegetable has a truly fresh taste. To prolong this superior fall flavor, some homemakers cook and freeze sweet potatoes then, for winter and spring pies. You can either bake or cook the unpeeled vegetable in salted water just until tender, then cool, peel, puree it, and package and freeze. Canned sweet potatoes can be used if desired.

2 cups sweet potato puree	½ teaspoon nutmeg
2 eggs, slightly beaten	1 teaspoon vanilla
¾ cup sugar	1⅔ cup light cream or evaporated milk
½ teaspoon salt	
½ teaspoon ginger	½ cup butter or margarine, melted

BAKE sweet potatoes until tender, peel, and mash. Make sure all lumps are removed. Mix all ingredients together and pour into an unbaked 9-inch pie shell. Bake at 400 degrees for 50 minutes or until firm.

little hope of finding out the description of her box. Luck was in Dan's favor as this certain young maiden had a brother about 10 years old who was willing to divulge information for a price. I don't remember this youngster's name, but I'm sure he became a successful businessman in later years. He traded the description of his sister's box for a flashy pinto pony.

Dan told me more details. "I'd given an Indian 10 hard-earned dollars for that paint horse. Then I had to bid 15 dollars for the box, which made me suspicious the derned kid had sold his information to a dozen other love-sick cowpunchers. Then to top it off, the pie was made of sweet potatoes and sweet potato pie is probably the only kind I don't like. It all turned out fine as I ended up marrying the maker of the sweet potato pie and she ain't ever baked another one since."

"Pie's fattening," some cooks say flatly in answer to their family's clamor for their favorite dessert. Well, true. But even if you have a whole family of overweights, pie now and then is a deserved reward after all those fruit cups and low-cal gelatin desserts.

Pies have won their way into our culture, and our sentiments. A doting grandmother may call a grandchild "Sweetie Pie," an expression of endearment. Husbands and wives use the same affectionate term. A hungry cowboy returning to the chuck wagon after a hard day in the saddle was likely to call it the pie box, if the roundup cook was known for turning out delicious concoctions called pie. Some women even baked birthday pies for their husbands or sons by request. These men liked to have lighted candles on pies rather than cakes.

"Cutting the pie" has come to mean dividing something good. And that's what I'm doing in this book, sharing some of my favorite pie recipes.

Remember that pies please men. Since men are the great pie eaters and promoters, I want to give a rancher friend the last word. His definition of his favorite dessert: "A triangle of pie is the best way ever discovered to round out a square meal."

Crisscross Cherry Pie

Cherry pie is one of the royal American desserts—it competes with apple pie for top honors. Here's a recipe for the classic—a simple, unadorned one.

2	1-pound cans of pitted tart cherries (water pack)	1	teaspoon lemon juice
2½	tablespoons quick-cooking tapioca	4	drops red food color
¼	teaspoon salt	1¼	cups sugar
¼	teaspoon almond extract	1	tablespoon butter or margarine

DRAIN cherries, reserve liquid. Measure ⅓ cup liquid into mixing bowl. Add tapioca, salt, almond extract, lemon juice, and food color. Then, add the cherries and 1 cup sugar. Mix and let stand while making pastry.

Fit pastry into bottom of 9-inch pie pan. Trim ½ inch beyond outer rim of pan. Fill with cherry mixture and dot with butter. Sprinkle with remaining sugar. Moisten rim with water, adjust lattice top, and flute edges.

To keep high rim from browning faster than crisscross strips, circle pie with a stand-up foil collar. Fold foil over rim and leave on during entire baking. Bake at 425 degrees, 40 to 50 minutes. Can be served warm if desired.

Apple Pie

If you have good, tart apples, it's hard to make a bad apple pie. I never use quick-cooking tapioca for thickening. I always mix flour with sugar and add to pie for thickening.

This pie is tart and good! Nothing insipid about it. And it's out of this world with ice cream heaped on top!

Many times I use equal amounts of brown sugar and white sugar, making slightly more than one cup. Sweetness depends on the apples; however, when using lemon juice, you may want to add slightly more sugar. Of course, you can make this pie without the cinnamon candies, but the candies make this different in such a way you'll get raves from all.

1	teaspoon cinnamon	3	tablespoons red cinnamon candies (red hots)
1	cup sugar	6	or 7 cups very thinly sliced peeled apples
2	tablespoons flour		
¼	teaspoon nutmeg		
¼	teaspoon salt	2	tablespoons butter or margarine
1	tablespoon lemon juice		

MELT candies on low heat in 1 or 2 tablespoons of water. Mix all ingredients with apples, toss lightly, and heap into pastry-lined 9- or 10-inch pie pan. Dot with butter or margarine. Adjust top crust and flute edges. Cut vents and sprinkle top lightly with granulated sugar. Bake at 425 degrees, 55 to 60 minutes. Some apples cook faster than others.

Fried Peach Pies

1 cup freestone peaches, chopped and drained	1 tablespoon flour
1/2 cup sugar	cinnamon candies

MAKE one recipe for fried pie pastry, roll out thin and cut disks by using the plastic cover to a 3-pound can of shortening for a pattern. Place about 2 tablespoons peaches on half the disk, leaving about an inch of space around edge for sealing. Mix together the sugar and flour. Sprinkle 1 teaspoon of sugar and flour mixture over peaches, then dot with 8 or 10 cinnamon candies. Moisten all around disk and fold half over. Press with fingers and use fork tines to seal. Dip tines in flour to keep from sticking to pastry.

Fry in deep fat at about 375 degrees until golden brown on each side, remove with slotted spoon, and place on paper towels to drain. Dust warm turnovers with powdered sugar if desired.

Be sure fat does not become too hot; nor should you crowd too many pies into kettle at once for fear of cooling grease too rapidly.

Fried Pies

Back in the mid-1930s I stopped by the Hashknife outfit's roundup wagon near Chevelon Butte, south of Winslow, Ariz., to visit my old friend Clair Haight, who was lord of the pots and pans that year. When I rattled to a stop in my Model A Ford, Clair made me welcome.

"Git down and come in," he called, waving his badge of office, a long-handled gonch hook. "Pour yourself some coffee," he said, pointing his chin to the steaming, 2-gallon pot resting on a small bed of coals near the fire. He offered me a seat on an upended water bucket just out of the fast lane between the chuck box and the fire pit. I could see Clair was busy as a bird dog in a stubble field, and soon my nostrils were assailed with the most wonderful smell that ever wafted through clear mountain air.

I raised up and peered into a 16-inch Dutch oven of smoking grease that sat on a bed of coals. I saw several little half-moon pies bubbling and bobbing in the boiling fat. I knew without being told that these small gems were filled with stewed dried fruit—in this case probably apples flavored with spices, sugar, and raisins—because I'd enjoyed Clair's specialty before.

While we visited, I watched Clair turn the pies, and when they were golden-hued on both sides, he lifted them from the fat with a slotted spoon and placed them reverently on some brown paper bags to drain. When they had cooled, he stacked them on edge in a large dishpan and covered them with a clean towel.

I knew he'd feed from 12 to 14 men that evening, and I also knew 3 or 4 of the pies for each man would barely be enough, even though each half-moon was so hefty a child would have to use both hands to hold it.

Clair was one of the few really clean roundup cooks, and at times was known to be cranky about his cooking area when some cowboy failed to measure up to his high standards of cleanliness. He began griping to me about the low-down, filthy habits of one of the men repping for the outfit. Clair told me this rep had the audacity that very morning to actually throw scraps from his plate into the fire pit. Unforgivable!

Clair angrily slung his grizzled head and snorted, "I fetched the shovel and handed it to the S.O.B. and told him to fish out the garbage and throw it into the brush where it belonged."

Beside the nasty habits of this certain cowboy, Clair was upset over the boss failing to provide him proper wood. Clair pointed out the skimpy pile of cedar logs—shredded bark still on, and ends oozing sap. The stuff was half-green, Clair fumed, and fit only to make a smudge to fight off mosquitoes, not to make long-lasting hot coals for baking biscuits or sourdough bread.

I knew Clair was the best bread baker in the country, and I felt it was truly a cardinal sin to expect a cook to bake anything without hardwood coals. Clair said a man had been up in the oak wood country the day before, but was too adle-brained to bring back a pickup load of good dry oak. He explained that was the reason he was making fried pies instead of baking a cobbler for dessert.

While Clair cleaned off the chuck-box lid, I listened to him quietly hum a little Indian chant. Clair had lived among the

Navajos and had adopted their ways, and when upset or seething in anger, Clair hummed this little ditty, as tuneless as the drone of a beehive.

I kept quiet, and figured the best I could hope for, considering his state of mind, was an offer for some more coffee. So when Clair motioned to the pan of fresh pies and invited me to help myself, I was elated. Warm fried pies are the most delectable treat there is.

Ramon Adams, in his good book *Come An' Get It*, tells in his chapter on chuckwagon desserts that cooks often made fried pies. Adams says the dough was made about like other pie dough, and writes: "The cook rolled out his dough with a vinegar bottle, and using an empty gallon-size can as a cutter, he filled half the small disks with fruit—anything he might have on hand—but it was usually dried apples or applesauce. In an average 16-inch Dutch oven, four or five little pies could be fried at one time."

Adams pointed out that, in the sandhills of Texas and Oklahoma, wild plums grew everywhere in the summertime, and when pitted and stewed to a thick mush, sweetened with sugar or honey, and some spices added, made a concoction that lent itself well to fried pie filling.

Maybe you've never fried pies, but, if your grandmother lived south of the Mason-Dixon Line, she rated turnovers from the kettle a great winter treat. Today's cooks often fry them in the electric skillet. A rather tart filling contrasts delightfully with the sugar-sprinkled, flaky crust. Serve the turnovers, often called half-moons, either hot or cold. Tuck them in a packed lunch for a much-appreciated treat.

Fried pies are good when filled with jam, mincemeat, or a mixture of chopped raisins, nuts, apples, and lemon rind, held together with beaten egg. You don't have to stick to cooked fruits. Pies made of chopped cooked chicken, beef, or pork, with some gravy, and even ones made with chili and beans, are delicious.

Pastry for Fried Pies

I've found that very rich pastry dough does not serve at all well when making fried pies. The rich dough, when rolled thin, breaks easily and will even fall apart in the hot fat. Canned biscuits are fine, and a fast way to make fried pies. One canned biscuit is just not enough, unless you want really little pies, so two of the canned biscuits, pressed together and rolled thin, is what I use.

3 cups flour	1/3 cup shortening
1 tablespoon baking powder	1 egg
1/2 teaspoon salt	1 1/4 cups buttermilk
1/2 teaspoon baking soda	

COMBINE dry ingredients; cut in shortening. Mix egg and buttermilk, and add to dry mixture; stir with fork until well blended. Form into 12 balls. Roll each ball thin to about the size of a large saucer. Fill one side with your favorite fruit, well drained. Do not place fruit too close to edge of pastry, leave about an inch to allow for sealing. Wet edges of dough and fold half over fruit and press with fingers, then use tines of fork to seal. Fry in hot fat until golden brown on each side. Drain on paper toweling.

Suitable fruit for filling: dried or fresh stewed apples, plums, peaches, apricots, cherries, rhubarb, apples and raisins combined, or apricots and crushed pineapple. Just be sure fruit is not too juicy or pies will ooze liquid into the hot fat. These pies are good keepers and should be stored in containers that do not sweat and make pies soggy. Wrapping them in toweling and storing in a regular bread box serves well. Don't worry; they won't last long anyhow.

Dried Apple and Raisin Half-Moons

3 cups dried apples	1/4 teaspoon cinnamon
sugar to taste	1 cup raisins
1 tablespoon flour	1 tablespoon butter or
1/4 teaspoon ground cloves	margarine

MAKE one recipe for fried pie pastry, roll out thin, and cut disks by using the plastic cover to a 3-pound can of shortening for a pattern.

Soak the dried apples overnight in 2 cups water. Next day cook the apples until tender but not mushy, about 25 minutes. Most of the liquid will boil away, but the slices should not lose their shape. Combine the sugar and flour; add to the hot apples, along with the spices and raisins. Spoon the fruit mixture onto half the pastry disks with slotted spoon, leaving the liquid in bowl. Moisten all around edges of circle and turn half over and press together with fingers. Seal edges with fork tines.

Fry each pie in deep fat at about 375 degrees and when brown on both sides place on paper towels to drain.

Be sure fat does not become too hot; nor should you crowd too many pies into kettle at once for fear of cooling grease too rapidly.

Stella's Pumpkin Pie

Because I seldom make this pie precisely, I measured all the ingredients to this recipe carefully. This is the way I've been making pumpkin pies for more than 50 years. No complaints yet.

1	1-pound can pumpkin	½	teaspoon ground cloves
¾	cup packed brown sugar	½	teaspoon ginger
¾	cup granulated sugar	½	teaspoon allspice
½	cup (or slightly less) of	½	teaspoon vanilla
	molasses or thick maple syrup	½	teaspoon salt or just a
1	can evaporated milk		smidgen more (nothing worse
5	large eggs		than a flat taste)
1	teaspoon cinnamon		

POUR one can of pumpkin in mixing bowl. Then add the sugars and syrup. Pour the can of milk into empty pumpkin can. Add eggs and beat with fork. Add spices, vanilla, salt, and beat well. Pour into pumpkin mixture. Then add a tablespoon water to the pumpkin can and scrape sides well; add to pumpkin mixture. Mix all well. Dot pies with real butter if you have it. This fills 2 deep-dish 9-inch pie shells to the brim. Bake at 350 degrees for 50 minutes.

Using the pumpkin can for mixing cuts down on dirty dishes. You end up with a measuring cup, mixing bowl, fork, and spoon to wash. This is a rich recipe, but so are all of them.

Pumpkin

Pumpkin can be used as a custard instead of a pie filling, and it's still the same mouth-watering concoction of milk, eggs, and spices. I made this discovery back in the early 1940s while camped with my husband, Mack, in a gawd-forsaken canyon south of Winslow, Arizona. The country was inhospitable, for sure, with wide, deep cracks in the solid rocks, many bottomless (or so the cowboys claimed). There were endless red dust storms, sidewinders, and only one scrubby juniper tree for shade.

It was a sorry camp with no cook tent—not even a fly—and only a 9 by 9 sheepherder's tent for privacy and sleeping. We had an old-time chuck box taken from the back of a real chuck wagon to serve as a work table and kitchen cupboard. Mack and one of the cowboys lifted this heavy contraption on to two pack boxes stood on end. This didn't bring the table of the chuck box high enough to keep me from breaking my back, but it was a derned sight better than sitting on the ground.

Mack was holding 800 head of cows on leased land for an estate, until the estate could be settled, so the cows could be sold and the heirs could start spending all that money. There were no buildings or corrals on this range, and mighty few fences that would hold cows from roaming a hundred miles in any direction. Mack and three cowboys rode all day, every day, and usually rode in just before dark—those bottomless cracks weren't conducive to night riding—so that meant I was alone in camp throughout the day. It was a "greasy sack" outfit, meaning there was little chuck aside from beans and salt pork, a couple Dutch ovens, and tin dishes. All meals were prepared on an open campfire, and it tried my culinary expertise (almost non-existent then) to come up with meals that weren't monotonous to the point of being nauseous, especially to me, because I was pregnant.

The administrator of the estate was trying to cut corners, and felt the first place to save lots of money was to spend as little on chuck as he could get away with. I did manage to buy some canned pumpkin, and on rare occasions bought eggs. And we had plenty of canned milk and sugar, so I experimented with baking pumpkin custard, rather than pies, because I thought baking pies in a Dutch oven would be impossible for me.

After the breakfast fire had died down to ashes, I'd mix a custard of pumpkin, sugar, milk, eggs, and spices, pour it into a Dutch oven, put on the lid, and bury the oven in hot ashes (not coals). The ashes would be too hot to put your hand in, but would not ignite a chip of wood. The main thing was to bake slowly, as though it was being done in a modern gas range with the oven set at about 275 degrees. At no time did I want the custard to boil or bubble, because it would separate and become watery.

In an hour or so the custard would be done, and could be taken from the ashes, the lid removed so the custard wouldn't sweat, and the oven covered with a towel and set on top of the chuck box to cool. This pumpkin custard was a welcome change from the usual dessert of stewed fruit, dried apples, or just sourdough biscuits with Tea Garden syrup.

Highpockets' Vinegar Cobbler

Back in the 1930s, Mack and I visited the roundup camp of the A Prod Ranch in northern Arizona. Our good friend, Dode Richards, was wagon boss for the outfit that year. Dode was getting along in years, but I hesitate to say he was worn out, because old cowpunchers and old mules can fool you, and go on being useful many years after their so-called retirement age. Anyhow, Dode ramrodded a bunch of cow-catchin' fools, and didn't eat anybody's dust on a long drive.

When we drove up and parked out aways from camp, I saw a tall, lanky, long-legged man looming above the Dutch ovens and knew Dode had a new cook. This one was so long-legged he looked like a sandhill crane in Levi's. Each time he bent over his pots, he looked like an extension ladder breaking in two.

Highpockets' Vinegar Cobbler

This is not a custard pie, and is best baked in Dutch oven in camp. Sourdough dumplin's can be used instead of pie crust. If you don't think it's good, just try it!

4	cups sugar	1/2	cup butter
2 1/2	cups water		nutmeg to taste
3/4	cup vinegar		dash of salt

PUT all ingredients in pan you are going to bake in—a bread pan if cooking on a stove, a Dutch oven if cooking on an open fire. Let mixture boil while you make pie dough (enough for two regular crusts). Roll out pie dough thin and cut into strips. Crisscross on top of hot vinegar solution. Bake in medium oven until crust is brown. If pie is thin, that's the way it should be.

Fresh Peach Cobbler

4	cups sweetened sliced peaches, use fully ripened freestone variety	1/2	cup water
		1	tablespoon butter
		1	tablespoon lemon juice
1 1/2	tablespoons cornstarch	1/4	teaspoon ground cloves
1/3	cup packed brown sugar		

MIX cornstarch, sugar, and water. Add peaches and cook until mixture is thickened. Add butter, lemon juice, and cloves. Pour into an 8-inch round baking dish.

Drop spoonfuls of batter topping on hot peach mixture, sprinkle with sugar. Bake at 400 degrees, 40 to 50 minutes. Serve warm.

Batter Topping:

1/2	cup flour	1/4	teaspoon salt
1/2	cup sugar	2	tablespoons soft butter
1/2	teaspoon baking powder	1	egg, slightly beaten

Combine all ingredients and beat with spoon until batter is smooth. It spreads over peaches during baking.

Slim's Tallow Suet Pudding

1	cup chopped suet	2	cups flour
2	cups raisins	1	teaspoon cinnamon
1	cup chopped nuts	1	teaspoon allspice
1	cup packed dark brown sugar	1	teaspoon nutmeg
1	cup chopped dried fruit (any	1	teaspoon salt
	kind—prunes, apples, figs, or	2	teaspoons baking powder
	apricots)	1½	cups milk

CHOP suet into very small pieces, no piece being larger than a bean. Combine with raisins, nuts, brown sugar, and chopped dried fruit. Then mix flour, spices, and salt with baking powder. Add gradually to fruit mixture with milk, beating well. Put in flour sack or tie in large square cloth. It's best to wet cloth and sprinkle well with flour before putting in the pudding. Put in kettle of boiling water and boil at least three hours, always keeping enough boiling water to cover pudding.

When done, remove pudding from water, and put on cloth to drain. After about 30 minutes, untie cloth and turn pudding onto dish. Chill. Slice and serve with hard sauce. This pudding will keep well and is similar to regular old-fashioned plum pudding. This was a great favorite with chuck-wagon cooks. It can be made with molasses instead of brown sugar, or can be made with white sugar.

"I never ate Dutch-oven fried steaks that were better, and his sourdough biscuits were feather light and browned to a golden hue."

The A Prod outfit was one of the few that still used a horse-drawn chuck wagon with high, iron-tired wheels. The cook was working from a regular old-time chuck box with the lid let down, serving as his work table. Some distance away from the wagon, scattered among the low cedar and juniper trees, were the cowboys' tepee tents. The crew had just ridden in, and when Dode saw us he hailed us over to his tent. Graciously, he dragged his cot out into the open and offered me a seat on his bed.

While Mack and Dode visited, I enjoyed that wonderful time of evening when the sun squats briefly on the horizon, making the sand bumps and Mormon Tea clumps cast shadows long and skinny. Which reminded me of the cook.

"Dode, who's your cook and where'd he come from?"

"Oh, you mean ol' Highpockets?" Dode pursed his sunburned lips toward the chuck wagon. "Why, he come down from Utah during the summer. Hit me up for a job . . . said he could cook. He weren't lying either. Puts out such good grub ain't a man quit all fall."

I looked over at the cook and saw his shadow was now a hundred yards long. "He must have the longest legs in the world," I mused aloud.

Dode was sitting on the ground, with his hands clasped behind his neck, leaning back on his saddle, completely relaxed. "He tells me his legs wasn't always that long," Dode said, chuckling softly. "In fact, he says he used to be called just Slim. It was only after his accident he got to be called Highpockets."

I knew better, but I asked anyhow. "What kind of accident?"

Dode's kind old eyes began to sparkle. "Well, he says back when he was just a young button, he was chasin' an ol' silly, wild cow, an' his horse ran into a bob-wire fence and fell. Threw Slim astraddle the fence and he slid down it for 50 yards, mowin' down posts an' rollin' up wire." Dode paused dramatically, for effect.

I could see what was coming a mile away, but I was already beyond the point of no return, and besides, why spoil Dode's fun? So I asked, "Did it hurt him?"

"Naw, not much. Just split him up to his brisket. But he got up, caught his horse, let his stirrups out to the last notch, an' went ahead and caught that ol' *sookey*."

Highpockets' meal made up for Dode's joke. I never ate Dutch-oven fried steaks that were better, and his sourdough biscuits were feather light and browned to a golden hue. For dessert he had made a vinegar cobbler in a 16-inch Dutch oven. This was my first taste of this homey dish, and I noticed the cowboys mopped up the last bite. They were generous in their praise, and one went so far as to swear his mother couldn't have done any better.

Nobody knows who made the first vinegar cobbler or pie, but it no doubt was a substitute for lemon pie. The cobbler was easier to make in camp, and called for things found in the chuck box, except for butter. Possibly in the fall, a roundup cook might have a crock of homemade butter, brought out from the home ranch, but any other time butter wasn't even considered.

Pudding

Blackie was a graduate of the school of "Dump and Throw" (see Chapter 2), so you'll have to figure out your own measurements according to the number to be served. This is his recipe for Tallow Pudding.

Put into a large granite pot several kinds of dried fruit: apples, peaches, apricots, and raisins (prunes are not desirable). Soak dried fruit overnight allowing plenty of room for swelling. This cuts down on cooking time. Chop white tallow into small, fine pieces (1 cup for 2 to 3 quarts fruit) and add to fruit. Add enough water to cover and cook until done. While cooking, if needed, add a little hot water to fruit to keep from scorching the pot. When fruit and tallow are done, add sugar and spices (cinnamon, cloves, or nutmeg) to taste. If the pudding is too soupy, the juice can be thickened by adding a little flour and water, or cornstarch. Pour the hot-cooked fruit into a Dutch oven and cover with a regular pie crust. Cut small slits for steam to escape. Heat the Dutch-oven lid on the fire irons. Place Dutch oven on a few hot coals, put on lid, and cover with more hot coals. In a conventional oven, bake at 375 degrees until the crust is light brown. Remove and let cool.

Blackie says this is a real tallow pudding. Some people think it has to be boiled in a sack but he likes this way best.

Speedy Rice Pudding

2	cups cooked rice	1/4	teaspoon nutmeg
1	can Eagle Brand milk (*not* condensed milk)	1	cup chopped nuts
		1/2	cup coconut
2	eggs, beaten	1	teaspoon salt
1	teaspoon vanilla	1/2	teaspoon cinnamon

MIX rice, milk, and eggs. Cook on top of stove until mixture coats metal spoon—only a few minutes. Remove from heat and add remaining ingredients. Serve with whipped cream. This recipe is fast and, oh, so good!

Brown Sugar Pudding

1	cup packed brown sugar		pinch of salt
1/2	stick butter or margarine	1	teaspoon cinnamon
2	cups boiling water	1	teaspoon baking powder
1/2	cup packed brown sugar	1/2	cup milk
1	tablespoon butter or margarine	1/2	cup chopped nuts
		1/2	cup raisins
1	cup flour	1	egg

MIX together 1 cup brown sugar, 1/2 stick butter or margarine, and boiling water in a saucepan; bring to boil. Combine remaining ingredients in a separate bowl, stirring until blended. Put boiling syrup in 9 by 9-inch pan and pour batter over hot syrup. Bake at 350 degrees for 30 minutes.

You can use any dried fruit you have on hand, even chopped fresh apple is good. Nuts improve it, but don't fret if you don't have any. This is good served hot or cold and, if you have cream or whipped cream, it improves it a lot. Can be made in camp in a Dutch oven with just hot coals on top to bake batter. This pudding isn't touchy so don't worry about making it in your kitchen or outdoors!

Shirley Blunt
Malta, Mont.

13 MORE FOR THE SWEET TOOTH

I've been known, on rare occasions, to follow some recipes to a T, but not so with cookie recipes.

Cookies

I've always been a lousy cookie maker. I don't know why because my mother was a cookie maker supreme. You'd have thought some of her expertise would have rubbed off on me. They say talent skips a

Illustration by Bill Culbertson

generation, and this may be so, because my daughter bakes cookies that are gems of the baker's art, and so delectable they melt in your mouth.

I've been known, on rare occasions, to follow some recipes to a T, but never have I been known to do so with a cookie recipe. I always think there's been a typographical error and, in spite of everything, I add more shortening, more sugar, more flour, *and* a lot of stuff the original recipe *doesn't* call for. The results are bad.

Betty McDonald, in her wonderfully funny book *The Egg and I,* tells about her grandmother's cookies:

"Gammy taught us when you make cookies to put in anything you lay your hands on. Scrapings from several jars of jam; leftover hot-cake batter; the rest of the syrup in the jug; a few grapes, cherries, raisins, plums, or dates; and always use drippings instead of butter or shortening. The results were terrible, and they were big and brown and over an inch thick and were full of seeds and pits."

Well, I'm a graduate of Gammy's school of cookie-makin'. Consequently, due to peer pressure and severe criticism from my children, I quit making cookies many years ago. But, that doesn't stop friends and grandchildren from encouraging me by giving me cookie jars for Mother's Day gifts. My kitchen is loaded with unusual cookie containers. Several are in the shapes of cows with mooney eyes, a wimpish bull, a cuddly puppy, a giant strawberry, a shiny red apple, and one that looks just like an old-timey sourdough jug. I really do keep my sourdough starter in this jug, which I have on top of my gas refrigerator because it's just the right temperature to keep the

Pumpkin Nut Cookies

I'm known far and wide as a notoriously horrible cookie maker. Just ask my children if you don't believe me. However, even *I* make these cookies and I've yet to see any going to waste.

1/2	cup shortening	1	teaspoon salt
1	cup sugar	2 1/2	teaspoons cinnamon
2	eggs, beaten	1/2	teaspoon ginger
1	cup pumpkin	1	cup raisins
2	cups all-purpose flour	1	cup chopped nuts
4	teaspoons baking powder		

CREAM shortening, adding sugar gradually. Add eggs and pumpkin; mix well. Sift flour, baking powder, salt, and spices together. Stir dry ingredients into pumpkin mixture and mix well. Add nuts and raisins. Drop by spoonfuls on greased cookie sheet. Bake 15 minutes at 350 degrees.

My grandsons check my cookie jars periodically, but always find they contain hair curlers, clothespins, canning lids, nuts, bolts, and screws.

dough alive and frothy.

One time this caused a minor furor when a friend wandered into my kitchen, and spying the cookie jar atop the fridge, he trustfully plunged his hand deep into the jar for some of grandmother's home-made cookies. On contact with the warm, slimy mess, he screamed like a woman. Everyone thought he'd been bitten by a rattlesnake.

Ever optimistic, my grandsons check my cookie jars periodically, but always find they contain hair curlers, clothespins, canning lids, nuts, bolts, screws, and several pressure gauges for cookers gone lo these many years.

So, because I hate to be a complete failure in my grandmotherly duties, in later years I've been known to purchase store-bought cookies to fill the empty cookie jars. However, I'm informed this isn't quite kosher.

During the second world war, I sent off numerous packages of cookies to Mack's younger brothers who were stationed in faraway corners of the world. I had a

Rice Krispies Cookies

1	cup shortening	1	teaspoon baking soda
1	cup packed brown sugar	1/2	teaspoon baking powder
1	cup white sugar	1/2	teaspoon salt
2	eggs, well beaten	2	cups quick oats
1	teaspoon vanilla	1	cup shredded coconut
2 1/2	cups flour	2	cups Rice Krispies

CREAM shortening and brown sugar first, then add white sugar and cream together. Add eggs and vanilla. Sift dry ingredients together and add to mixture. Add oats and coconut. Fold in Rice Krispies last so as not to break them. Drop on greased sheet and bake 12 minutes in a 350-degree oven. Makes 6 dozen.

Oatmeal Macaroons

1	cup packed brown sugar	1 1/2	cups flour
1	cup white sugar	1	teaspoon baking soda
3/4	cup butter, melted and cooled	1	teaspoon baking powder
2	eggs, lightly beaten	1/2	teaspoon salt
1	teaspoon vanilla	3	cups oatmeal

IN a mixing bowl, combine the sugars, butter, eggs, and vanilla; blend. Sift together all dry ingredients except oatmeal. Add to egg mixture. Stir in the oatmeal. Drop by teaspoonfuls onto cookie sheet. Bake at 350 degrees until golden brown. Makes 10 dozen or more macaroons depending on how many cookie snatchers are lurking nearby.

Mincemeat Cookies

3/4	cup shortening	3	cups flour
1 1/2	cups sugar	1	teaspoon baking soda
3	eggs	1	pinch salt
1	cup mincemeat	1	cup broken nut meats

CREAM shortening and sugar; add eggs, beat well; add mincemeat. Sift dry ingredients together and add to sugar mixture; blend. Stir in nuts. Drop by spoonfuls onto greased cookie sheet. Bake at 350 degrees for about 15 minutes. Makes a bunch.

Old-Fashioned Sorghum Cookies

1½	cups lard	2	tablespoons ginger
1	cup sugar	2	tablespoons cinnamon
2	cups sorghum	2	teaspoons salt
6	eggs, lightly beaten	6	cups flour
2	tablespoons baking soda		

COMBINE lard, sugar, and sorghum in a saucepan; bring to a boil. Stir until sugar is dissolved; remove from heat and cool. When cool, blend with eggs. Sift dry ingredients together. Add egg batter to dry ingredients and blend. If the dough is not stiff enough to roll out, add a little more flour. Turn dough out onto a lightly floured board, roll out to ¼-inch thickness. Cut into any shape desired. Arrange on lightly greased baking sheet and bake at 375 degrees until brown. Lift off with spatula when done, cool. When cold, pack in tin box with wax paper between layers. Cover tightly. The flavor improves if these are left several days before eating. Makes 8 to 9 dozen cookies according to the cook's and cookie snatchers' willpower.

Paint Pony Cookies

1	cup sugar	2	teaspoons nutmeg
1½	cups shortening	2	teaspoons cinnamon
½	cup molasses	1	teaspoon cloves
2	eggs	2	teaspoons ginger
4	cups flour	4	teaspoons baking soda
2	teaspoons salt	1½	cups candied fruit, cut in bits

CREAM sugar and shortening. Add molasses and eggs. Sift together all of the dry ingredients and blend into sugar mixture. Stir in the candied fruit. Roll in balls the size of walnuts. Bake about 8 minutes at 375 degrees. It's better to undercook than to overcook.

favorite recipe I used that described the cookies as being "chewy and good keepers." They certainly did keep—for weeks at a time—until they became more flinty than chewy. And it was this recipe I used in my food packages. It called for a lot of raisins and dates, and wartime shortages being what they were, I often had to substitute with dried apples and apricots.

Faithful brothers-in-law wrote back and dutifully thanked me, but said it took so many weeks in transit that the cookies were ruined. The truth be known, they were unfit to eat before they ever left my kitchen.

Also, during the war, I used my precious sugar, which was rationed, in making clunky, anemic-looking cookies with a lone satsuma raisin plastered in the center. I sold these to the Hopi trader, who in turn sold them to his customers. Incredible as it seems, they were snatched up by the Hopis, who always seemed to have a sweet tooth that needed a fix.

The Paint Pony recipe originally came from the old Paint Pony Lodge in Show Low, Arizona. These cookies are winners at any season, but because of the colored candied fruit, I call them Christmas cookies. My daughter-in-law, Patti Hughes, makes these every year during the holidays and I almost founder on them. *Please* don't leave out anything or add a single ingredient.

My favorite cookie recipe described the cookies as being "chewy and good keepers." They certainly did keep—for weeks at a time—until they became more flinty than chewy.

Salted Nut Roll Bars

⅔	cup packed brown sugar	1	12-ounce package miniature marshmallows
½	cup butter	½	cup butter
2	egg yolks, beaten	12	ounces peanut butter chips
1½	cups flour	2	teaspoons vanilla
½	teaspoon salt	2	cups peanuts
½	teaspoon baking powder		
½	teaspoon baking soda		

CREAM together brown sugar, butter, and egg yolks. Sift together all dry ingredients; combine mixtures. Pat in 9 by 13-inch pan and bake at 350 degrees for 12 to 15 minutes. Add miniature marshmallows to crust; bake 2 minutes until melted. Let cool.

In separate saucepan over low heat cook the butter, peanut butter, and vanilla. Pour over entire pan of candy. Sprinkle peanuts on top while still warm. Refrigerate to set, then cut in squares. Each square wrapped in clear plastic keeps candies from sticking and helps pack with other kinds of candy for gift packages.

Chocolate Christmas Candies

1 cup butter or margarine	1 cup chopped walnuts
½ cup creamy peanut butter	1 6-ounce package semi-sweet
2½ cups graham cracker crumbs	chocolate pieces
2 cups sifted powdered sugar	1 2-ounce piece paraffin wax
2 cups flaked coconut	

COMBINE butter and peanut butter in saucepan. Cook over medium heat, stirring constantly, until melted. Remove from heat. Combine graham cracker crumbs, powdered sugar, coconut, and walnuts in bowl. Pour peanut butter mixture over; toss until blended. Shape into ½-inch balls. Place on waxed paper-lined baking sheets. Cover with aluminum foil and chill in refrigerator.

Combine chocolate pieces and paraffin wax in top of double boiler. Place over hot water and stir until melted. Dip balls in chocolate and place back on waxed paper-lined baking sheets. Let stand until chocolate is set. Cover with aluminum foil and store in refrigerator. Makes 2 pounds or about 8 dozen.

A picture of Skeeter Bill, the "little cowboy," taken about the time of Christmas 1943 on the Hopi Reservation.

Christmas With The Hopi

In 1943 and '44, Mack and I, along with our two small children, lived at Oraibi, a pueblo village on the Hopi Reservation in northern Arizona. Mack was a range rider with the U.S. Department of Interior. We lived in a government house at the base of a sandstone cliff at the edge of the village.

This was wartime, and many foods, as well as gasoline, were rationed. It was 80 miles, all except 10 over poorly maintained dirt roads, to the nearest town on the railroad. Rarely did we make this trip more often than once a month, but when we did, the stores always seemed to be fresh out of luxuries—candy being one of them. Oh, we could buy war candy, but it was awful . . . filled with grain cereals, or was it sawdust?

The owner of the trading post near our house went to town every Wednesday to obtain supplies from the wholesale grocer. Sometimes he was able to buy several cartons of real Hershey bars, Baby Ruths, Almond Joys, and Milky Ways. When the hour approached for the trader's return, a long "candy line" formed just outside the store.

The situation was handled in a democratic manner: The candy was sold strictly first-come, first-served. There was a limit of five candy bars per person, no matter whether you were chief of the tribe or chief dishwasher at the government day school. I usually sent our 5-year-old son,

Dried Apricot Candy Roll

3 cups sugar	1 cup chopped raisins
1 cup cream	1 cup chopped nuts
½ teaspoon salt	2 teaspoons vanilla
1 cup chopped dried apricots	

COMBINE sugar, cream, salt, apricots, and raisins. Boil to soft ball stage; stir occasionally. Cool to lukewarm. Stir in nuts and vanilla. Pour out onto very lightly floured board, grease hands with butter, knead until smooth. Shape into roll and cool in refrigerator for at least 3 hours. Cut into slices.

Skeeter Bill, with his quarter in hand, to stand in line.

There was never any problem until the day Skeeter failed to return from the store after I saw the trader's truck unloading its cargo. I watched Hopi children passing our house, happily munching on candy bars; still no Skeeter. Finally, exasperated, I went to the store and asked if they'd seen the "little cowboy," as they called Skeeter. *Ah, yiss,* he'd been there, but had gone to so-and-so's house, which was pointed out to me, clinging to the side of the mesa.

When I did find Skeeter, he had a following of Hopi boys, but not a sign of any candy. I towed Skeeter home by his hand and questioned him along the way. Just what had become of his candy?

"I shared it with my freens," Skeeter said. His generosity was commendable, but I

During November I'd made extra money for Christmas by baking cookies, cupcakes, and fruitcakes, which I sold to the trading post. I'd used almost all my sugar ration stamps and had none to make candy for Christmas. Unless there was a modern-day miracle, we'd have few sweets for the holiday.

Marshmallow-Pecan Fudge

¼ pound sweet butter	1½ cups semi-sweet chocolate bits
1 14-ounce can evaporated milk	2 cups small marshmallows
5 cups sugar	1 teaspoon vanilla
pinch of salt	1½ cups chopped pecans

COMBINE butter, milk, sugar, and salt in a saucepan and cook over low heat, stirring constantly, until sugar is dissolved and butter melted. Increase heat and boil 8 minutes without stirring. Meanwhile, combine chocolate bits and marshmallows in a greased bowl. When syrup is done, pour immediately over chocolate mixture. Do not scrape the pan. Stir until chocolate is dissolved. Add vanilla and pecans. Spread on a buttered platter and let cool completely. Cut into squares.

was burned up for I was sure Skeeter had none for himself, as his *freens* were twice his size. I berated him for not coming home right away.

"I wouldn't care if you'd just gotten some," I complained as we walked along the dusty road.

"I did, I did," Skeeter assured me. When I looked doubtful, he opened his mouth wide and, using a grubby finger, pulled his lips as far as they would stretch. I could see signs of chocolate and bits of nuts clinging to his molars. Defeated, I had to laugh.

As Christmas approached, I had little faith that our trader could supply the demand for holiday goodies. I sent off a large order from the Sears, Roebuck catalog. From past experiences, I knew half the items shown would be unavailable, but I trustfully marked each item, "Substitute with whatever you have. Just send *something.*"

From the skimpy pages of candy offerings, I ordered some of everything pictured. I mailed the order off with crossed fingers, but derned little good it did me. When the packages arrived, there was no candy of any kind.

During November I'd made extra money for Christmas by baking cookies, cupcakes, and fruitcakes, which I sold to the trading post. I'd used almost all my sugar ration stamps and had none to make candy for Christmas. Unless there was a modern-day miracle, we'd have few sweets for the holiday.

The Hopi are a religious people and their lives center on their centuries-old religion. Most participate in their many seasonal ceremonies. Skeeter became a steady visitor to the *kiva*, where the Hopi priests stayed, and which was strictly off

limits for me. However, Skeeter was most welcome and in a little over a year's time learned to speak Hopi. The *kiva* was so close to our house I could hear the drums and chanting through the night.

Hopi ceremonies for the public were held in the plaza just beyond the store. I wasn't surprised when, just 2 days before Christmas, I saw a great many people gathering there. Trucks full of Indians were parking everywhere. Even horse-drawn wagons, loaded to the sideboards with oldsters and children, rattled off the mesa from Old Oraibi and stopped at the store. Skeeter began begging to attend, and when I gave my permission, he left, riding his stick-horse on a dead run.

Soon I heard the squawking sounds of a loudspeaker, and then a recording of "Silent Night" began to play. This was something I had to see for myself. I dressed the baby for cold weather and went to investigate. Well, I found no regular Hopi ceremony, but instead a huge Christmas party sponsored by a missionary group from Gallup. They spared nothing in presenting treats for everybody.

I watched the missionaries hand out candy canes, gumdrops, packages of gum, oranges, apples, and sacks of peanuts. There were even toys, some of them new. There were boxes of used clothing and I saw warm coats, heavy jackets, woolen sweaters, and stocking caps handed to eager recipients. Another truck held hundreds of loaves of bakery bread, boxes of crackers, cases of canned tomatoes, bags of flour, and sacks of beans and rice. It was all distributed in an orderly manner while recordings of Christmas carols played over the loudspeaker.

Skeeter ran up to me, his eyes shining

and his arms full of candy and fruit. He returned to get bags of candy for his baby sister and even one each for Mack and me. I returned home with enough candy to last the holidays. Glory be!

Doughnuts

Not all doughnuts have holes, but the ones that do have become more American than apple pie. And it may not come as a surprise that doughnuts did not originate in this country (a heck of a lot of things didn't), but Americans can take credit for the hole.

It seems in about 1847 a sea captain named Hanson Gregory from Camden, Maine, suggested that his mother leave a hole in the center of doughnuts she made, because they were often doughy on the inside. Following her son's advice, she made holes with her thimble, and the resulting doughnuts were so delicious that all doughnut makers soon copied her method, and the doughnut with a hole in it has been with us ever since.

In the far West, women were practically unknown in the lonely cow camps, scattered over the open range from Canada to the Mexican border. Good cooks were as scarce as women, and the ranchers and cowboys cooked their own monotonous meals of beef and biscuits, with perhaps a treat of sweetened, dried applesauce occasionally.

Andy Adams, in his book *Log of a Cowboy*, tells about a winter camp on the Cherokee Strip in the 1880s where several cowboys were spending the Christmas holidays, alone and far from loved ones. Gloom hovered over this bachelor camp like a shroud.

Several days before Christmas, one of the old-timers drifted in from the Cheyenne country. He had worked on the range before, and they all knew him. In the course of the first evening's conversation around the cook stove, this old-timer mentioned he'd become an artist on making doughnuts, commonly called "bear sign" by the cowboys. He modestly admitted he could turn them out, browned to a turn, and as toothsome as those any mother could make.

Right there, the boss of the outfit told one of the men to throw the old-timer's horse into the big pasture next morning. For as the boss said, "He stays right here until the first green grass in the spring."

The next morning, after breakfast, the boss rolled a barrel of flour into the kitchen from the storehouse, got 20 gallons of lard, 100 pounds of sugar, and told the doughnut maker to go at it.

"About how many do you think you'll want?" asked the old-timer.

Spud Doughnuts

2	cups milk	1/2	teaspoon baking soda
1/2	cup shortening	1/2	teaspoon baking powder
1/2	cup sugar	1/2	teaspoon vanilla
1/2	cup mashed potatoes	2	eggs, beaten
2	packages dry yeast	1	teaspoon salt
1/2	cup lukewarm water	6	cups flour

CREAM the milk, shortening, and sugar together. Bring to fast boil and let cool; add the mashed potatoes. Dissolve dry yeast in the lukewarm water and stir into mixture. Add the baking soda, baking powder, and vanilla. Let batter rise until foamy, about 30 minutes. Then add eggs, salt, and about 6 cups of flour. Mix well and let rise until doubled in size.

Roll out on well-floured board about 1/4 inch thick and cut large doughnuts. Let rise again. Fry in deep fat until golden brown.

Glaze:

1/2	cup water	vanilla to taste
3 1/2	cups powdered sugar	

Bring water to boil; stirring constantly, mix in powdered sugar and vanilla. Remove from heat and dip doughnuts while still warm. Place on paper towels.

"It says, 'Time to make the doughnuts.'"

And don't forget to fry the doughnut holes—some people claim they're the best part of the doughnuts.

"That big tub full won't be too many," answered the boss. "Some of these fellows haven't had anything like this since they were little boys. If news of this gets out, I look for men from other camps."

By 10 o'clock the doughnut maker began turning out gems of the baker's art, like he said he could. By dinnertime, the initial taste had made the cowboys ravenous for more. After dinner, the bear-sign man settled down to doughnut making in earnest.

During the afternoon, a boy rode by on his way to the railroad with an important letter. He said he could only tarry a moment, but after eating doughnuts for a solid hour, he filled his pockets and rode away. One cowboy called after him, "Don't you go blabbin' an' tell anybody what we got."

Late that evening, the boss told the doughnut maker to knock off, as he had been at the stove since morning.

The next day, the old-timer set up his production line once more. About 10 o'clock, two men whom the boy with the letter had passed the day before rode in from the north. Both men made a beeline to the bear-sign tub—that was a dead giveaway they were onto the racket. An hour later, another man showed up on a lathered horse, having ridden 25 miles since early morning. Making his way to the tub, he refused to sit down like a civilized man, but stood up close and picked out ones that were a pale brown.

Early in the afternoon, three more men rode in. The doughnut maker's fame was circulating faster than a secret among women. The old-timer never let up, yet by nighttime he had never covered the bottom of the tub. When he finally quit for the night, the remaining doughnuts were soon gobbled up.

The next day was Christmas, and the doughnut maker stirred up a large batch of dough before breakfast. It was a good thing he did, because early that morning a rancher and four of his men rode in from the west. They said they'd simply come over to spend Christmas, but there was no doubt that the word had gotten to them, as they wasted no time in bellying up to the tub.

As they were all sitting down to dinner, in came two men from 30 miles south of the Cimarron. Like the rest, they used the excuse of dropping by because it was Christmas. The boss called the doughnut maker behind the house and told him he

---

Pinto Bean Doughnuts

3 cups sifted all-purpose flour	¼ cup butter or margarine, melted
4 teaspoons baking powder	1 cup mashed, cold, unseasoned pinto beans
1 teaspoon nutmeg	¼ cup milk
1 teaspoon salt	
3 eggs	
1 cup sugar	

SIFT flour with baking powder, nutmeg, and salt; set aside. At high speed, beat eggs, sugar, and butter until very light and fluffy (about 2 minutes). On low speed add beans, half the dry ingredients and milk, then the rest of the dry ingredients. Cover and refrigerate for 1 hour.

Place one half the chilled dough on a floured board or pastry cloth. Coat with flour on all sides. Roll out flat to ⅓ inch thick and cut with floured doughnut cutter. Repeat with remaining half. Fry in hot fat at 375 degrees until brown on both sides. Frost as desired or serve plain.

Cake Doughnuts

2 eggs	1 tablespoon baking powder
1 cup sugar	1/2 teaspoon nutmeg
2 tablespoons butter, melted	1/4 teaspoon mace
1 cup milk	5 cups flour (approximately)

BEAT the eggs and sugar until thick and light. Add butter and milk. Sift together the baking powder, nutmeg, mace, and 4 1/2 cups of flour. Stir the dry ingredients lightly into the egg mixture, adding enough additional flour to make a soft dough. Cover the dough and refrigerate for about an hour. Roll the dough to a thickness of 1/2 inch on a lightly floured board and cut with a doughnut cutter.

Heat fat to a depth of 3 inches in a deep fryer, kettle, or electric skillet. When the fat has reached a temperature of 360 or 375 degrees, drop in the doughnuts, 3 or 4 at a time, and fry them, turning once, until golden brown on both sides. Drain on paper towels. The doughnuts may be dusted with sugar and cinnamon if desired. Makes 24 doughnuts.

Is there anything more reminiscent of country kitchens than that wonderful aroma of frying doughnuts?

could quit if he wanted to, but the old-timer wouldn't do it, and right after dinner he turned out another batch.

The new arrivals hadn't near satisfied their craving by bedtime that night, but sometime the next day, the doughnut maker finally filled his tub. Too bad no one bothered to keep tally. Worse yet, no one took time to write down the recipe.

Is there anything more reminiscent of country kitchens than the wonderful aroma of frying doughnuts? No barn raisings, cider pressings, square dances, or holidays could have been complete without batches of sugar-coated doughnuts piled high in the center of the dinner table.

Doughnuts fall into two classes: one kind is leavened with yeast, the other with baking powder. The yeast-leavened ones are called raised doughnuts. Their dough, like bread, is not very sweet. They derive their sweetness from sugar dipping or a topper of glaze or frosting. The baking powder-leavened kind are called cake doughnuts. Their dough is sweet, but that doesn't prevent us from shaking them in a bag of confectioner's sugar or cinnamon sugar, or giving them a glaze or frosting treatment.

Raised doughnuts may be the old familiar, round-with-a-hole-in-the-middle type, or they may be long and eclair-shaped, or twisted, or square, or round but without a hole so they may be filled after frying with jam or jelly or a smooth cream custard. Cake doughnuts are often round, but inside the crispy brown crust can lurk any number of flavors: nutmeg, chocolate, chopped nuts, crushed hard candy, or candied fruits.

Raised doughnuts must rise before they are fried. Cake doughnuts can be fried at once, but it is a good idea to let the dough cool in the refrigerator an hour to firm it up. Then, very little flour is needed to roll them out.

Be certain that the fat you use for frying is the proper temperature, which is 365 degrees Fahrenheit for most doughnuts. And don't forget to fry the holes—some people claim they're the best part of the doughnuts.

119

14 BREAK TIME

Coffee is to a cowboy what gasoline is to a car—they just don't run without it.

Beverages and Dips

Them words "Arbuckle Brothers" on a
    sack of coffee beans,
Saved the West an' all of Texas, from the
    Injuns an' their schemes.
When the wagon left headquarters for the
    roundup, Spring an' Fall,
It was sure to carry with it lots of coffee
    for us all.
The boys shore liked their coffee ever'
    mornin' an' night.
An even in between times when the
    wagon was in sight.

—*Carter "Tex" Taylor*

When I visited the roundup camps during the years Mack was manager of the tribal herd for the San Carlos Apaches, there'd always be a big pot of coffee burping away on a bed of hot coals near the cook's fire. All were welcome to help themselves to this brew, day or night, and *never* was the coffee weak. I've always believed it was the Apache's code of honor, when making coffee, to save water and splurge on coffee, and never, never throw out the grounds during the day, no matter how many times the pot is added to. I'd have been disappointed had it been otherwise. I like what I'm used to.

Or, at least I thought I did until one afternoon I visited the camp of a fence crew in Bonita Canyon. It was late in the day and the 2-gallon pot had been on the coals since early morning. The coffee that lurched sluggishly from the spout was bottle-green in color, somewhat resembling that of a once-black serge suit that had become sunfaded with age. One cup of this witch's potion and I had enough caffeine to keep me awake for a year and a half.

When ordering supplies for the roundup, Mack purchased coffee by the case; each case contained a dozen 3-pound cans. The cook could run out of almost anything, even flour, and the outfit could manage for a day or so until the truck could go to town. But not coffee. No cowboy expected to be served a meal without coffee and plenty of it. I never knew of but one Apache cowboy who didn't drink coffee, and that was Mack's big strawboss, Marco Davis. Marco drank hot water for breakfast, and because he was well over 6 feet tall and weighed a solid 215, he took little if any kidding

120

Cow-Sale Coffee

2½ pounds ground coffee   muslin bag
29 gallons water

BRING 29 gallons of water to a boil in a 30-gallon container. A big, clean oil drum works fine. Drop a muslin bag filled with the coffee grounds into the boiling water. Reduce heat and place a clean stick across the top of the drum. This will keep coffee from boiling over. Let coffee reach the gently bubbling stage; then, to settle the grounds, add a pint or so of cold water. Coffee is now ready to serve. If coffee is to be served most of the day, 5 or 10 gallons at a time can be poured into milk cans and lids placed on lightly. Hot coals under the cans keep coffee hot for hours. Makes 250 cups of coffee, give or take a few.

"Man at the pot!" If a man gets up to refill his coffee cup and hears this yell, he is duty-bound by camp etiquette to go around with the pot and fill the cups held out to him. This rule is never broken.

about his strange habit.

Of the many brands of coffee available at the trading post, Folger's was favored by the Apaches. Sometimes a cook would order MJB or Hills Bros., but I believe it made little if any difference, just so the coffee was strong and hot and they never ran out. Few of the Apaches used cream or sugar in their coffee and made fun of their neighbors to the north, the Navajo, who were wont to boil coffee with plenty of sugar added.

Although the United States is known today as one of the heaviest coffee-drinking nations in the world, coffee came late to the American table. Oh, sure, it was known and available if you had the money, but its luxury prices denied it to the majority of people. In the early 1800s a pound of green coffee beans sold for as much as 45 cents a pound, a price considered so exorbitant, housewives blanched at the thought of spending so much money for coffee when the same amount would buy flour for a family of five to last a week.

Before the Civil War, coffee beans were packed green. The coffee beans were placed in a pan and roasted to the exact doneness, then they were ground in a coffee mill. Handfuls of the freshly ground coffee would be thrown into a pot of cold water and boiled until the desired strength. The longer the boiling, the stronger the brew. Most early-day coffee drinkers liked their coffee sweetened, and many used cream as well.

Most poor people made their own breakfast drink, their substitute for coffee being made of roasted wheat, corn, acorns, sweet potatoes, and even okra seeds. One early-day pioneer told of roast-

Six-Shooter Coffee

(a.k.a. bellywash)

1½ pounds ground coffee   1 gallon water

PUT coffee grounds into pot with a gallon of water and boil the hell out of it. Do not worry about boiling too much for there is no such thing. Set it aside for a few minutes for the grounds to hit bottom before you pour.

ing potato peelings and cornmeal for their ersatz coffee. The early Mormons in Utah made a nutritious drink by grinding wheat and sometimes corn, mixing it with egg white and sorghum molasses, then toasting in the oven or skillet. Like instant coffee, they blended it with hot water, adding thick cream, making a hot eye-opener. Some homesteaders in North Dakota told of toasting bread until it became a deep brown, then soaking the toast in hot water until the water was colored. Then it was strained and served with cream and, if they had it, sweetened with sugar or honey.

When the Civil War came along, thousands of young men who had never tasted coffee found it supplied in their rations. Along with their flour (they did their own cooking), they received salt pork, cornmeal, sugar, and coffee. The coffee and sugar were assigned in given amounts—so much per 100 men. The daily amount of roasted and ground coffee was 8 pounds. It was up to the sergeant in each company to see that his men got their fair share. Every soldier had a bag of some sort to put his coffee in. Some mixed their sugar ration right in with their coffee and this way had their coffee sweetened without any fuss when they found a moment to boil

Chili con Queso

(dip)

1 large onion, minced	1 can chopped green chili peppers
2 tablespoons butter	1 pound Velveeta cheese
1 clove garlic, chopped	salt to taste
1½ cups canned tomatoes	hot pepper sauce to taste

IN a pan or skillet brown the onion and garlic slowly in butter. When the onion is just turning brown, add the tomatoes. Mash with a fork as the juice cooks away. When very thick, add chili peppers and cheese cut in small chunks. Cook over very low heat, stirring frequently, until all the cheese is melted. Add salt and hot pepper sauce to taste. Keep hot in chafing dish to use as a dip for tostadas, corn chips, crackers, or bread sticks. Store in refrigerator, covered, until needed. Reheat gently before serving. This may also be used as a sauce over hamburgers or with hot dogs.

their pint or so of coffee.

Is it any wonder then, upon their return to civilian life, the boys in blue or gray were not inclined to kick their coffee habit cold turkey? They had become such devoted coffee drinkers that, price or no price, they demanded coffee when they got back home. Coffee companies rushed to comply to their great new demand. There followed a tremendous rush of coffee importing and roasting apparatus inventions, plenty of far-fetched advertising, and "coffee wars." This led to considerable under-the-table adulterations.

Honest coffee roasters, wholesalers, and retailers were plagued by many unscrupulous competitors who pushed adulterated

"Will you have sugar and cream in your coffee?" asked the waitress.

The cowboy said, "Nope, I don't want nothin' in mine but water, and mighty little of that."

Guacamole (Avocado Dip)

There are hundreds of recipes for guacamole, but once you've made this one, you'll probably throw all the others out. It's *good!*

2 ripe avocados	1 hard-cooked egg
1 small onion, grated	⅓ stick butter, melted
1 4-ounce can chopped green chilies	2 tablespoons mayonnaise

PEEL, pit, and mash the avocados. Stir in the onion and chilies. In a separate bowl, grate the *warm* egg over the butter and work in the mayonnaise with a fork. Gradually add the contents of the other bowl; taste and salt. It's easy to double this recipe.

Pinto Bean Dip

1 cup mashed pinto beans	1 tablespoon sugar
1 cup ketchup	¼ teaspoon savory salt
½ cup minced sweet pickles	¼ teaspoon garlic salt
1 teaspoon minced onion	¼ teaspoon celery salt

COMBINE all ingredients thoroughly. Serve with chips.

Illustration by Keith Walters

Potato Chip Mixture

2	hard-boiled eggs	1	whole pimiento, minced
1	tablespoon minced ripe olives	1	cup mayonnaise
½	teaspoon salt		Tabasco to taste
1	tablespoon minced sour pickle		potato chips

PEEL eggs and mash with fork until crumbly. Add olives, pickle, salt, and pimiento; mix thoroughly. Add mayonnaise and Tabasco. Stir thoroughly and serve with potato chips.

Before the 20th century, coffee was termed an insidious destroyer of health, and debates were held on coffee vs. alcohol.

Clam Dip

1	7-ounce can minced clams	10	drops Tabasco
6	ounces cream cheese	½	small onion, finely grated
1	pint cream-style cottage cheese	¼	teaspoon garlic powder
1	teaspoon Worcestershire sauce		dash of salt

DRAIN clams and set liquid aside. Blend all other ingredients thoroughly. Pour clam juice a little at a time into mixture until about the consistency of thick cream.

coffee at lower prices. All sorts of grains, nuts and shells, and chicory root were used as extenders. Some additives composed as much as 70 percent of the product packaged. There was even a machine invented and patented that was used in shaping substances such as chicory root powder into coffee-berry shape. Some manufactured "coffee extract," a popular compound, containing little pure coffee, allowing the user to do his own adulterating. It was used extensively in cheap boarding houses by mixing it with real coffee.

Pure coffee or adulterated, no matter, the brew had its detractors. Seventeenth-century England believed wholeheartedly that coffee drinking caused leprosy. American preachers, reformers, and extremists, even into the 20th century, were predicting results almost as dire. Coffee detractors made wild claims of men who drank coffee for any length of time becoming imbeciles or dying of consumption. Coffee was termed an insidious destroyer of health, and debates were held on coffee vs. alcohol.

Taking advantage of the growing sentiment against the evils of coffee, several people began developing substitutes. One, O.F. Woodward of New York, concocted a drink of roasted cereal grains. It was very similar to those early settlers and farmers had made for themselves. Woodward capitalized on the "evils of coffee" and made a fortune with his Grain-O, which he put out in packages labeled "A Table Beverage Which The Children As Well As Adults May Drink Without Injury."

Charles William Post later developed a hot drink called Postum Cereal and in a few years came out with Instant Postum. His advertising read "toothsome, palatable and delicious Postum Cereal Food Coffee." Post's new drink promised to make a "new man of a coffee wreck." It made a millionaire of Mr. Post.

Unabashed by the imitators, the real coffee companies continued plugging their coffees. The Oriental Tea Company in Boston hit the advertising jackpot when they brought out, in 1868, a "Male-Berry Java Coffee." The male berry, they claimed, was "the round or fully developed bean, picked from the ordinary flat coffee by hand, in Java," and was in their opinion and that of everyone who had tried it, "the best coffee in the world." As late as 1873, they were warning their customers through advertisements to beware of imitations.

Other companies worked hard to combat this "Male-Berry" appeal. The first branded coffee in 1869 was Osborn's Celebrated Java Coffee, which was packaged in 1-pound foil paper; cases of 30 and 50 pounds; wholesale price, 18 cents per pound. Their advertisements were headed "No Prize Packages, No Orders For Spoons Or Dolls, But A Coffee Really Worth Its Price."

Maxwell House Coffee was developed in Nashville, Tenn., by Joel Cheek, who hailed from Kentucky. After developing his famous blend of coffee over a period of years, he had it tested at the Maxwell House in Nashville, one of the South's finest hotels at the time. The guests, who included the elite of the country, liked it— and the rest is history.

In 1864, Caleb Chase started a coffee

The food on some ranches might be weak tastin', but the coffee's strong enough to bring up the average.

Jello Punch for a Bunch

2 large packages gelatin, any flavor
9 cups boiling water
4 cups sugar
4 cups boiling water

2 46-ounce cans pineapple juice
2 cups lemon juice
2 tablespoons almond extract
2 quarts ginger ale

COMBINE gelatin and 9 cups hot water. Dissolve, stirring well, set aside to cool. Dissolve sugar in the 4 cups boiling water and set aside to cool. Mix all ingredients together except ginger ale and freeze. About 2 to 3 hours before serving, take out of freezer and let thaw until snow cone consistency; add ginger ale. Keep very cold while serving.

Margarita

2 1½-ounce jiggers tequila
1 jigger Cointreau (Triple Sec, Controy, etc.)
½ jigger fresh lime juice

ice
salt
½ fresh lime

MIX the 3 liquids well with ice. Spread the salt on the plate, rub the edge of a cocktail glass with the half lime and twirl the damp edge of the glass in the salt. Carefully strain the iced cocktail into a glass, so as not to disturb the salted edge. Serves 1.

"Stop me if you've heard this one . . ."

business in Boston, and soon joined forces with young James Sanborn. Their firm was the first to pack roasted coffee in sealed cans. Chase and Sanborn have been familiar household names ever since.

Arbuckle & Co. had a patented process for coating or glazing their coffee, after it was roasted, with egg white and sugar to seal in its fresh flavor. The purchaser only had to grind the polished beans in order to brew a fine cup of coffee. Besides this, the Arbuckle folks were shrewd merchandisers, for they packed the coffee with coupons redeemable for razors, alarm clocks, "silver" spoons, and dolls. For several years, they included sticks of peppermint candy in each bag. Anyone with a sweet tooth could claim the candy if they ground the coffee.

It has been said that Arbuckle was the coffee that "kept the West awake." This may be true, but it's my opinion that Arbuckle captured the trade of the West by packing their coffee in very sturdy wooden boxes with handholds in each end; boxes so indestructible that people living in the lumber-shy West, if they had the brains of a gnat, never threw one away. They were used as kitchen cupboards, chairs, bedside tables, and they even made fine chests for clothes. In the chuck wagon, they were filled with spices, kitchen tools, medicines, horseshoes, nails, and rivets. No blacksmith shop was complete without several Arbuckle boxes, and down at the bunkhouse there was a box, or even two, under each cot. The

Sneaky-House Punch

46 ounces Hawaiian Punch (any red fruit)
6 ounces frozen orange juice
6 ounces frozen lemonade
1 quart Bacardi Light Rum
strawberries (optional)
1 block of ice

MIX all ingredients in large punch bowl with block of ice.
Slice strawberries and add to punch. Then watch out!
It's sneaky.

Joyce House
Kingman, Arizona

An eastern lady once asked a cowboy how many cups of coffee he drank in a day? He said, "As many as I can get . . . about 20." "Don't it keep you awake?" she asked. He replied, "It helps."

rancher dismantled the boxes and built line shacks, chickenhouses, doghouses, and outhouses. One woman, telling of her life on an early ranch, said her father built her an elegant doll house from Arbuckle Brothers boxes that was the envy of every child in the country.

A great tome of a book (1,044 pages), *The Trail Drivers of Texas,* contains 157 first-person accounts of the great cattle drives to northern markets. It is a wonderful source of material for the serious student of western history. Time and again the authors mention coffee and its importance to the cowboys. Coffee was always high on the list when purchasing supplies for the long trek. One drover said, "We were low on grub and sent for coffee and sugar." D.H. Snyder of Georgetown, Tex., had this to say in his memoirs: "We purchased coffee, flour, bacon, beans, and dried fruit. Three-quarters of a pound of bacon and the same of flour being allotted to each man for each day. Coffee beans, in sacks, were purchased in such quantity so that at no time would we run out." Another wrote: "We parched coffee and ground it, enough to last for several days at a time." Still another had this to say: "We came in off the drive and lost no time getting on the outside of some hot coffee, pone, and sowbelly, and back to the herd."

The first trail drivers up the trail after the Civil War found the Indians a great nuisance, begging for "tobac and sugar." But the following year, the Indians had added an important item to their list of wants, and that was "Kaw-fee." The Texans might part with sugar and "tobac," but they were most reluctant to share their precious coffee with the Redskins, and were apt to offer to cut out a sore-footed steer instead.

Illustration by Joe Beeler

JUDGED COMPETITIONS

Chuck-wagon cooking competitions have become very popular.

Getting Started

IT'S A DARNED good thing I didn't know how ignorant I was when I started to assemble an old-time chuck wagon, the kind the Texas trail drivers took north with their herds of Longhorns, headed for market back in the late 1860s. If I'd known what a difficult task it would turn out to be, I'd have thrown up my hands and quit on the spot!

It all started out innocently enough back in the spring of 1968 when the Ari-

zona State Cowbelles appointed me co-chairman of beef promotion. I was to be in charge of the booth at the Arizona State Fair in Phoenix that fall. This was months away and would allow me ample time to carry out my plans of using an old-time chuck wagon as my theme.

For starters I had a team of old mare mules, Maude and Molly, a set of service-able harness, and a complete camp outfit including Dutch ovens of every size, pots, pans, fire irons, a sourdough keg, a wooden water barrel, and kerosene

Stella Hughes, Bob Hedrick, and John Wolf in 1990 as judges at the first Chuck Wagon Cook-Off in Ruidoso, New Mexico.

Photo by Dudley Barker

lanterns. Well, that was still a long way from having a *wagon*!

Luck was with me, as only a hundred miles from home I found running gears and wheels, along with five hardwood wagon bows, all from a junk dealer who was willing to part with this treasure trove for a mere $135. I did not realize until later the five wagon bows were as rare as finding a gold mine in the middle of my kitchen floor. I ordered a wagon sheet from a company in Texas and was on a roll.

I had a carpenter build a wagon box and a chuck box, and I traded for a wagon seat with springs and brackets from an antique dealer. That was the only time I'd ever seen a perfect wagon seat for sale. Beginner's luck!

With lots of paint, axle grease, and tightening of bolts, I was ready for parades and fairs throughout Arizona. Well, not quite ready.

Maude and Molly were brought out of retirement and conditioned for parade work. Perhaps we overconditioned them, as the first parade in Phoenix got a bit western. The old gals objected to popping balloons, band music, flying banners, screaming crowds, and the crosswalk markers at each intersection. Things turned out fine, though, and we were awarded the first-place trophy in our class. I entered six more parades and won first place in each before fair time in September.

A few days before the fair I loaded the wagon (dismantled) in my four-horse trailer, along with all my camp outfit. I even took some oak wood (for display only), and I filled a tub with hardwood coals to use to illustrate how a Dutch oven looked with biscuits baking.

I had a committee of hard-working Cowbelles, and the first thing they did was take my pickup out into the desert and haul back a load of sand and gravel, sagebrush, and a few cactus. They even collected a few authentic cow chips to scatter around. The overactive sourdough dribbled down the sides of the crock, the kerosene can had a potato stopper, and a granite wash basin was filled with dirty water—we all washed our hands and then dried them on the flour sack towel. There was a bar of homemade soap, galvanized water bucket and dipper, wash tubs, and lard cans.

Wolf Wagon Works rebuilt this Bain wagon for Cecil Scott. It carries the brand of the Four C Crescent Ranch, San Angelo, Texas.

A good wagon after restoration by John Wolf of Crossroads, New Mexico.

127

Gillette Ranch chuck wagon at the Ranching Heritage Museum in Lubbock, Texas. At the rear of the wagon are, from left, Pipp and Guy Gillette and Ron Conatser.

You may add other items for cooking, but they must be authentic to the period of the 1870s to early 1920s.

Someone had made a plaster hindquarter of beef and painted it. We rented a mannequin, dressed him in period clothes, and put a butcher knife in his hand. The mannequin was young and pink-cheeked, so we bought a mask of an old man and that took care of the problem, even if he did look like death warmed over. Or at best, like he'd had a big night on the town!

Equipping Your Wagon

John Wolf owns Wolf Wagon Works & Mercantile Co., Box 927, Crossroads, NM 88114; 505-675-2480. He has been restoring and judging wagons for years. Here are some items he suggests you need to turn a ranch wagon into an authentic chuck wagon:
- Chuck box (no plywood)
- Dutch oven boot (optional)
- Wooden water barrel with hinged lid
- Iron pot rack, with at least four "S" pot hooks and two gonch hooks
- Two wooden props with wagon sheet fly, when it is positioned to shade area, with ropes and stakes
- Cast-iron cook pots
- Dutch ovens . . . one 16-inch diameter, two 14-inch, one 12-inch, one 10-inch, one 6½-quart bean or stew pot
- Two or more large coffee pots, capacity 1 gallon or more
- Large granite kettle with lid for hot water

Bill Dakan, Eldorado, Tex., has won several authenticity awards for his wagon.

- Enough tin or enamelware cups, plates, knives, forks, spoons for 12 cowhands
- Various cook spoons, big forks, butcher knives, ladles, and pancake turners
- Large flour pan for mixing biscuits
- One sourdough crock or keg, approximately 1-gallon size, with lid, or saucer for lid
- Meat cutting board, meat saw, and meat cleaver
- Shovel (perhaps one flat-bottomed for coals and one spade for digging fire pit)
- Two galvanized wash tubs, one for washing dishes and one for rinsing
- One galvanized water bucket and dipper
- A side-mill coffee grinder mounted on board to hang on sideboard of wagon
- Kerosene lantern and kerosene can
- A wind-up alarm clock
- Ax
- Bar soap (no liquids or powder)
- Dish cloths and towels of cotton material only
- Axle grease, a wagon jack, a team harness draped on wagon tongue for display for authentic chuck-wagon competition
- Dinner gong or bell (optional)

You may add other items for cooking, but they must be authentic to the period of the 1870s to early 1920s. Avoid plastic, stainless steel, and aluminum.

129

Stella Hughes and John Wolf at Eldorado, Tex., in 1987.

How Judging Works

I helped judge my first Chuck Wagon Cook Off contest in April of 1987 at Eldorado, Texas. That's when I first met John Wolf, who was also a judge. We judges had a few skimpy rules to go by. There were 50 points to be given for perfection: 25 points for taste and texture, 20 points for appearance and authenticity, and 5 points for showmanship. This contest was complicated by being divided into chuck-box cookers as well as chuck wagons. We did the best we could and got out of that one alive.

John and I met again 3 years later when we judged at the 1st Lincoln County Cowboy Symposium at Ruidoso, N.M., in October 1990. This time, besides John and me, Bob Hedrick also judged. Well, I'd met Bob at Eldorado, as he was one of the chuck-box cookers. We three made the rules used at this cook-off that are being used in almost all contests today.

The rules established at that symposium read:

Due to the increasing popularity in chuck-wagon cooking competitions, it is apparently essential that a set of basic rules and regulations be established to assist both the competitors and the judges and sponsors.

As the preservation of our past heritage is the primary purpose of these activities, it is suggested that the type of wagon in use 50 years or more ago be adopted as the typical wagon.

The original old-time chuck wagon was still in use until right after World War II, up until about 1948, when cattle-hauling trucks took over the movement of cattle to market. Prior to that time cattle were still being driven across country or to the railroads by trail herd. The chuck wagons on these drives were on the move twice a day, after breakfast and after dinner, staying ahead of the moving herds. This is the type of wagon that these guidelines are based on.

Guidelines

The wagons should be customary old-style ranch wagons, authentically restored or authentic replicas, driveably sound, with wagon bed at least two sideboards high, painted or unpainted, with or without Dutch oven boot or possum belly; no iron-wheeled farm wagons, no rubber-tired wagons; wagon equipped with the following:

1/ A complete brake system.

2/ Spring seat mounted on the wagon.

3/ Complete wooden tongue assembly, with tongue cap, neckyoke or tongue chains, doubletree and singletrees, wheel wrench, and stay

Stella driving Jake and Pete to an authentic chuck wagon in 1976. Husband Mack seems to be riding the brake. Stella and Mack replaced the pipe bows on the wagon with hardwood.

Cook has preference of pot rack, grill, or both; shovel and ax to be at fireplace.

chains. No iron or pipe tongues or iron farm-wagon-type doubletree or singletrees.

4/ One set of team harness (two-horse or two-mule hitch) displayed on wagon tongue.

5/ Four or five wooden wagon bows mounted on wagon; a canvas wagon sheet with wagon. No iron or pipe bows.

6/ Wooden water barrel mounted on wagon.

7/ Old chuck-wagon-style coffee grinder.

8/ Old-style kerosene lantern.

9/ Old-style chuck box, preferably not of plywood.

Scoring System

10 - Excellent	6 - Satisfactory	2 - Fairly Bad
9 - Very Good	5 - Sufficient	1 - Bad
8 - Good	4 - Insufficient	0 - Not in Place
7 - Fairly Good	3 - Poor	

Camp Layout

A/ Camp layout to be neat and functional; fireplace located for the cook's convenience at rear or side of wagon, not more than 25 feet from the chuck box. Cook has preference of pot rack, grill, or both; shovel and ax to be at fireplace.

B/ Cooking utensils used are to be of the authentic type, made of cast iron; no plastic or stainless steel.

C/ Cooks and helpers should be courteous and considerate, their clothing of period type—no shorts, T-shirts, tennis shoes, or baseball caps.

Further Suggestions

1/ Limit the number of wagons to 15 wagons for each set of 3 judges.

2/ Have the sponsors, wagon cooks, and judges hold a meeting, preferably the evening before the competition, to set the time for the wagons to be in place, the cook-off judging to

Lots of hooks and big coffeepots over a fine, hardwood fire.

Silver trophy buckles or belts are a no-no, as are tennis shoes and sunglasses.

begin, and to work out various other details.

3/ Have wagons and camp layout judged 1 or 2 hours before food is judged.

4/ Four foods to be judged: bread, beef, beans, and dessert.

5/ Post the winners' scores after judges' score sheets are turned in to the sponsor.

6/ This one is for the ranch-rodeo-type cook-offs only: Due to the difficulty in judging the various modern types of chuck wagons being used now in the ranch rodeo cook-offs, it is suggested that the score sheet used in judging old-time wagon authenticity be eliminated and competitors with modern chuck wagons be judged on camp layout and cooking only.

My Pet Peeves

When I'm judging a chuck-wagon cook-off, I have several peeves. I give low marks for beans cooked in Dutch ovens. I firmly believe the iron pots give them a metallic taste and darken them. I believe beans should be cooked in a granite kettle with a lid, which also has a bail or handles.

The rules require that the cook and helpers wear clothes of the period. There should be no wrist watches, diamond rings, wallets in hip pockets, baseball caps, or shirts with snaps or of loud splashy prints. Silver trophy buckles or belts are a no-no, as are tennis shoes and sunglasses.

Branding irons in a cook's fire pit? At no time was the cook's fire used to heat branding irons, for heaven's sake! It's okay to be proud of your brand, but hang the irons on the wagon or stack them under the wagon.

Stella Hughes driving Maude and Molly in 1972 in Globe, Arizona. This was Stella's first wagon, and would not meet today's requirements. Stella wore a wig, authentic riding skirt, and added a Colt .45.

Contents of the chuck box often break rules. A mishmash of containers I've seen at different events throughout the country include plastic or Tupperware bowls, microwave glassware, modern fruit jars with sealing caps, rolls of toilet paper, paper towels, cartons of milk, and a bottle of hand lotion.

Cook-off rules vary widely. Many say no aluminum, when in fact aluminum was in use before 1900. By 1915 aluminum was used in every household—teakettles, double boilers, sauce pans, roasters, and dishpans.

Stainless steel? If you want to play it safe, refrain from using any stainless steel. Most cook-off rules ban its use entirely, even though stainless steel was patented in 1911, and in use widely by 1920. This cuts contestants a lot of slack, timewise, and judges had better be fairly expert on antiques. Few are!

John Wolf's Pet Peeves

I hate to see auto filler used in wagons. Cracks and age are beautiful to me.

I hate coolers "hid" inside wooden trunks.

Possum bellies for wood should be rawhide and not processed hides.

Biscuits should be cut with a cup and not a cookie cutter.

Nobody should walk between the cook and the fire. People should wait to be called; never help themselves.

I give low marks to cooks who overflow the Dutch oven lids and allow ashes into the food.

When the cook's wood supply is too close to the fire, it is a hazard and gets in the way of the judges.

Special Helps

All temperatures used in recipes are given in degrees Fahrenheit.

Equivalent Measures

1 ounce = 2 tablespoons
Dash or pinch = less than $1/8$ teaspoon
1 tablespoon = 3 teaspoons
$1/4$ cup = 4 tablespoons = 2 ounces
$1/3$ cup = $5 1/3$ tablespoons
$1/2$ cup = 8 tablespoons = 4 ounces
1 cup = 16 tablespoons = 8 ounces
1 pint = 2 cups
1 quart = 4 cups = 2 pints
1 gallon = 4 quarts
1 peck = 8 quarts
1 bushel = 4 pecks
1 pound = 16 ounces

Temperature

250°-275°   very slow oven
300°-325°   slow oven
350°-375°   moderate oven
400°-425°   hot oven
450°-475°   very hot oven
500°-525°   extremely hot oven

Substitutions

Baking powder. 1 teaspoon = $1/4$ teaspoon baking soda plus $1/2$ teaspoon cream of tartar.
Chocolate. 1 square = 3 tablespoons cocoa plus 1 tablespoon shortening.
Cornstarch. 1 tablespoon = 2 tablespoons flour (as thickening).
Buttermilk. Use 1 teaspoon sugar, $1/2$ teaspoon salt, and 3 tablespoons vinegar to 1 cup canned milk, and measure desired amount.
Sour milk. 1 cup = 1 cup lukewarm milk (less 1 tablespoon) plus 1 tablespoon vinegar. Let stand 5 minutes.
Ketchup. Use 1 cup tomato sauce, $1/2$ cup sugar, 2 tablespoons vinegar, and measure desired amount.
Lemon juice. Vinegar may be substituted in small quantities.

INDEX

WHERE COVERS COME FROM

We unanimously agreed that the hat had to go.

Bert Anderson tries aerial photography, Kathy Kadash shoots a low angle, Brenda Goodwin uses the straight-on approach, and Joyce uses a tailgate for a director's chair. (Hillside and chuck wagon by Tom and Betty Watt.)

After many months of work, primarily by Stella and Editorial Assistant Brenda Goodwin, our staff thought the prospect of taking the cover pictures for this book seemed like a picnic. And, it turned out to be just that much fun.

However, the project needed to be completed during the infamous "Springtime in the Rockies," when the Colorado weather does flashbacks to winter while lurching toward summer. Stella and daughter Joyce House had driven from greater metropolitan Eagle Creek, Ariz., and they planned to be in Colorado Springs for only 3 days. That would be enough time for Stella to review the almost-final stages of the book. However, since the best picture-taking light is in the mornings, we were a little nervous about getting the photography done.

Although we couldn't control the weather, we were all confident that the location and the chuck wagon were perfect. Both were provided by Tom and Betty Watt,

who live north of Colorado Springs. Their collection of rolling stock is magnificent, and the light in Stella's eyes when she saw the chuck wagon was the final benediction.

The weather teased us a little on the first morning, but there was plenty of good light. The shooting crew included Brenda Goodwin, Bert Anderson, Kathy Kadash, and Gary Vorhes. Tom Watt, WH Publisher Randy Witte, and Joyce kept an eye on the activities as the gunners went through 11 rolls of color film and quite a lot of Stella's patience.

A little suspense arose later that day when the weather gloomed over and the forecast held more clouds. It took a day to find out if the first effort had been successful. By that time it was raining and it didn't look as though there would be good picture-taking light for several days.

But the first batch of film did the job. There were lots of good shots to choose from, and the back cover shot came from Brenda Goodwin, the cover from Gary Vorhes.

Stella and Brenda give up on getting serious.

Daughter Joyce certainly inherited a big part of Stella's disposition.

Stella cracked up the crew by slapping some flour on herself. She said she always ends up getting flour all over, so she likes to get it over with right away.

When you're around Stella, you're going to get straightened out occasionally.

Update

In September 1997, Mack and Stella Hughes sold their ranch near Eagle Creek, Ariz., where they had lived 42 years, and moved to Wikieup, Ariz., where their daughter, Joyce House, lives. Mack Hughes died in 1998.

—Brenda Goodwin
February, 1999

NOTES

Books Published by
WESTERN HORSEMAN®

ARABIAN LEGENDS by Marian K. Carpenter
280 pages and 319 photographs. Abu Farwa, *Aladdinn, *Ansata Ibn Halima, *Bask, Bay-Abi, Bay El Bey, Bint Sahara, Fadjur, Ferzon, Indraff, Khemosabi, *Morafic, *Muscat, *Naborr, *Padron, *Raffles, *Raseyn, *Sakr, Samtyr, *Sanacht, *Serafix, Skorage, *Witez II, Xenophonn.

BACON & BEANS, by Stella Hughes
144 pages and 200-plus recipes for delicious western chow.

BARREL RACING, Completely Revised by Sharon Camarillo
128 pages, 158 photographs and 17 illustrations. Teaches foundation horsemanship and barrel racing skills for horse and rider, with additional tips on feeding, hauling and winning.

CALF ROPING by Roy Cooper
144 pages and 280 photographs. Complete coverage of roping and tying.

CHARMAYNE JAMES ON BARREL RACING
by Charmayne James with Cheryl Magoteaux
192 pages and over 200 color photographs. Charmayne shares the training techniques and philosophy that made her the most successful barrel racer in history. Also included are vignettes of horses and riders that illustrate Charmayne's approach to indentifying and correcting problems in barrel racing, as well as examples and experiences from over 20 years as a world-class competitor in this exciting event.

COWBOYS & BUCKAROOS by Tim O'Byrne
176 pages and over 250 color photographs. The author, who's spent 20 years on ranches and feedyards, explains in great detail the trade secrets and working lifestyle of this North American icon. Readers can follow the cowboy crew through the four seasons of a cattle-industry year, learn their lingo and the Cowboy Code they live by, understand how they start colts, handle cattle, make long circles in rough terrain and much, much more. Many interesting sidebars, including excerpts from the author's personal journal offering firsthand accounts of the cowboy way.

CUTTING by Leon Harrel
144 pages and 200 photographs. Complete guide to this popular sport.

FIRST HORSE by Fran Devereux Smith
176 pages, 160 black-and-white photos, numerous illustrations. Step-by-step information for the first-time horse owner and/or novice rider.

HELPFUL HINTS FOR HORSEMEN
128 pages and 325 photographs and illustrations. WH readers and editors provide tips on every facet of life with horses and offer solutions to common problems horse owners share. Chapters include: Equine Health Care; Saddles; Bits and Bridles; Gear; Knots; Trailers/Hauling Horses; Trail Riding/Backcountry Camping; Barn Equipment; Watering Systems; Pasture, Corral and Arena Equipment; Fencing and Gates; Odds and Ends.

IMPRINT TRAINING by Robert M. Miller, D.V.M.
144 pages and 250 photographs. Learn to "program" newborn foals.

LEGENDS 1 by Diane Ciarloni
168 pages and 214 photographs. Barbra B, Bert, Chicaro Bill, Cowboy P-12, Depth Charge (TB), Doc Bar, Go Man Go, Hard Twist, Hollywood Gold, Joe Hancock, Joe Reed P-3, Joe Reed II, King P-234, King Fritz, Leo, Peppy, Plaudit, Poco Bueno, Poco Tivio, Queenie, Quick M Silver, Shue Fly, Star Duster, Three Bars (TB), Top Deck (TB) and Wimpy P-1.

LEGENDS 2 by Jim Goodhue, Frank Holmes, Phil Livingston, Diane Ciarloni
192 pages and 224 photographs. Clabber, Driftwood, Easy Jet, Grey Badger II, Jessie James, Jet Deck, Joe Bailey P-4 (Gonzales), Joe Bailey (Weatherford), King's Pistol, Lena's Bar, Lightning Bar, Lucky Blanton, Midnight, Midnight Jr, Moon Deck, My Texas Dandy, Oklahoma Star, Oklahoma Star Jr., Peter McCue, Rocket Bar (TB), Skipper W, Sugar Bars and Traveler.

LEGENDS 3 by Jim Goodhue, Frank Holmes, Diane Ciarloni, Kim Guenther, Larry Thornton, Betsy Lynch
208 pages and 196 photographs. Flying Bob, Hollywood Jac 86, Jackstraw (TB), Maddon's Bright Eyes, Mr Gun Smoke, Old Sorrel, Piggin String (TB), Poco Lena, Poco Pine, Poco Dell, Question Mark, Quo Vadis, Royal King, Showdown, Steel Dust and Two Eyed Jack.

LEGENDS 4
216 pages and 216 photographs. Several authors chronicle the great Quarter Horses Zantanon, Ed Echols, Zan Parr Bar, Blondy's Dude, Diamonds Sparkle, Woven Web/Miss Princess, Miss Bank, Rebel Cause, Tonto Bars Hank, Harlan, Lady Bug's Moon, Dash For Cash, Vandy, Impressive, Fillinic, Zippo Pine Bar and Doc O' Lena.

LEGENDS 5 by Frank Holmes, Ty Wyant, Alan Gold, Sally Harrison
248 pages, including about 300 photographs. The stories of Little Joe, Joe Moore, Monita, Bill Cody, Joe Cody, Topsail Cody, Pretty Buck, Pat Star Jr., Skipa Star, Hank H, Chubby, Bartender, Leo San, Custus Rastus (TB), Jaguar, Jackie Bee, Chicado V and Mr Bar None.

LEGENDS 6 by Frank Holmes, Patricia Campbell, Sally Harrison, GloryAnn Kurtz, Cheryl Magoteaux, Heidi Nyland, Bev Pechan, Juli S. Thorson
236 pages, including about 270 photographs. The stories of Paul A, Croton Oil, Okie Leo Flit Bar, Billietta, Coy's Bonanza, Major Bonanza, Doc Quixote, Doc's Prescription, Jewels Leo Bar, Colonel Freckles, Freckles Playboy, Peppy San, Mr San Peppy, Great Pine, The Invester, Speedy Glow, Conclusive, Dynamic Deluxe and Caseys Charm

NATURAL HORSE-MAN-SHIP by Pat Parelli
224 pages and 275 photographs. Parelli's six keys to a natural horse-human relationship.

PROBLEM-SOLVING, Volume 1 by Marty Marten
248 pages and over 250 photos and illustrations. Develop a willing partnership between horse and human — trailer-loading, hard-to-catch, barn-sour, spooking, water-crossing, herdbound and pull-back problems.

PROBLEM-SOLVING, Volume 2 by Marty Marten
A continuation of Volume 1. Ten chapters with illustrations and photos.

RAISE YOUR HAND IF YOU LOVE HORSES by Pat Parelli w. Kathy Swan
224 pages and over 200 black and white and color photos. The autobiography of the world's foremost proponent of natural horsemanship. Chapters contain hundreds of Pat Parelli stories, from the clinician's earliest remembrances to the fabulous experiences and opportunities he has enjoyed in the last decade. As a bonus, there are anecdotes in which Pat's friends tell stories about him.

RANCH HORSEMANSHIP by Curt Pate w. Fran Devereux Smith
220 pages and over 250 full color photos and illustrations. Learn how almost any rider at almost any level of expertise can adapt ranch-horse-training techniques to help his mount become a safer more enjoyable ride. Curt's ideas help prepare rider and horse for whatever they might encounter in the round pen, arena, pasture and beyond.

REINING, Completely Revised By Al Dunning
216 pages and over 300 photographs. Complete how-to training for this exciting event.

RIDE SMART, by Craig Cameron w. Kathy Swan
224 pages and over 250 black and white and color photos. Under one title, Craig Cameron combines a look at horses as a species and how to develop a positive, partnering relationship with them, along with good, solid horsemanship skills that suit both novice and experienced riders. Topics include ground-handling techniques, hobble-breaking methods, colt-starting, high performance maneuvers and trailer-loading. Interesting sidebars, such as trouble-shooting tips and personal anecdotes about Cameron's life, complement the main text.

RODEO LEGENDS by Gavin Ehringer
Photos and life stories fill 216 pages. Included are: Joe Alexander, Jake Barnes & Clay O'Brien Cooper, Joe Beaver, Leo Camarillo, Roy Cooper, Tom Ferguson, Bruce Ford, Marvin Garrett, Don Gay, Tuff Hedeman, Charmayne James, Bill Linderman, Larry Mahan, Ty Murray, Dean Oliver, Jim Shoulders, Casey Tibbs, Harry Tompkins and Fred Whitfield.

ROOFS AND RAILS by Gavin Ehringer
144 pages, 128 black-and-white photographs plus drawings, charts and floor plans. How to plan and build your ideal horse facility.

STARTING COLTS by Mike Kevil
168 pages and 400 photographs. Step-by-step process in starting colts.

THE HANK WIESCAMP STORY by Frank Holmes
208 pages and over 260 photographs. The biography of the legendary breeder of Quarter Horses, Appaloosas and Paints.

TEAM PENNING by Phil Livingston
144 pages and 200 photographs. How to compete in this popular family sport.

TEAM ROPING WITH JAKE AND CLAY by Fran Devereux Smith
224 pages and over 200 photographs and illustrations. Learn about fast times from champions Jake Barnes and Clay O'Brien Cooper. Solid information about handling a rope, roping dummies and heading and heeling for practice and in competition. Also sound advice about rope horses, roping steers, gear and horsemanship.

TRAIL RIDING by Janine M. Wilder
128 pages and over 150 color photographs. The author, who's ridden in all 48 states, Hawaii and the Yucatan over the last 20 years, has compiled a comprehensive guide that covers all the bases a trail rider needs in this fast-growing sport. She offers proven methods for developing a solid trail horse, safe ways to handle a variety of terrain, solutions for common trail problems, plus tips and resources on how to travel with horses. Interesting sidebars document her experiences on the trail.

WELL-SHOD by Don Baskins
160 pages, 300 black-and-white photos and illustrations. A horse-shoeing guide for owners and farriers. Easy-to-read, step-by-step how to trim and shoe a horse for a variety of uses. Special attention is paid to corrective shoeing for horses with various foot and leg problems.

WESTERN TRAINING by Jack Brainard
With Peter Phinny. 136 pages. Stresses the foundation for western training.

WIN WITH BOB AVILA by Juli S. Thorson
Hardbound, 128 full-color pages. Learn the traits that separate horse-world achievers from also-rans. World champion horseman Bob Avila shares his philosophies on succeeding as a competitor, breeder and trainer.

Western Horseman, established in 1936, is the world's leading horse publication. For subscription information: 800-877-5278.
To order other *Western Horseman* books: 800-874-6774 • *Western Horseman*, PO Box 470725, Fort Worth, TX 76147
Web site: **www.westernhorseman.com.**